MW01079050

SUPER CHARACTER DESIGN & POSES
Vol.2 HEROINE

製品ID MPCSCD2552H

※小社ホームページからユーザー登録をする場合に必要です→http://www.mpc-world.co.jp/

Introduction to

**SUPER CHARACTER / DESIGN & POSES
Vol.2 HEROINE**

by You Kusano ⓒ
Copyright ⓒ 2001 by MPC Publishing Co., Ltd.
1-10-1, Uchi-kanda, Chiyodaku Tokyo 101-0047. Japan

ISBN4-87197-552-5

SUPER CHARACTER DESIGN & POSES
Vol.2 HEROINE

スーパー・キャラクター
デザイン&ポーズ
② ヒロイン編

草野 雄 著

Special
CD-ROM
included!
for Windows
& Macintosh

この本のメインテーマは「ハードでタフなスーパーキャラクターを制作する」ということです。魅力的なオリジナルキャラクターを創造するための基本的な考え方や、発想の仕方、また人物の表情やコスチューム、武器などの小物のバリエーション、さらには具体的な描き方を紹介しています。オリジナルな作品を描くための参考資料となるように、ポーズ集も充実させました。また、すべての掲載イラストを収録したCD-ROM（Windows &Macintosh両対応）も付属していますので、ぜひご活用ください。

The main theme of this book is how to draw tough and hard-boiled characters and thier expressions, costumes, and arms.
The collection of pauses might be a reference guide for drawing your original work.
The CD-ROM is included. It contains all the graphic data which this book shows. You can use both Windows and Macintosh.

WORKS

この項では、新しいキャラクターを作るための過程を紹介しています。ひとつのテーマをもとにラフスケッチからフィニッシュまで仕上げて行きます。何とかわかりやすくまとめたつもりです。各ジャンルのスーパーヒーローたちを「ハード」というテーマに沿ってバリエーションを出してまとめてあります。

This chapter shows the process for creating a new character. Based on a theme, this section focusses on the rough sketch until the finish. I have tried to summerize it so it is easily understood. I have included a variation of heroes from different genres and tried to recreate them as "hard" characters.

BODY

ここからは、キャラクターを作るための基本段階の項目になります。スーパー・キャラクターに必要不可欠なかっこいい身体の描き方のポイントをまとめてみました。目、鼻、顔、髪のバリエーションや描き方のポイント等を、比較しながらわかりやすく、効果的にまとめてあります。

This chapter explains the basic stages of how to create a character. It includes how to draw the smart body indespensable to "super" characters. I have simply and effectively compared different variations of eyes and nose, and included paints regarding face and hair.

PEN&TECHNIQUE

必要最低限なペン画のテクニックをまとめました。
ページ数は少ないですが、必要な基本的な技術を、最小の努力で得られるようにまとめてみました。

Although this chapter seems small, we have edited it to include the necessary fundamental techniques which can be obtained easily with minimum effort.

POSES

この項目は、その名の通りポーズ集です。ハードでタフなスーパーヒーローたちのさまざまなポーズを集めてみました。
本書のいちばんの魅力は、このPOSEとテクニックを合体させたことだと思っています。普段描きにくいポーズやよく描かれるポーズを約200点掲載しています。参考になるポーズが必ず見つかることを確信しています。私自身も描き手なので、こんなポーズ集があればいいなという気持ちで描き揃えたつもりです。
このポーズ集に登場する人物は、なるべく服を着用しないようにし、Tシャツかタンクトップの姿で描きました。身体の動きや形をわかりやすくするためです。これらのキャラクターにジャケットなどを着用させて、オリジナルの作品を完成させてください。

This chapter as the name suggests, is a collection of poses. I think what makes this book attractive is the unification of technique and poses. This includes poses which are usually difficult to draw and about 200 commmonly drawn poses. As I am an illustrator, when I compiled this collection of poses I kept in mind "wouldn't it be great to have a collection of poses like this". Where possible, the characters that appear in this collection do not wear clothes. I have drawn them with a T-shirt or tank top so you can easily understand the body motion and form. You can add clothing and complete your own characters.

02093_01

付録 CD-ROMの使用方法

How to use this CD-ROM

●The purpose of this CD-ROM
This CD-ROM is mainly for graphic designers, CG designers, and game designers. Please use this CD-ROM to support your inspiration and to create your own characters.

●Contents of this CD-ROM
This CD-ROM contains all the illustrations shown in this book, as digital data.
The illustration data can be downloaded onto Windows or Macintosh. However, application software is necessary to read the following data files. Please refer to user's manuals of your softwares.

●Data files
JPEG (grayscale/1200dpi) BMP(Windows only/Black and white/350dpi)
PICT(Macintosh only/Black and white/350dpi)
To get the file number, please refer to the numbers by the illustrations in this book.

●Compatible OS
Windows 95/98/Me/2000
Macintosh (MacOS8.1 or later)

●Copy right
The copy right of all the CD-ROM data is reserved by MPC Publishing Co., Ltd.
This data is for private use only. Permission is required for usage for business purposes (eq advertising, flyers etc).

NOTICE

The CD-ROM does not include application software programs, it contains illustration data only. In order to use this data, graphic software, word processing software, etc, is necessary.

CD-ROMの内容

●本CD-ROMの目的
本書付録CD-ROMの目的は、主にグラフィックデザイナーやCGデザイナー、ゲームデザイナー等を目指す方々の一助となることです。オリジナルキャラクターを創る上の資料として、インスピレーションソースとして、ご活用ください。

●CD-ROMの内容
本CD-ROM内には、本書に掲載しているすべてのイラストがデジタルデータとして収録されています。イラストデータはWindows、Macintosh等のパソコン上に読み込むことができます。ただし、下記のデータ形式が読み込み可能なアプリケーションソフトが必要となります。お持ちのソフトのマニュアルを参照してください。

●収録データ形式
JPEG（グレースケール／1200dpi）、BMP（Windowsのみ／モノクロ2値／350dpi）、PICT（Macintoshのみ／モノクロ2値／350dpi）。
ファイル番号は、本書掲載のイラストの脇に記載されている通し番号を参照してください。

●対応OS
Windows 95/98/Me/2000。Macintosh(MacOS8.1以上)。

●著作権について
付録CD-ROMに収録されているデータの著作権は、株式会社エム・ピー・シーが管理します。私的利用の場合はご自由にお使いいただけます。商用目的にお使いの場合(広告や大量部数のチラシなどに利用の場合)は、使用申請が必要になります。詳しくは本書p.126をご参照ください。

★★★★★★★★★注　意★★★★★★★★★
本CD-ROMにはアプリケーションソフト等のプログラムは入っておりません。イラストデータのみが収録されております。イラストを使用するためには、グラフィックソフト、ワープロソフト等が別途必要になります。

How to load graphic data

Please notice that this CD-ROM doesn't contain any application programs. Therefore, nothing will happen if you just put this CD-ROM in your computer. You must use software such as Adobe Photoshop or Microsoft Word to load the graphic data in the CD-ROM as instructed below.

イラストデータの読み込み例

本CD-ROMには、オートラン形式のプログラム等は入っておりません。従って、CD-ROMをドライブに入れただけでは何も起こりませんのでご注意ください。Adobe Photoshop等のグラフィックソフトやMicrosoftWord等のワープロソフトから、下記例のように直接CD-ROM内のイラストを読み込んでお使いください。

Adobe Photoshop

You can load and edit all the data this CD-ROM contains.

●How to load

1 Start Photoshop and put CD-ROM in your computer.
2 Choose File and go to Open from Menu.
3 Refer to the book and confirm the file number of the illustration you need.
4 Go to CD-ROM and find the same file number as in the book and then click open.

Adobe Photoshopの場合

Photoshopでは、本CD-ROM内のJPEG、BMP(Windows)、PICT(Macintosh)すべてのデータの読み込み・加工・編集ができます。

●読み込み方法例

①Photoshopを起動して、本CD-ROMをドライブに挿入。
②Photoshopのメニューから「ファイル」→「開く」を選択。
③本書を参照して、必要なイラストのファイル番号を確認。
④必要なイラストファイルを選択して、「開く」を実行する。

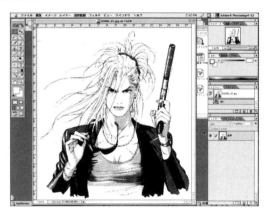

Microsoft Word

Word can load all the data this CD-ROM contains, but you should use BMP for Windows or PICT for Macintosh rather than JPEG which is heavy.

●How to load

1 Start Word and put CD-ROM in your computer.
2 On the Insert menu, point to Picture, and then click From File.
3 Refer to the book and confirm the file number of the illustration you need.
4 Go to CD-ROM and find the same file number as in the book and then click open.

Microsoft Wordの場合

Wordでは、本CD-ROM内のJPEG、BMP(Windows)、PICT(Macintosh)すべてのデータの読み込みができますが、本CD内のJPEGは非常に重いデータですので、通常の用途にはBMP(Windows)かPICT(Macintosh)をお使いになることをお薦めします。

●読み込み方法例

①Wordを起動して、本CD-ROMをドライブに挿入。
②Wordのメニューから「挿入」→「図」→「ファイルから」を選択。
③本書を参照して、必要なイラストのファイル番号を確認。
④必要なイラストファイルを選択して、「開く」を実行する。

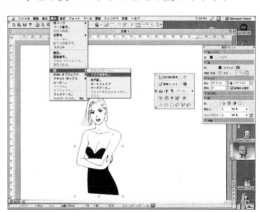

02094_03

CONTENTS

02101_02

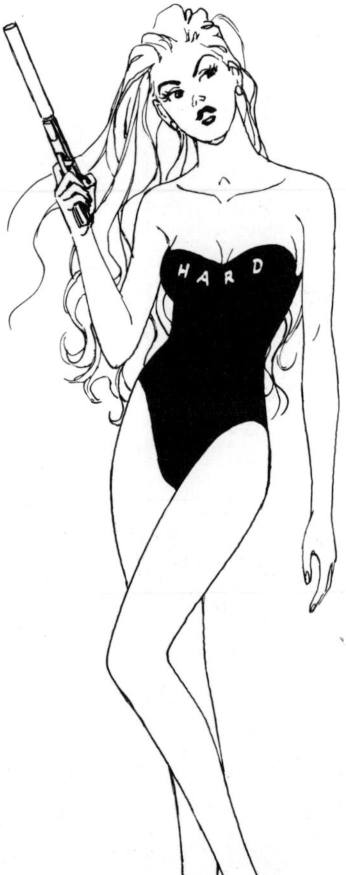
HARD
02092_02

制作テーマ

WORKS

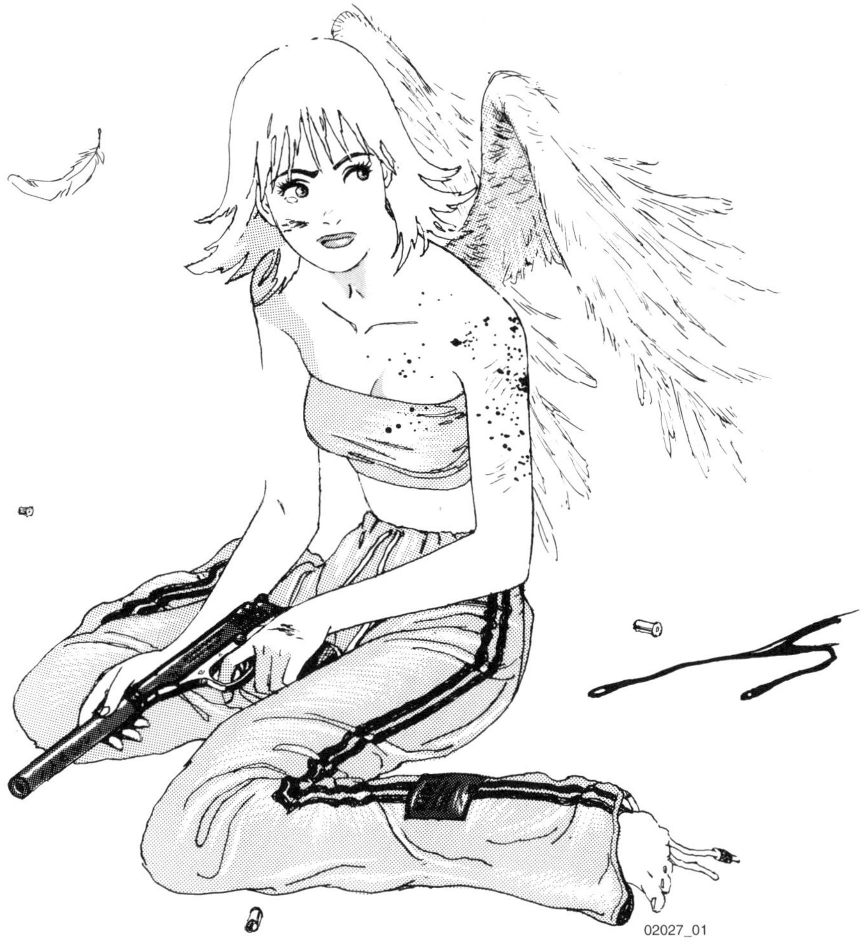

02027_01

■制作テーマ■

KAREN
カレン

クールな美少女の殺し屋だ。ある秘密組織に属した凄腕の殺人マシーンという設定だ。20歳くらいでクールな表情をしたキャラクターを制作する。現代の女性らしく。

This cool girl is a professional killer. She is a killing machine who belong to a certain secret organization. She is about 20 years old and has a cool expression. She is a modern day lady.

1 one クールな美少女。これがメインテーマだ。
A cool beautiful girl. This is the main theme.

頭の幅を狭くして、髪型もストレートヘアにした。シャープな雰囲気にしたかったからだ。
I wanted to give her a sharp look so I narrowed the width of her head and gave her a straight hairstyle.

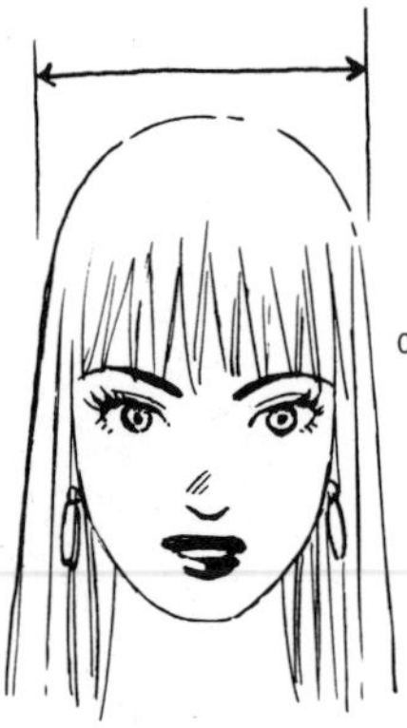

02012_01

長いストレートでブロンドのヘア。そしてクールな表情。決定だ。
She has long straight blond hair with a cool expression. It's decided!

2 two ファッショナブルな服を着せれば、このキャラクターの場合は完成といえるだろう。
If we dress her in fashionable clothes this character is complete.

おしゃれな小物やシーンがよく似合う。
Stylish props and senses suit her.

この手の主人公にはシーンによりいろいろとファッショナブルな服を着せられて楽しい。
It is fun to dress her in various fashionable outfits for different scenes.

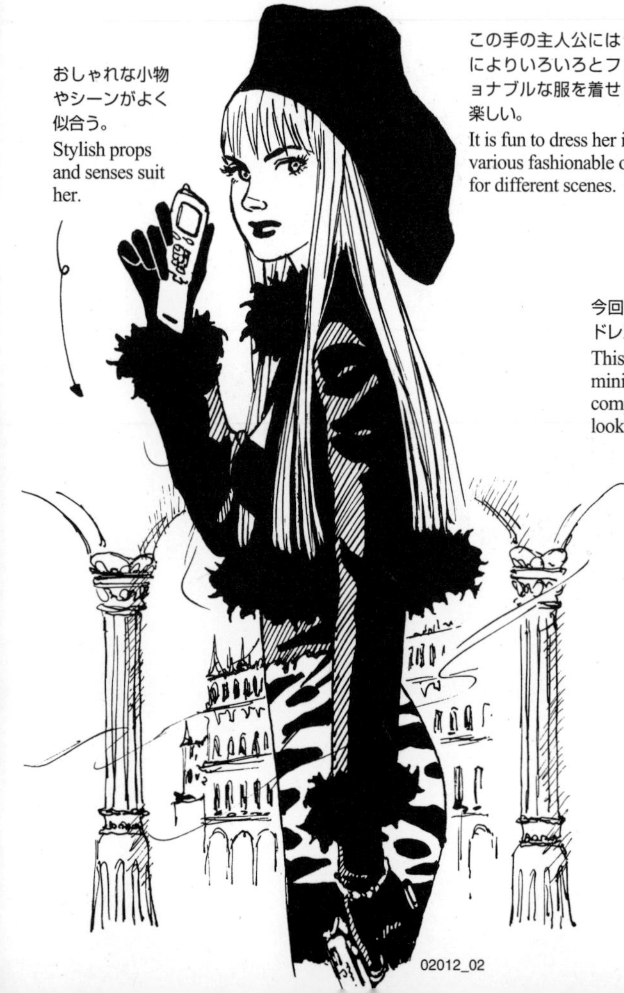

02012_02

3 three 完成。
Completion.

今回は黒のミニのドレスで完成。
This time a black mini dress completes her look.

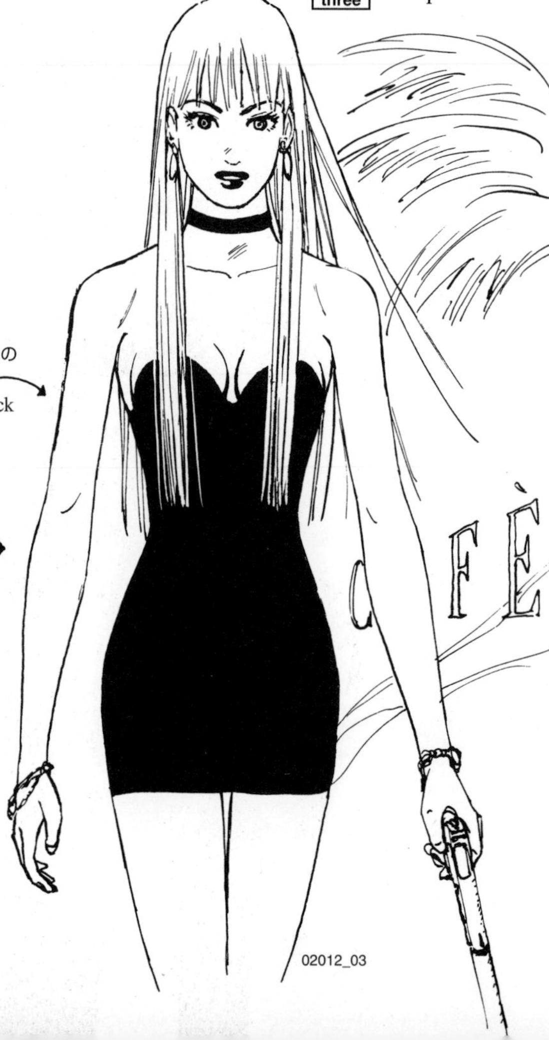

02012_03

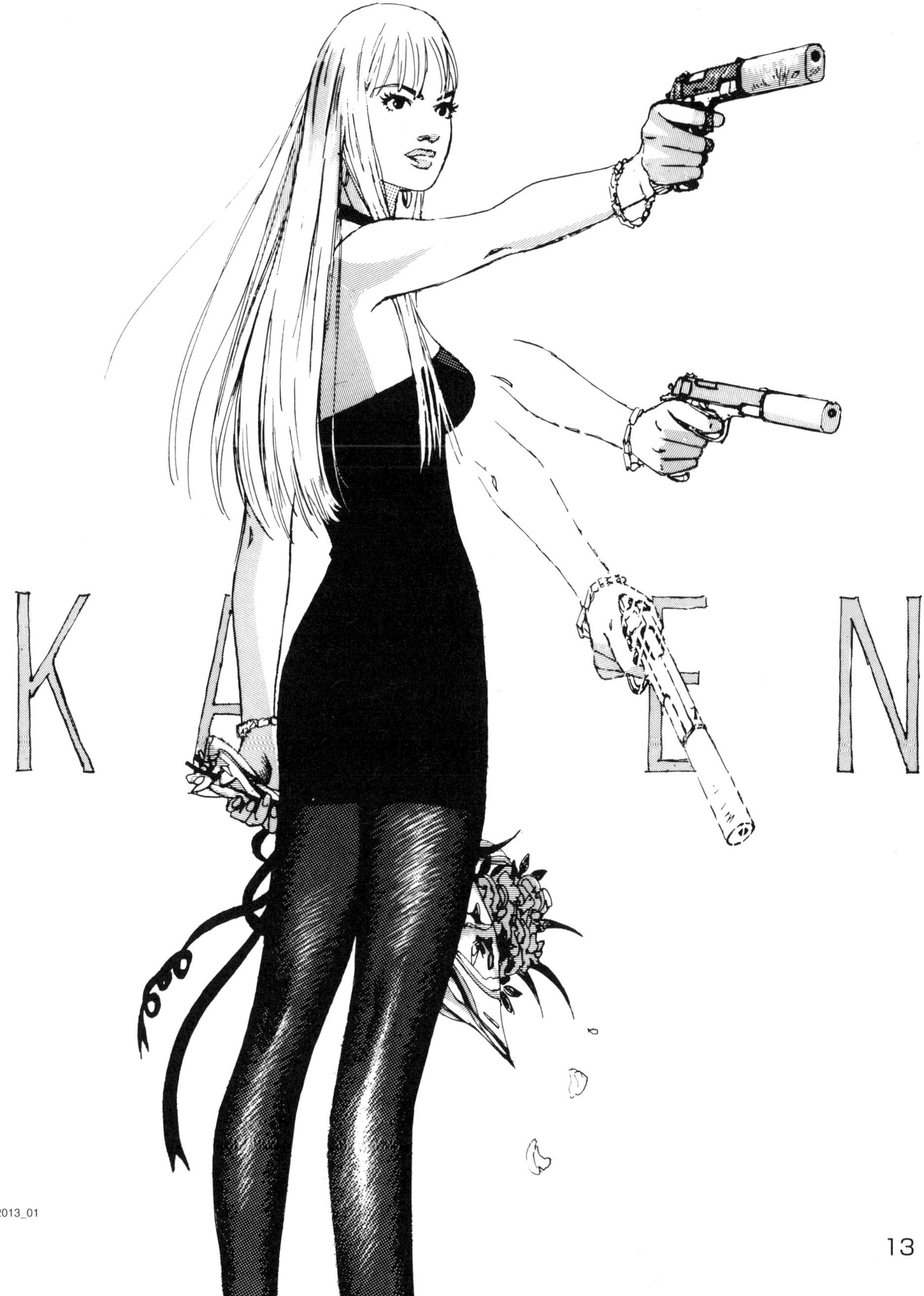
K A E N

02013_01

■制作テーマ■

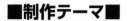

HARD COP

ハード・コップ

ハードものの定番のうちの一つ。かっこいいハードアクションの女刑事である。クールな一匹狼で、権力を嫌い正義を愛するヒロインを制作しよう。

She is one of the stereotype "tough" heroines. She is a hard action female detective. Let's create a heroine who is a lone wolf. She loves justice and hates authority.

1 one ヘアスタイルはブロンドの美しい髪。これで決まり！

She has beautiful blond hair. That is it!

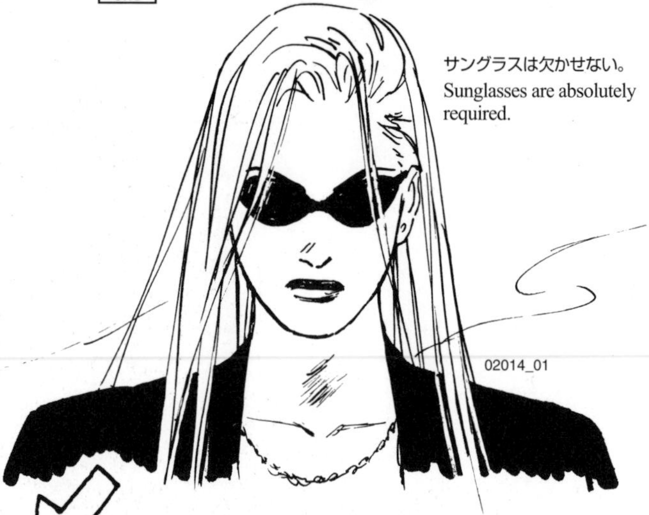

サングラスは欠かせない。

Sunglasses are absolutely required.

02014_01

2 two 服装は私の頭の中では既に決まっていた。黒のコートに革のパンツだ。悩んだのはインナーだ。ハイネック、タンクトップといろいろある。クルーネックのシャツに決めた。

Her clothes were already decided in my mind. Leather trousers and a black coat. I worried about what to put underneath a high neck, tank top, there is lots to choose from. I decided on a crew neck.

02014_02

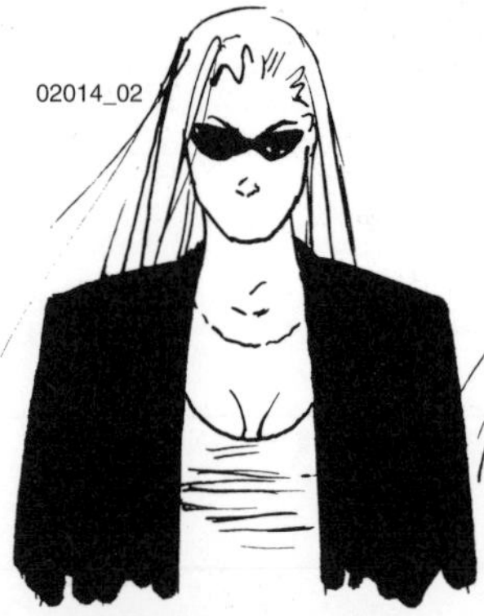

胸の開きの広いタンクトップ。一番セクシーだ。

A tank top with an open front. It is the sexiest.

02014_03

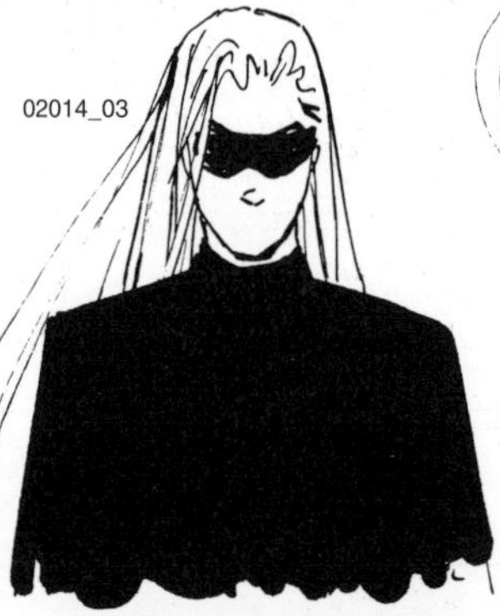

ハイネックもかっこいいがセクシーではない。

A high neck is smart but not sexy.

好みの問題もあるだろうが、結局、右のようなTシャツにした。

Although everyone has their own preference I decided on the T-shirt on the right.

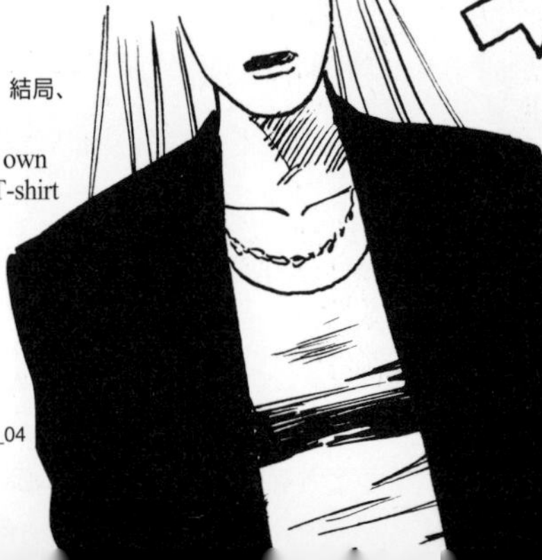

02014_04

02014_05

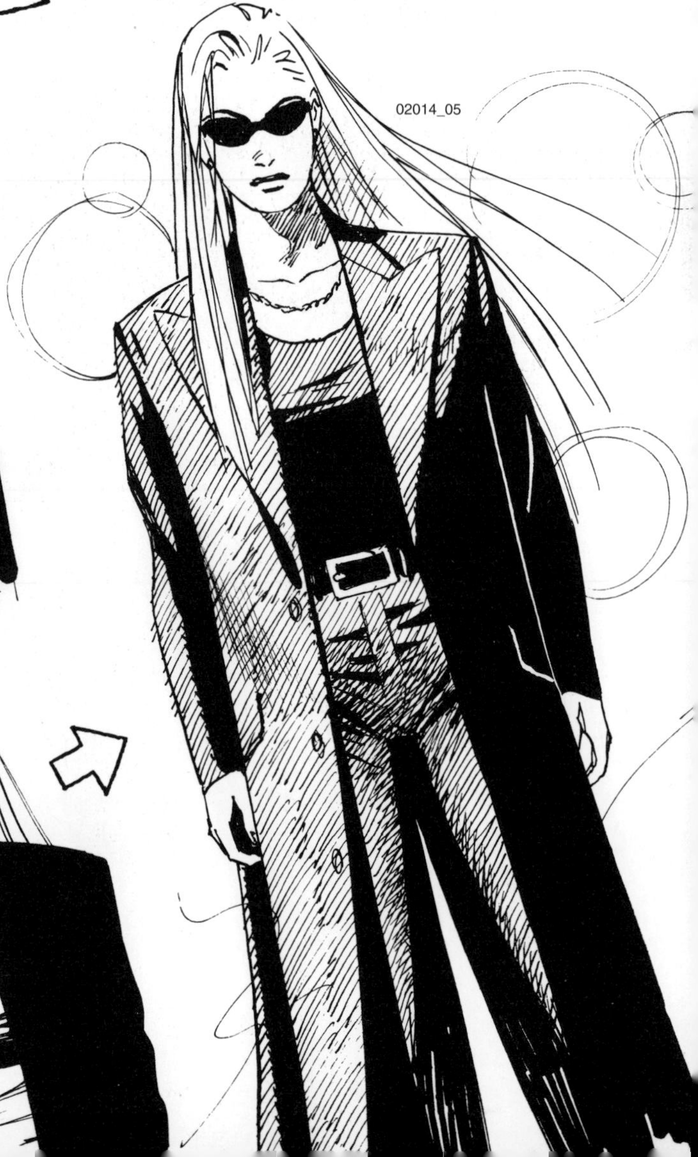

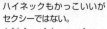

HARD COP

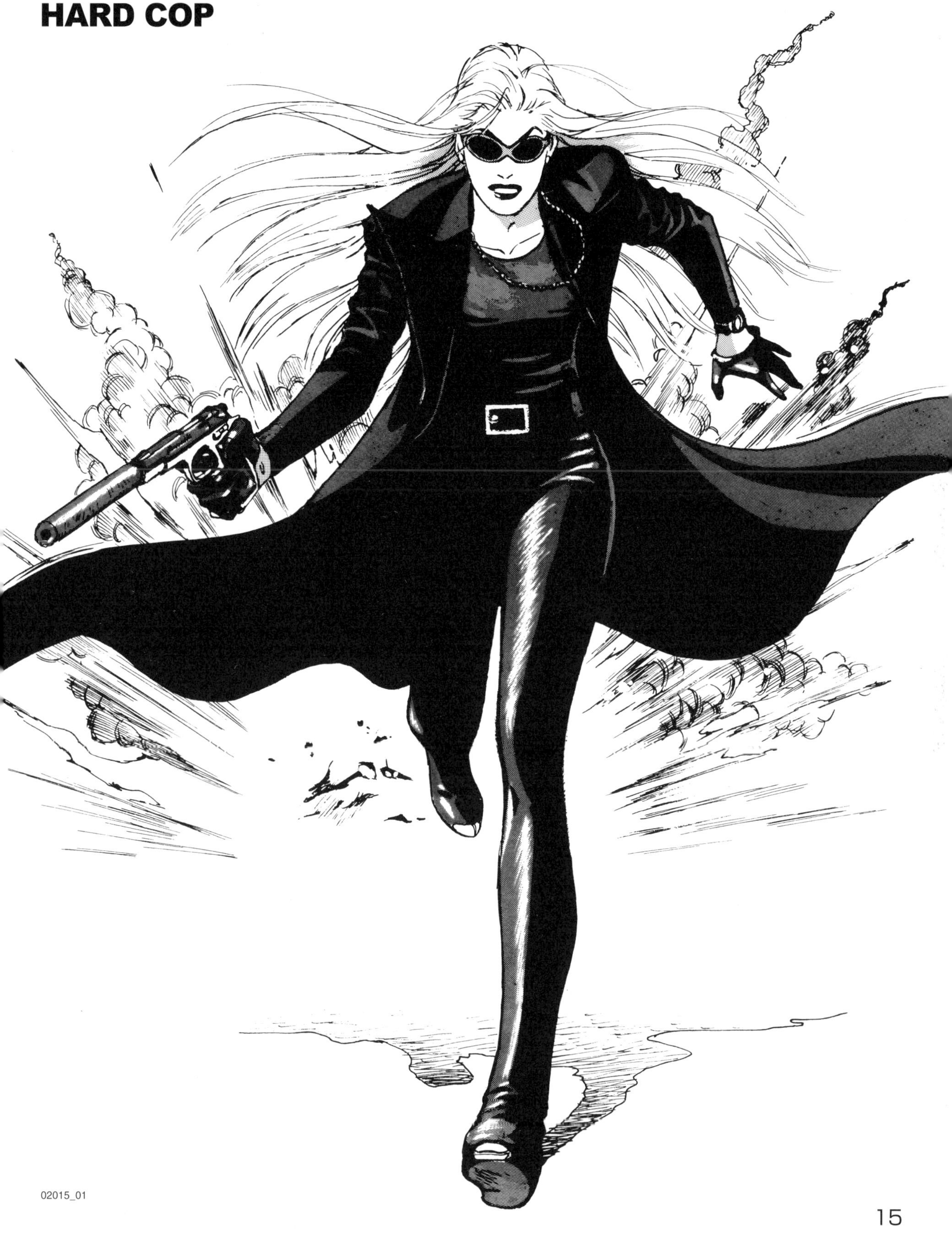

02015_01

SF HARD
SFハード

スターウォーズのようなサイエンス・フィクションのヒロインの制作。年齢は18歳くらいの設定。ある秘められた能力の持ち主で、人類を救う鍵となる。自ら戦闘服を着て指揮を執るリーダーシップも持ち合わせている。未来版ジャンヌ・ダルク。

I made a heroinefor a science fiction like Star Wars. She is about 18 years old. She is a hidden ability which enables her to save mankind. She wears a combat uniform.

1 one
18歳という年齢に気を配ろう。
チャーミングでありながら気丈なイメージを。
Pay attention to her age. She is 18 years old.
She has a charming but fearless image.

02016_01

02016_02

少し平凡で輝きがない。
It is somewhat common and there is no brightness.

少しつり上がった目でセクシーさを強調。こちらに決定。
Sexiness is emphasized by her eyes lifted up a little. I chose this one.

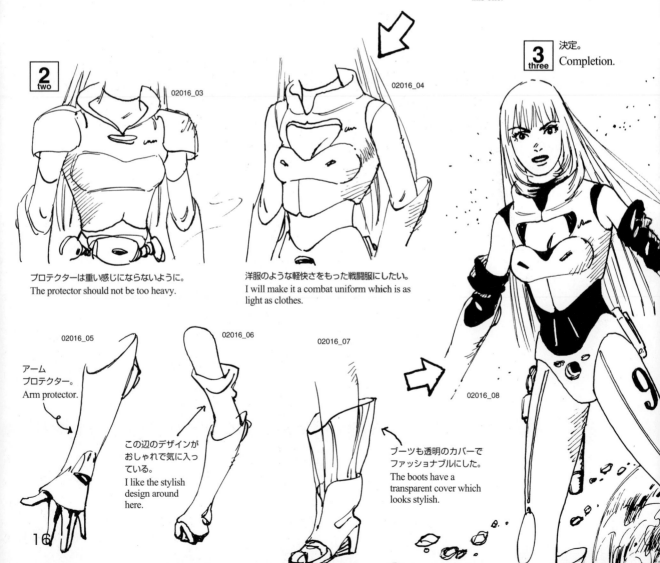

2 two
02016_03

プロテクターは重い感じにならないように。
The protector should not be too heavy.

02016_04

洋服のような軽快さをもった戦闘服にしたい。
I will make it a combat uniform which is as light as clothes.

3 three
決定。
Completion.

02016_05

アームプロテクター。
Arm protector.

02016_06

この辺のデザインがおしゃれで気に入っている。
I like the stylish design around here.

02016_07

ブーツも透明のカバーでファッショナブルにした。
The boots have a transparent cover which looks stylish.

02016_08

Sci-Fi HARD

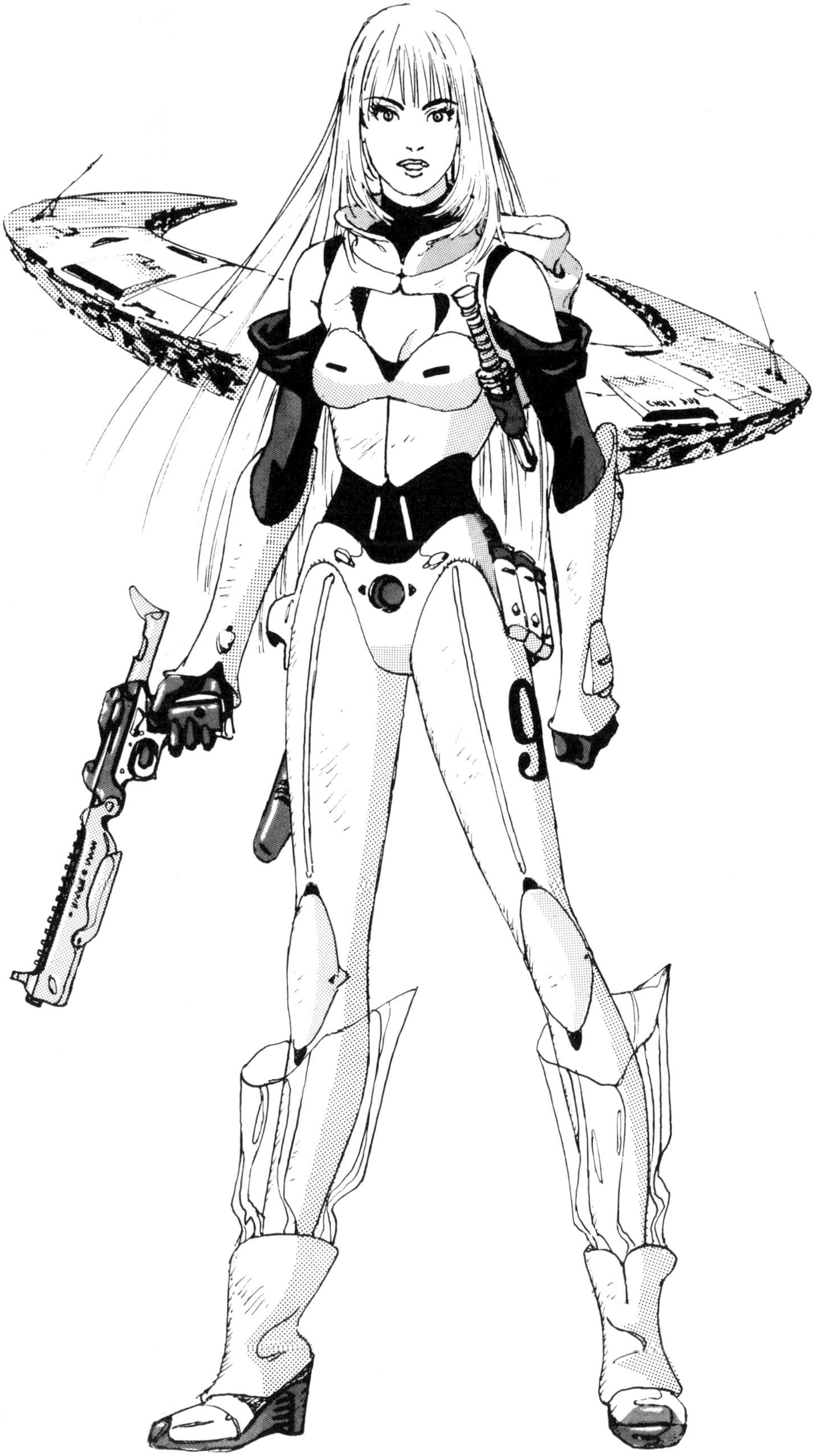

02017_01

■制作テーマ■

PAPILLON

怪盗パピヨン

女性版怪盗ルパン。女の「怪盗パピヨン」とでも名付けようか。セクシーでかっこいいキャラクターを制作する。

A female version Lupin. Let's call her "Thief Papillon". A sexy and smart character is made.

1 one

怪盗パピヨン。ゴージャスな雰囲気が欲しい。マスクをつけようと考えている。個性的な特徴になりそうだ。

I want her to be gorgeous. I am thinking about giving her a mask. It will most likely become her distinctive feature.

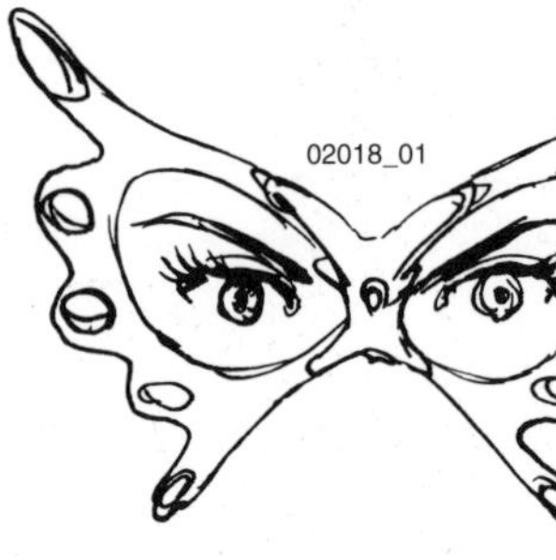

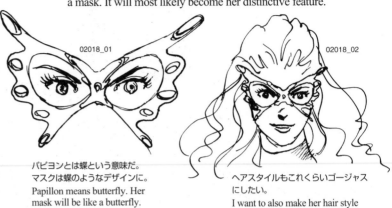

02018_01

パピヨンとは蝶という意味だ。マスクは蝶のようなデザインに。

Papillon means butterfly. Her mask will be like a butterfly.

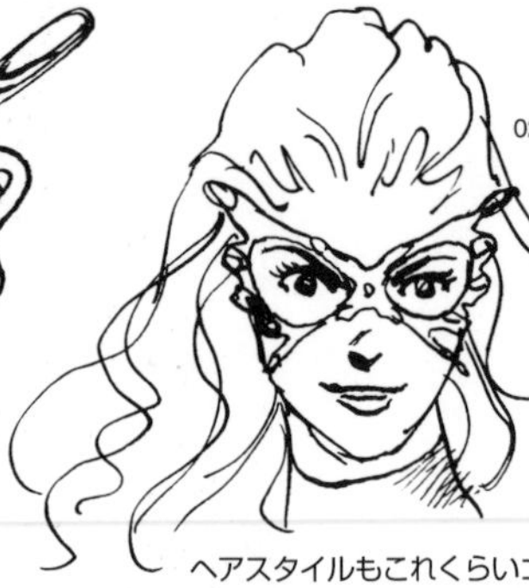

02018_02

ヘアスタイルもこれくらいゴージャスにしたい。

I want to also make her hair style as gorgeous as this.

2 two

問題はコスチュームだ。セクシーでパンチのあるコスチュームにしたい。

The problem is her costume. I want her costume to be sexy but to have punch.

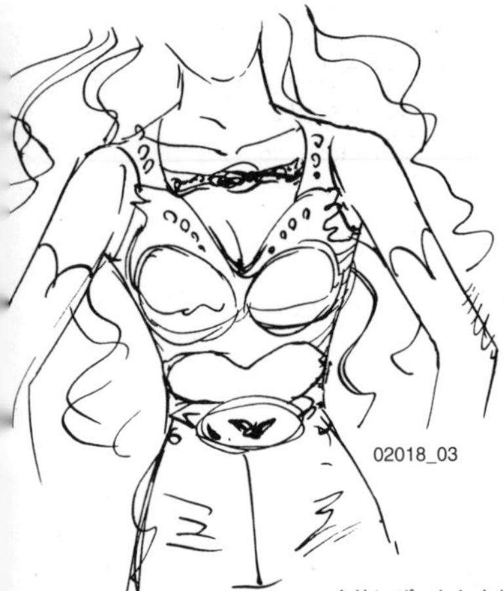

02018_03

金属的な装飾を部分的に入れる。

Add metal ornaments in some parts.

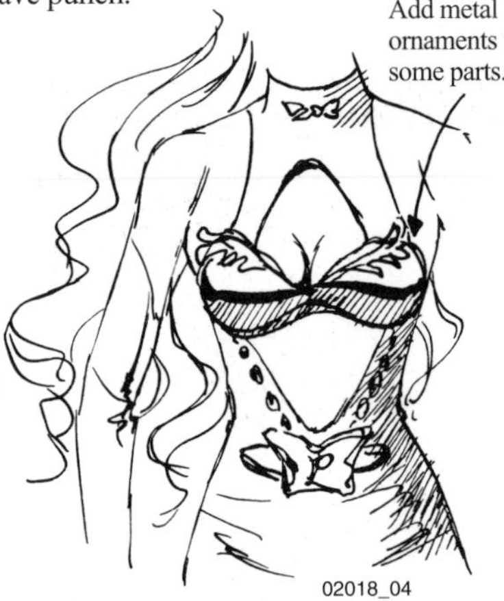

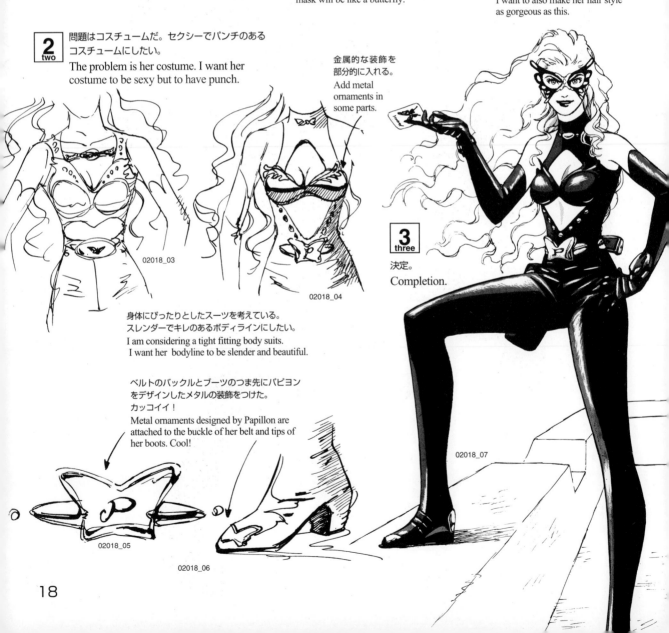

02018_04

身体にぴったりとしたスーツを考えている。スレンダーでキレのあるボディラインにしたい。

I am considering a tight fitting body suits. I want her bodyline to be slender and beautiful.

ベルトのバックルとブーツのつま先にパピヨンをデザインしたメタルの装飾をつけた。カッコイイ！

Metal ornaments designed by Papillon are attached to the buckle of her belt and tips of her boots. Cool!

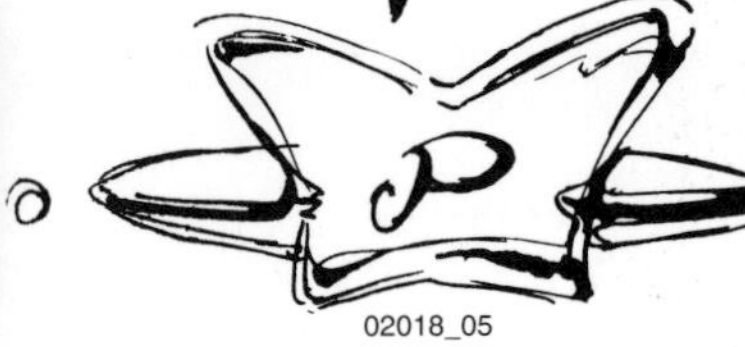

02018_05

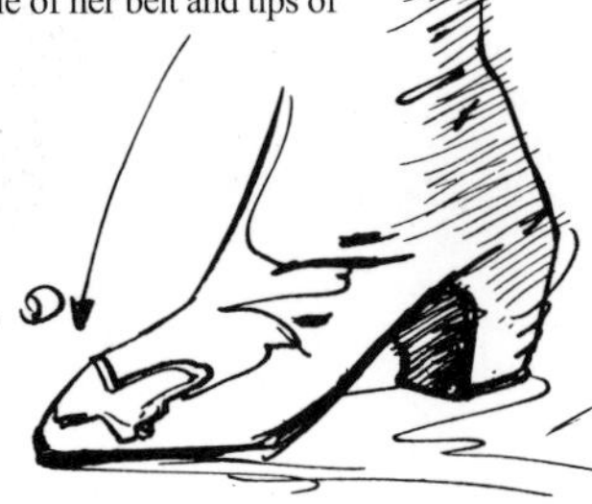

02018_06

3 three

決定。

Completion.

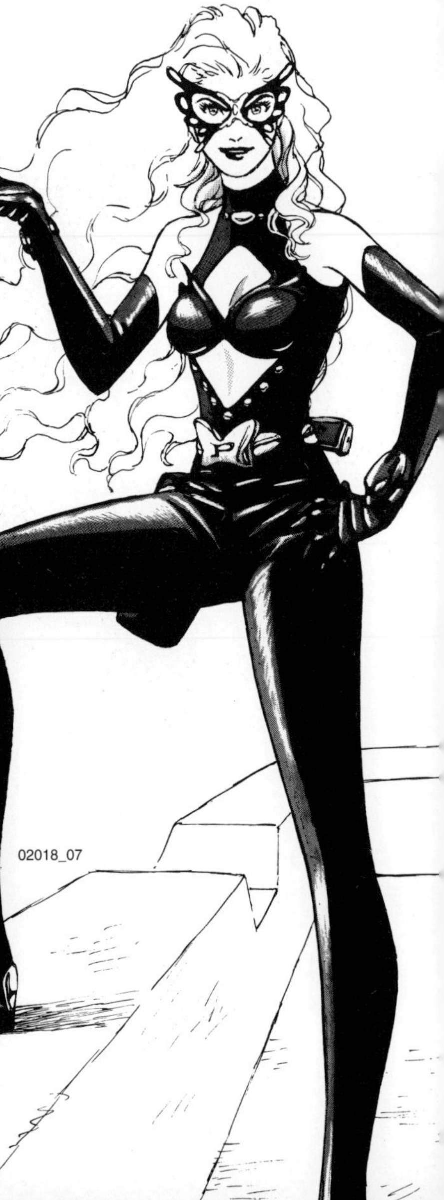

02018_07

PAPILLON

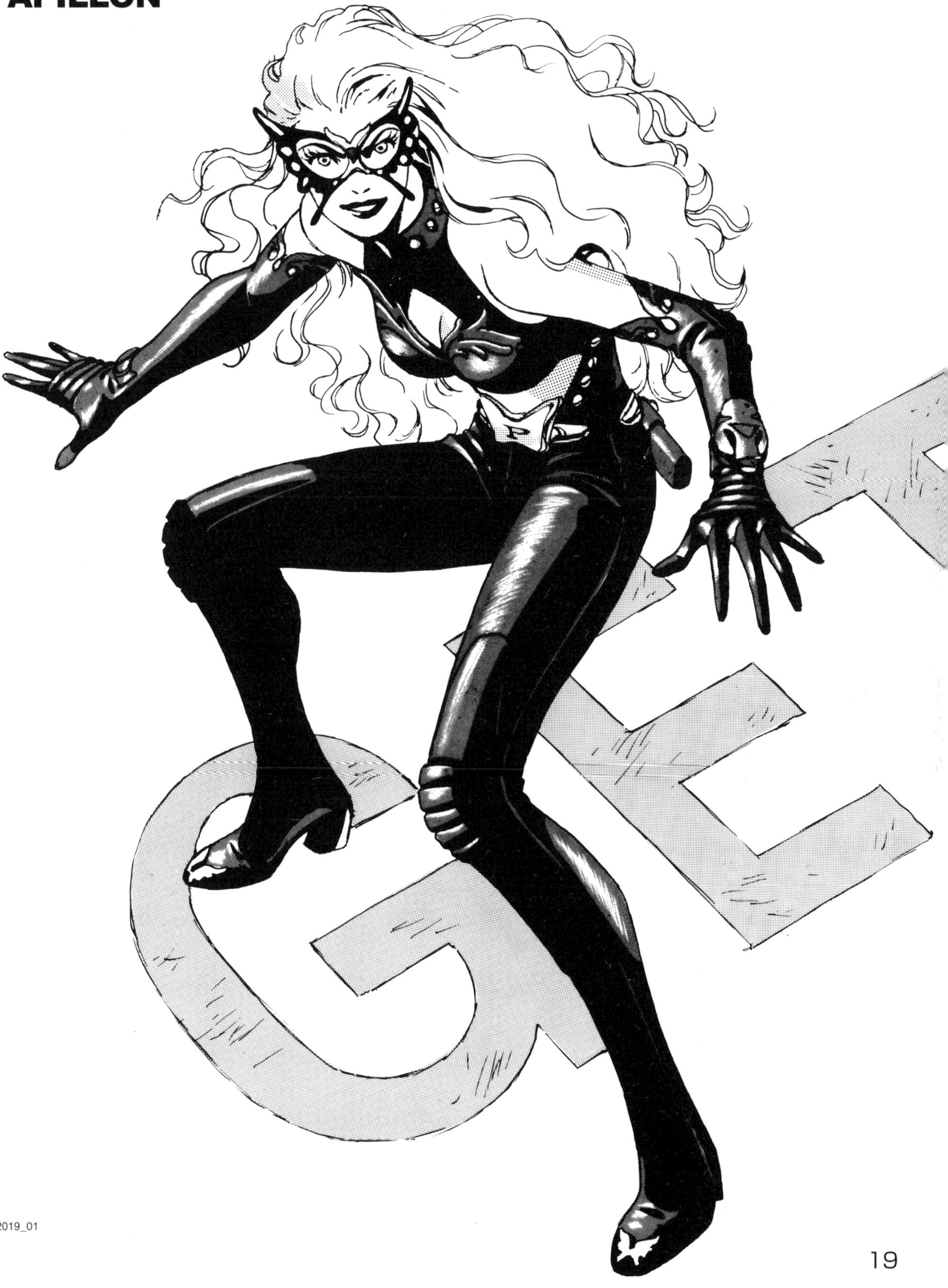

02019_01

■制作テーマ■

WILD GIRL

ワイルド・ガール

近未来、滅亡した地球で生きながらえた数少ない人類とエイリアンとの戦いの物語。主人公は一匹狼でエイリアンと戦っていくヒロインだ。ロケーションは荒野が舞台となるが、地下都市もある。

This is a tale set in the near future of a war between aliens and the remaining survivors after earth was destroyed. The heroine is a lone wolf who fights the aliens. Although this is set in the wilderness there is also an underground city.

1 one

ワイルドというと男っぽいキャラクターを考えがちなので、顔はセクシーにしてみた。

When you think of a wild person, you tend to imagine a manlike character, so I made her sexy.

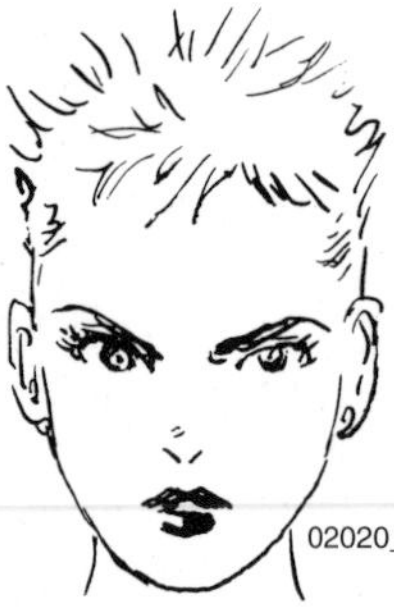

02020_01

こちらのタイプもいいが。

This type is also good.

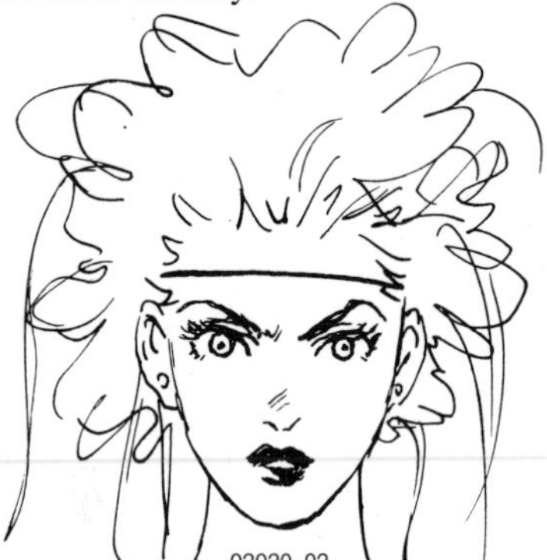

02020_02

マリリンモンローのイメージがコンセプトとなった。

I used Marilyn Monroe's image as my concept.

2 two

ジャケットも考えたが女性を強調してタンクトップ姿をベースにした。

I considered a jacket but based on a tank top to emphasize the woman.

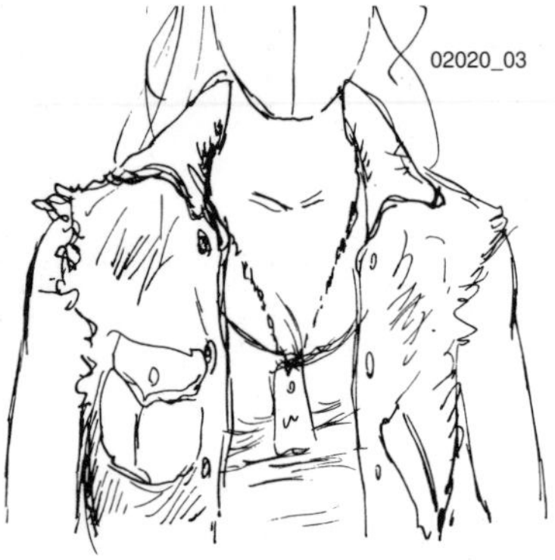

02020_03

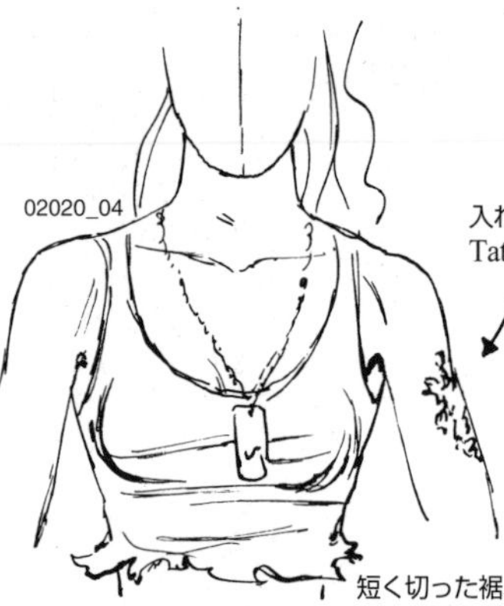

02020_04

入れ墨。
Tatoo.

短く切った裾。
The shirt is cut short.

パンツはぶかぶかのワークパンツ風に。

Trousers are baggy work trousers.

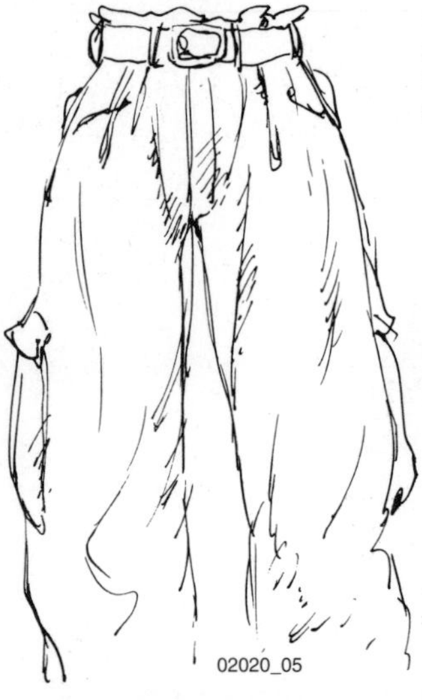

02020_05

男性用のアーミーパンツを見つけてはいているという設定。物質不足の世界を表現している。

She finds some men's army pants and wears them. It shows a world where material things are insufficient.

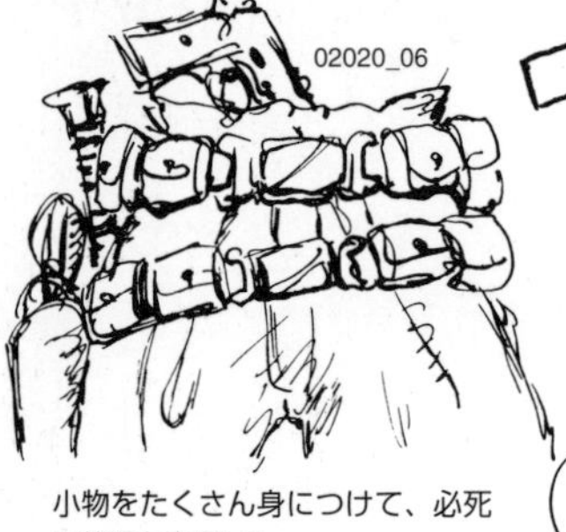

02020_06

小物をたくさん身につけて、必死な状況を表現した。

Many accessories are attached to the body to show how desperate the situation is.

3 three

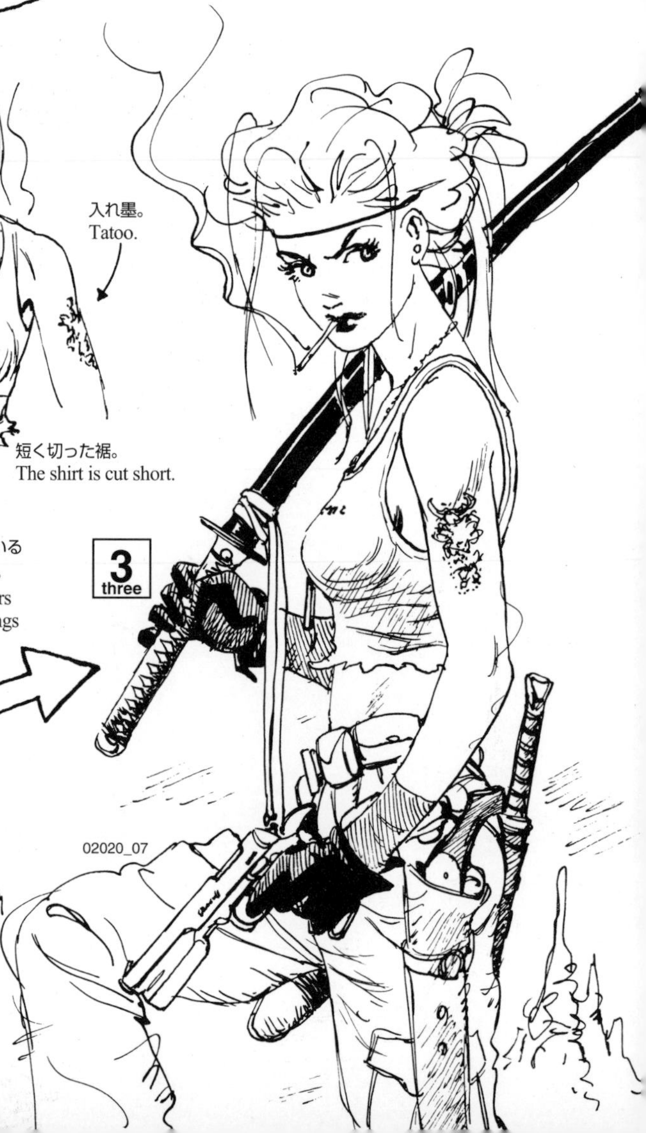

02020_07

WILD GIRL

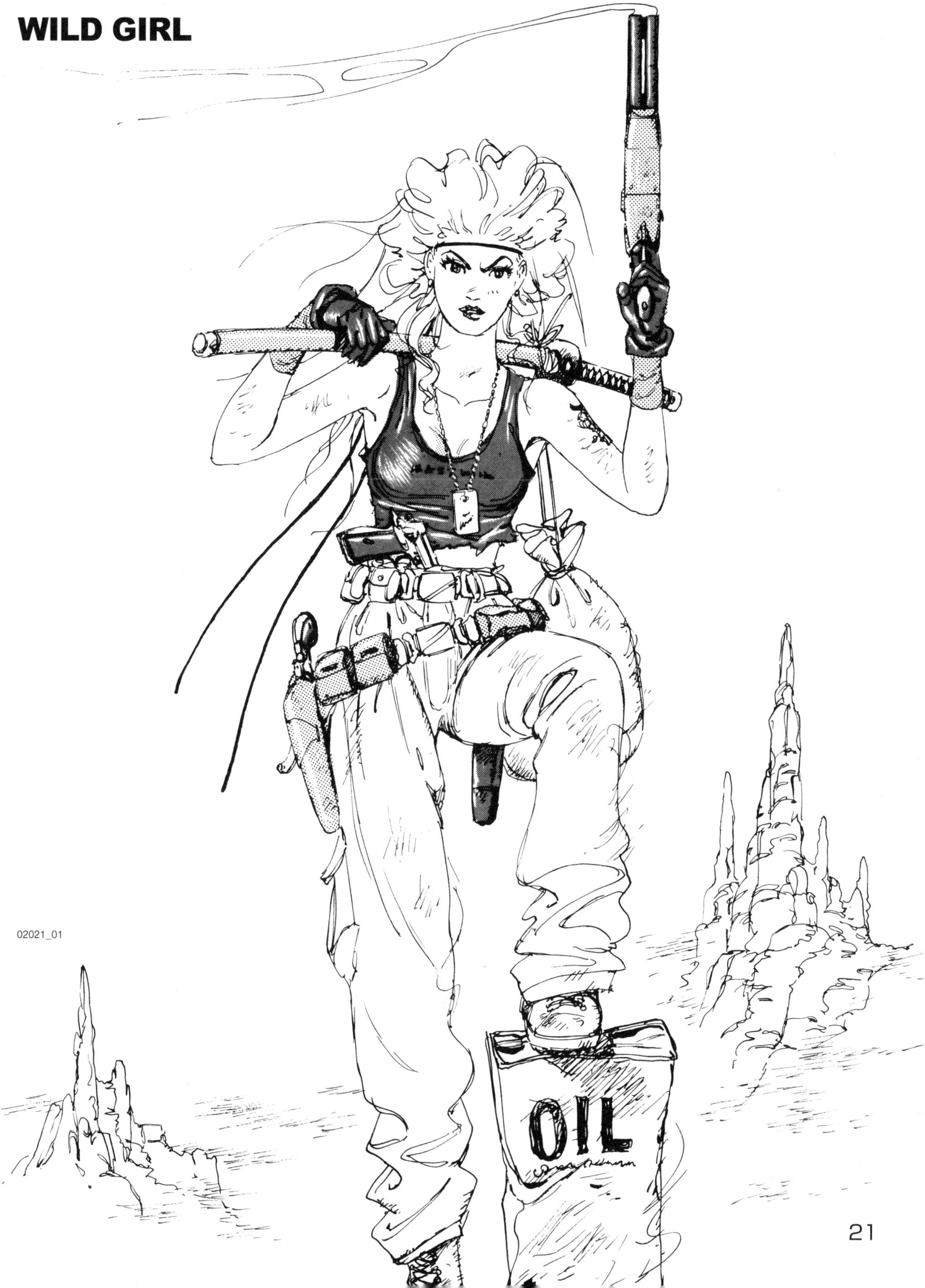
OIL

02021_01

■制作テーマ■

STREET GANG

ストリート・ギャング

マフィアのような巨大組織を嫌っている。少人数で活動することもあるが、基本的にはどこにも属していない一匹狼という設定。

She detests big oaganizations such as the mafia. She is a lone wolf who fundamentally doesn't belong to any particular gang but she does team up with small gangs sometimes.

1 one

顔は意志の強い性格が表れた表情にしたい。

I want to create a face which shows her strong willed personality.

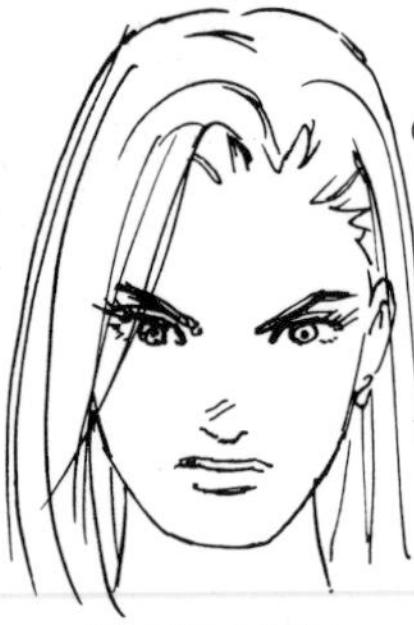

02022_01

少し正統派すぎる。

This ia too legitimate.

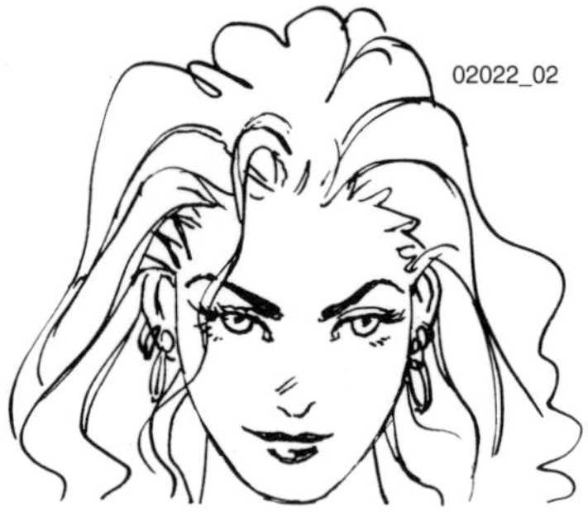

02022_02

ゴージャスなヘアスタイルのこちらの顔に決定。アクセサリーも少し派手目にしてみた。

I decided to go with this face and this gorgeous hair. Her accessories are flashy.

2 two

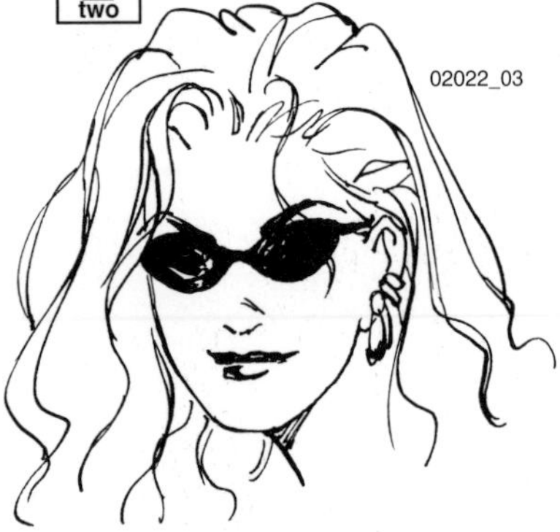

02022_03

サングラスでは平凡すぎる。

Sunglasses are too common.

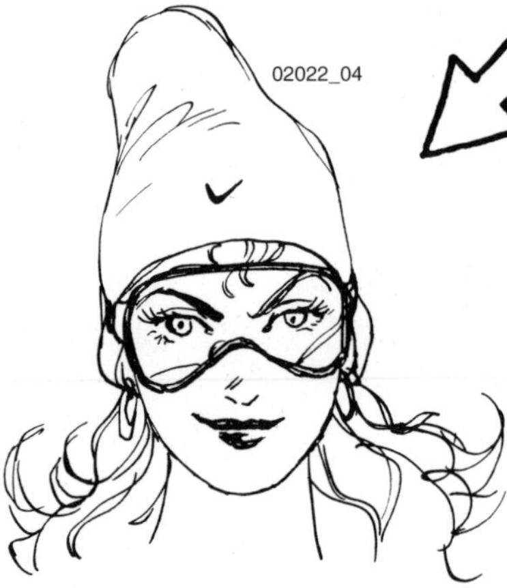

02022_04

何枚も描いているうちにキャップとゴーグルの組み合わせに決めた。鼻にピアスをするのもいい。

While drawing many sketches I decided on the conbination of a cap and goggles. A pierced earing in her nose would also be good.

ストリート系のラインパンツ、タンクトップ、Tシャツを組み合わせた。

I combined a T-shirt, tank top and track pants.

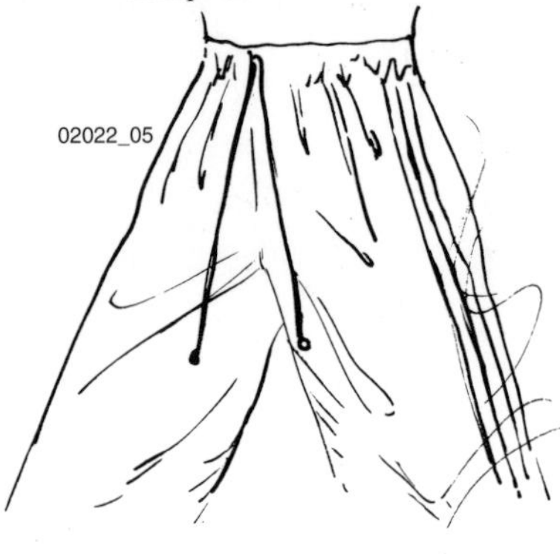

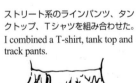

02022_05

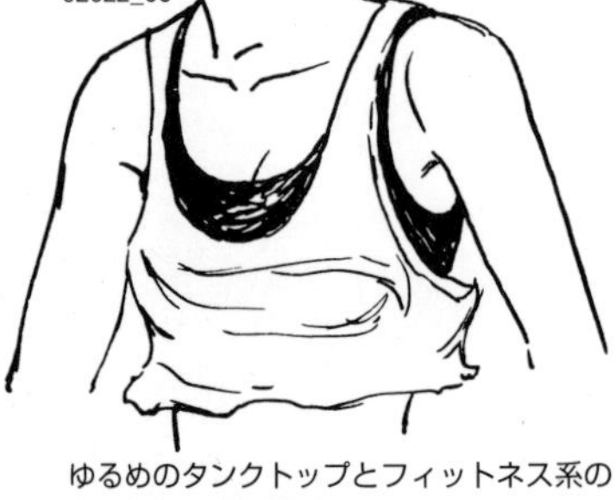

02022_06

ゆるめのタンクトップとフィットネス系のタンクトップを重ねた。

I combined a tight fitted workout tank top with a loose tank top on top.

3 three

決定。

Completion.

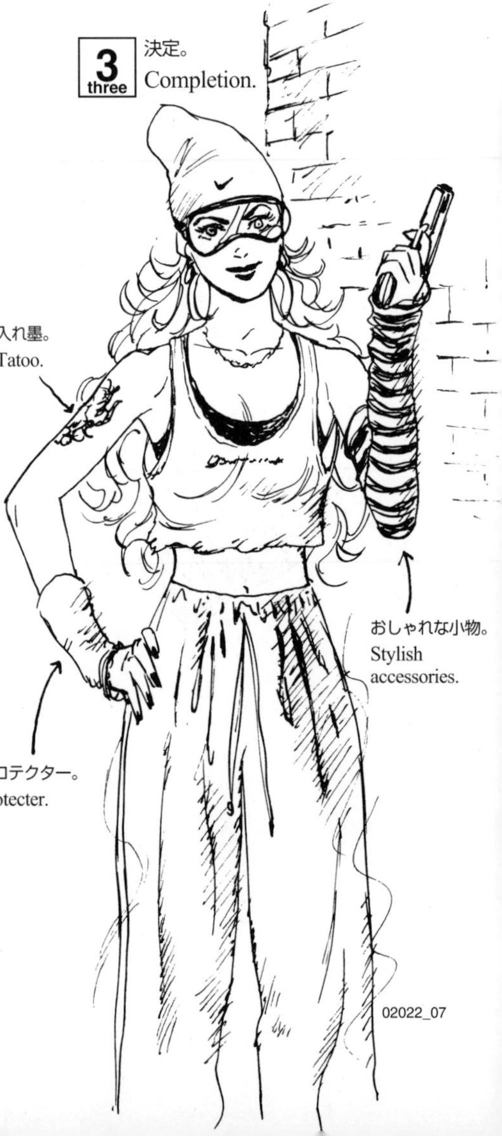
入れ墨。
Tatoo.
プロテクター。
Protecter.
おしゃれな小物。
Stylish accessories.

02022_07

STREET GANG

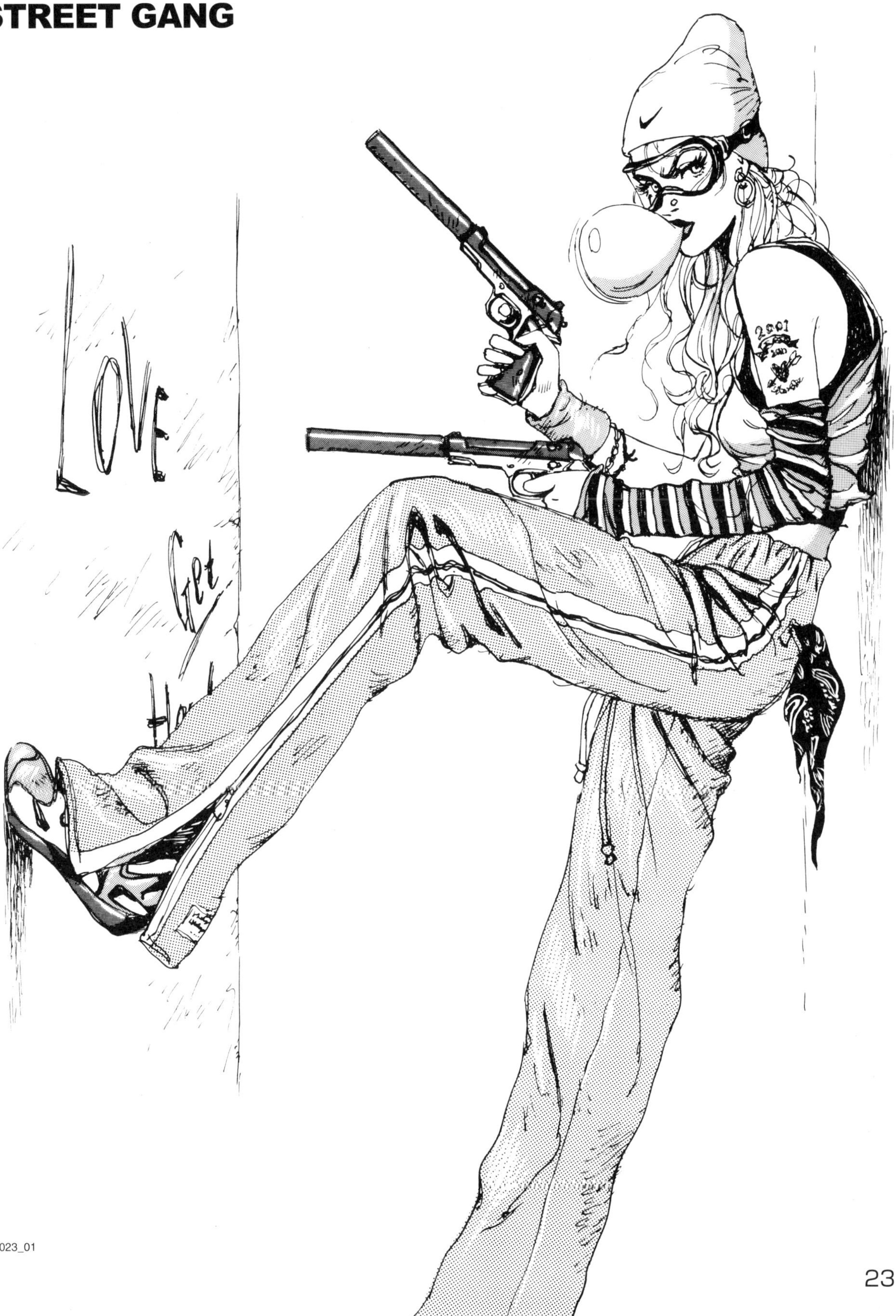

LOVE
Get

02023_01

■制作テーマ■

LOVELY GIRL

ラブリー・ガール

SFストーリー。タイムトラベルが自由にできる時代。宇宙にある中継駅でBARでもある一つの空間のヒロインのストーリー。駅長であり店長でもある彼女は尻尾を持っていて、そこに秘められたパワーがある。コスチュームは駅長の姿にしたい。セクシーでおしゃれだけどハードなストーリー。

This SF story is set in a time when time travel is done freely. This is a heroine story set in space on relay station which is also a bar. She is the station master as well as the bar manager. She has a tail which has hidden power. This is a hard story which is sexy and stylish.

1 one

セクシーでおしゃれ。そして駅長らしくという設定にも注意して描いていく。

Sexy and stylish. Be sure to incorporate a stationmaster's image.

02024_01

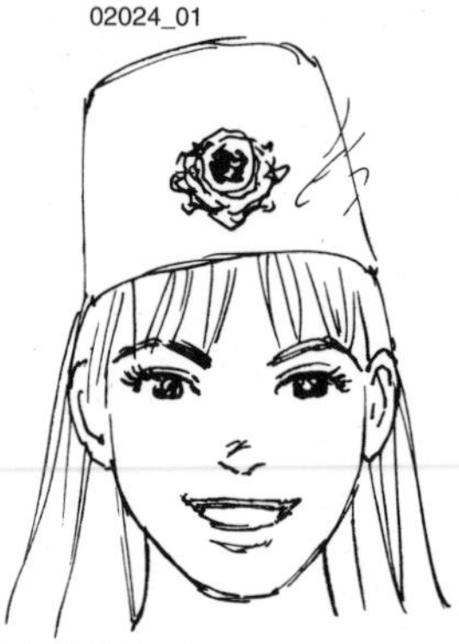

制帽が絵のポイントになりそうだ。

A regulation cap will probably be an element of her image.

02024_02

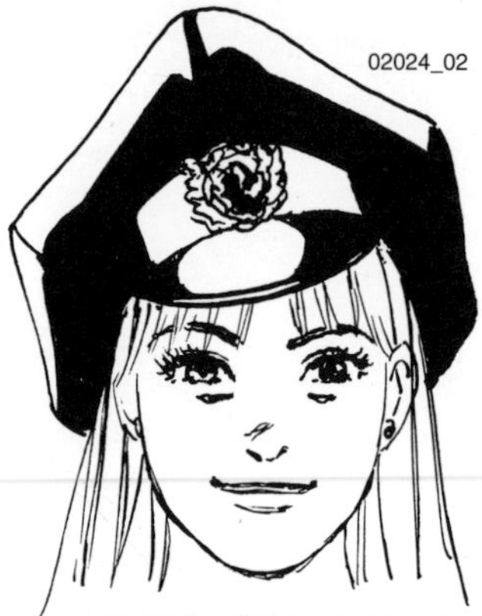

アメリカのポリスのようなスタイルにしてみた。カッコイイ。

I tried an American police cap. Very cool!

2 two

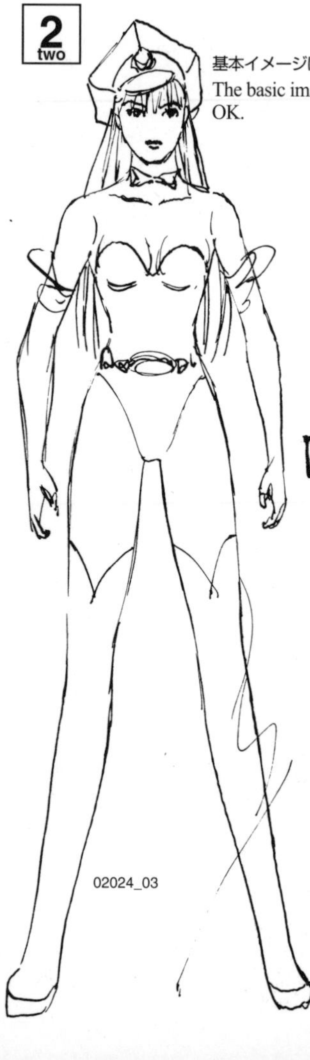

基本イメージはOK。

The basic image is OK.

02024_03

02024_04

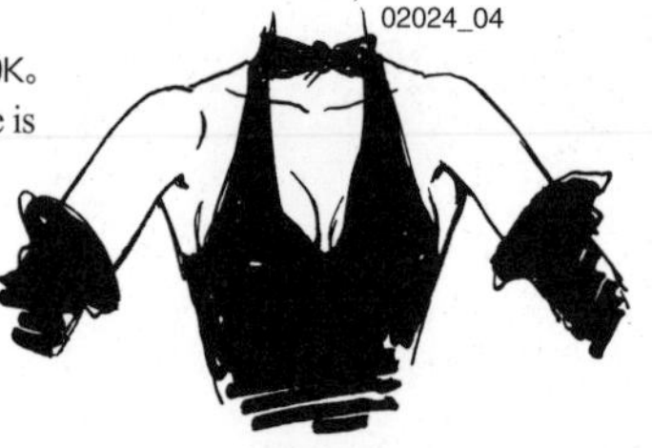

上着もいろいろ描いてみる。数点ラフを重ねた。

Various coats are drawn. I went through several rough sketches.

02024_05

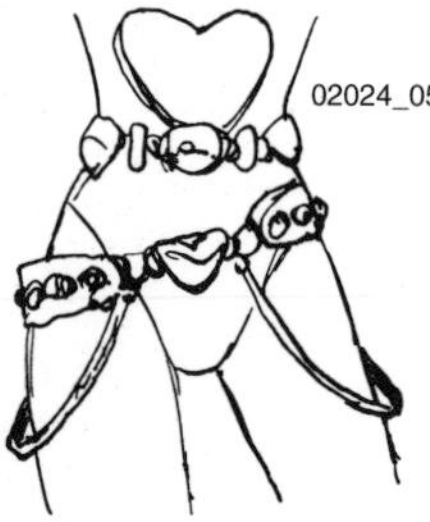

少しハードすぎる。

It is a little too hard.

尻尾はポイントになるのでいろいろ考えた。

Since her tails is an important element, I tried various designs.

02024_06

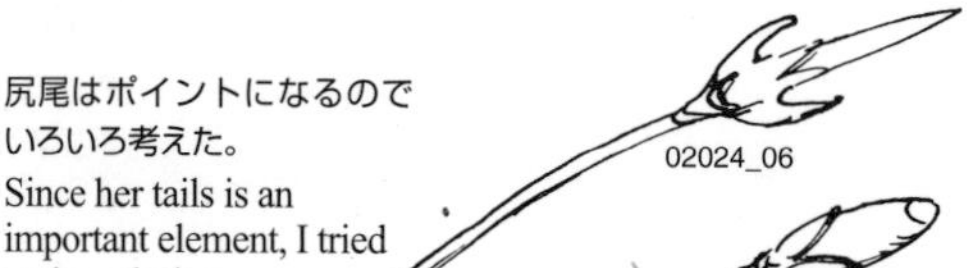

02024_07

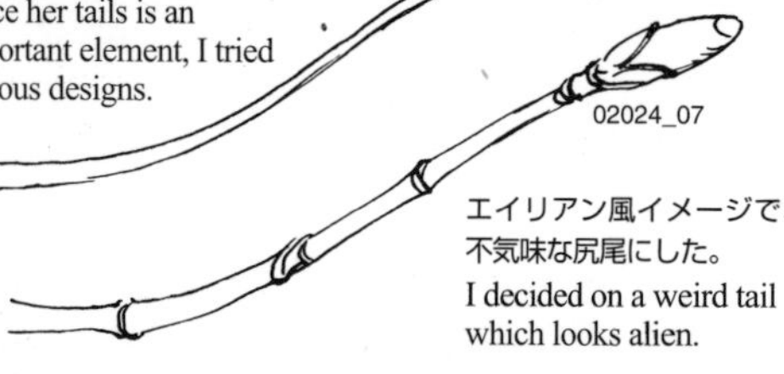

エイリアン風イメージで、不気味な尻尾にした。

I decided on a weird tail which looks alien.

3 three

完成。

Complete.

02024_08

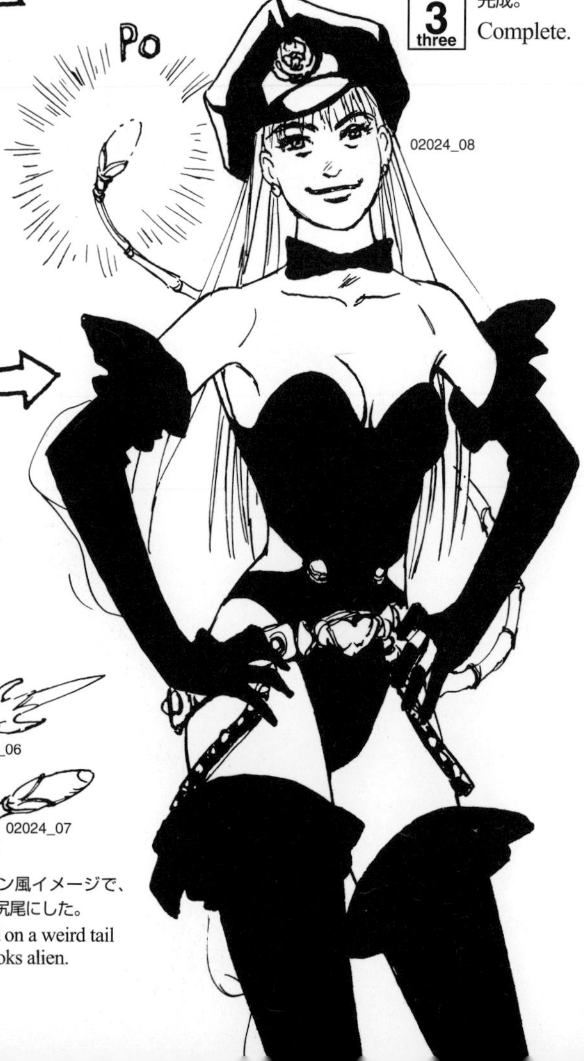
Po

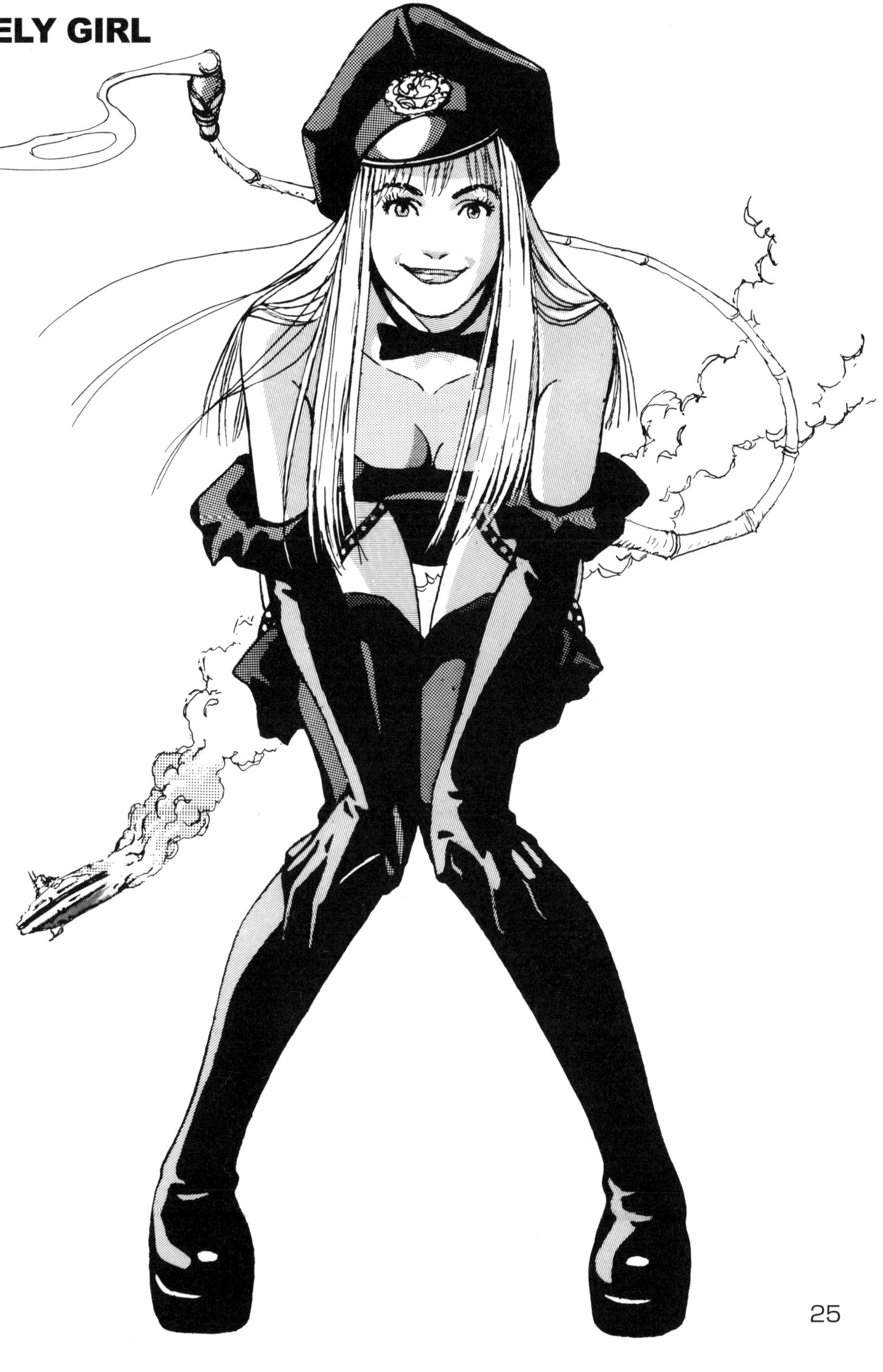

02025_01

■制作テーマ■

FANTASY

ファンタジー

天使のような一人の少女が、マフィアとのトラブルに巻き込まれ、運命的なストーリーが展開されるという物語。時代設定は現代。ヒロインは18歳くらいで純粋な優しい少女。明るく健康的で普通のキャラクターでOK。

This is a fateful story about an angel-like girl who gets into trouble with the mafia. It is set in the present day. The heroine is a gentle innocent girl about 18 years old. It's OK to create on ordinary, bright and healthy girl.

1 one

普通の女子高生をイメージ。明るく健康的な少女。

I amgined an ordinary, bright and healthy high school girl.

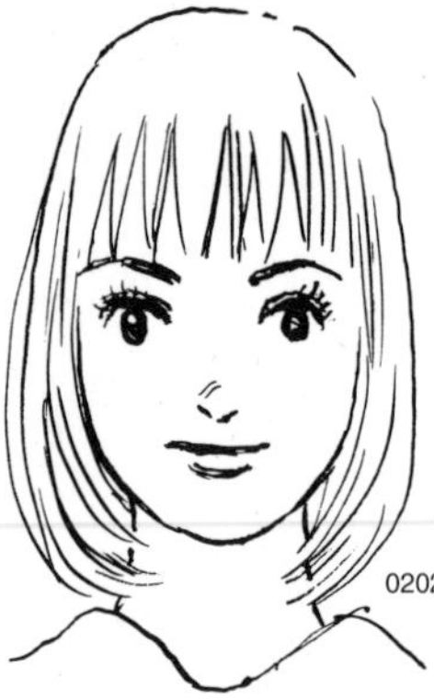

02026_01

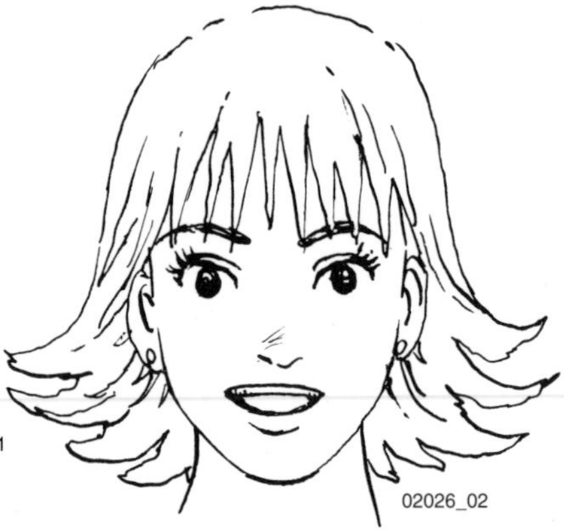

02026_02

少しお嬢様すぎた。

This image is too young.

目は優しいイメージに。あまり化粧っ気が感じられないようにした。こちらで決定。

Her eyes are gentle and she doesn't wear much make-up. I chose this one.

2 two

コスチュームは日常的な18歳の少女のファッションにした。

She wears everyday 18 year old clothes.

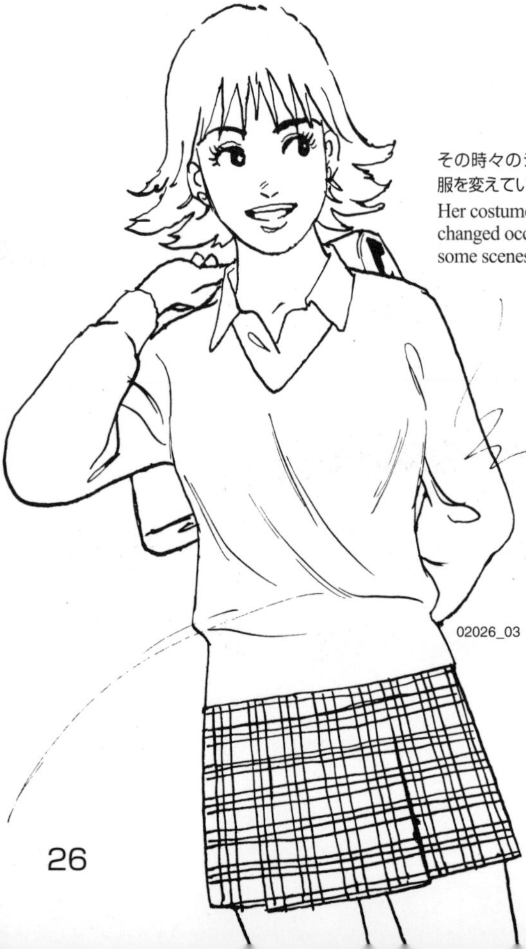

02026_03

その時々のシーンによって服を変えていくことにする。

Her costume will be changed occationally for some scenes.

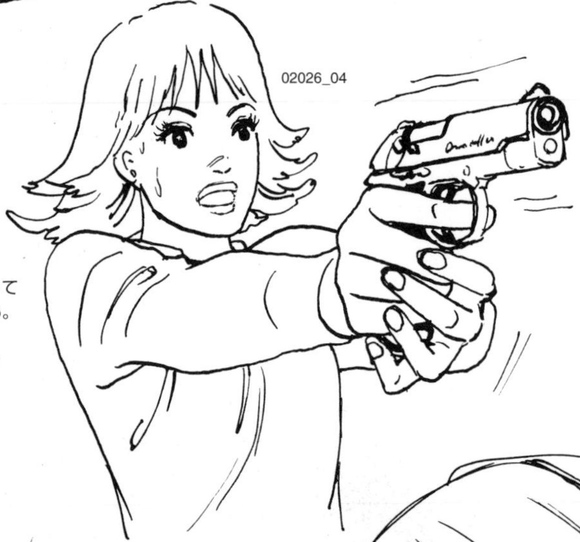

02026_04

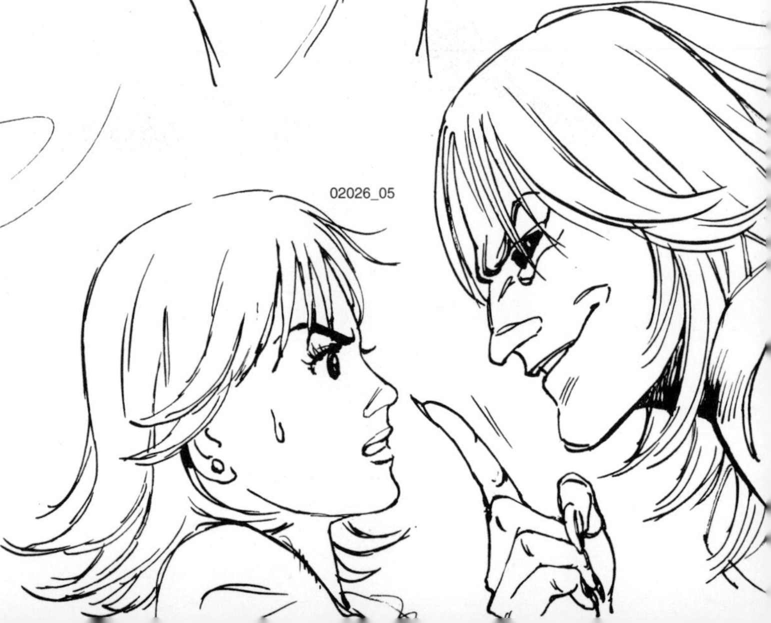

02026_05

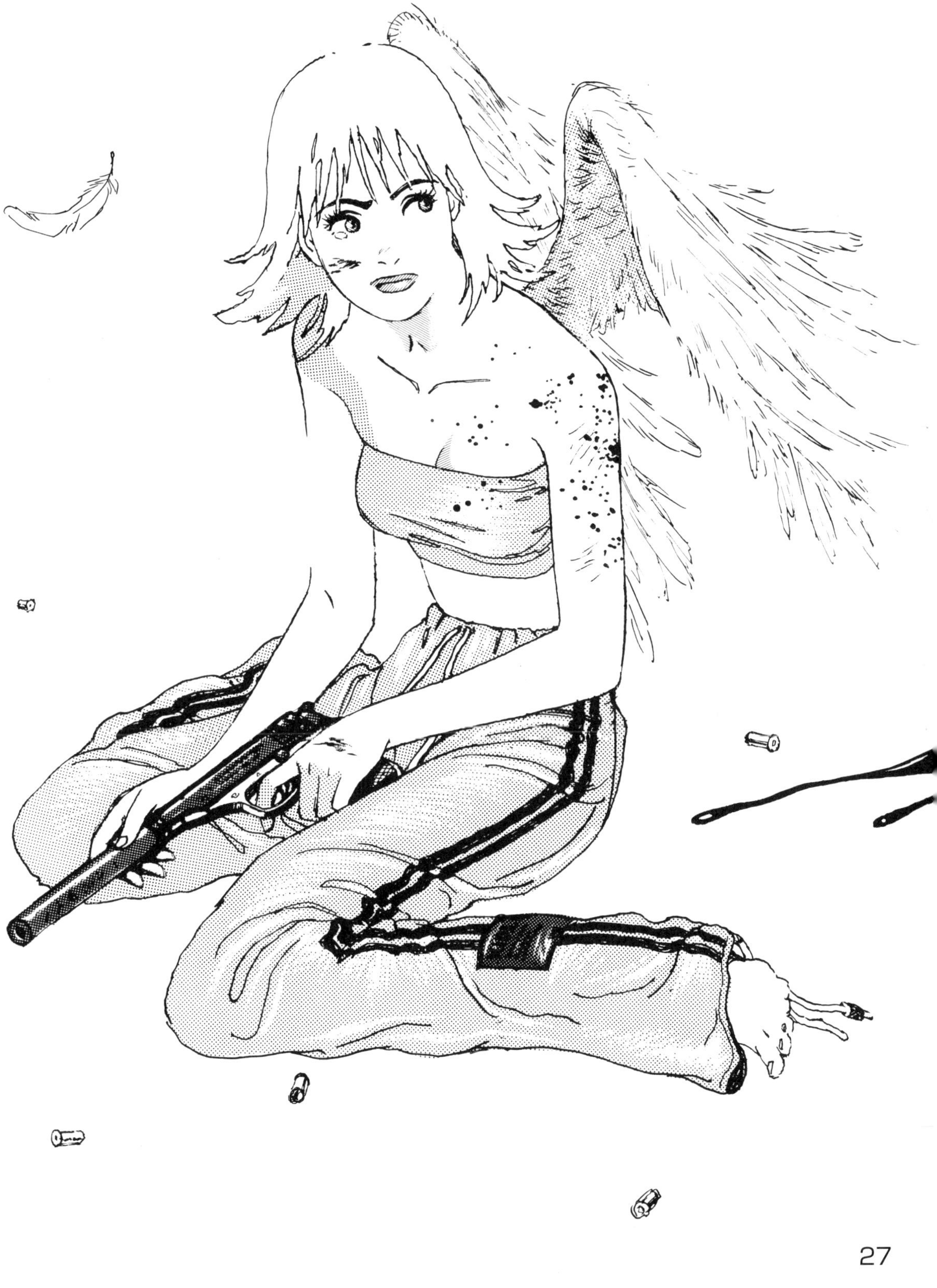

02027_01

■制作テーマ■

SEALA THE WITCH

魔女シーラ

その名前の通り魔女である。とはいっても、鼻の曲がった年寄りの魔女ではなく、若く美しい魔女である。ワイルドな雰囲気を持ったセクシーな魔女を制作する。

As the title suggests, she is a witch. She is not an old witch with a bent nose. She is a young and beautiful witch. She is wild but sexy.

1 one

ワイルドでセクシーな魔女がメインテーマだ。ヘアースタイルがかなり大切なポイントになるだろう。

The main theme is a wild but sexy witch. I think her hairstyle is an important element.

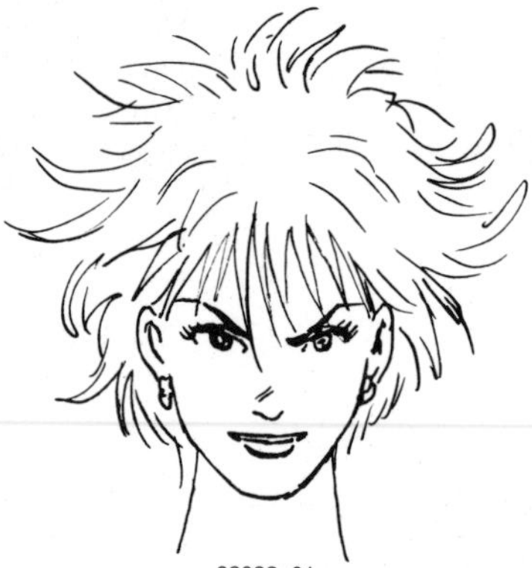

02028_01

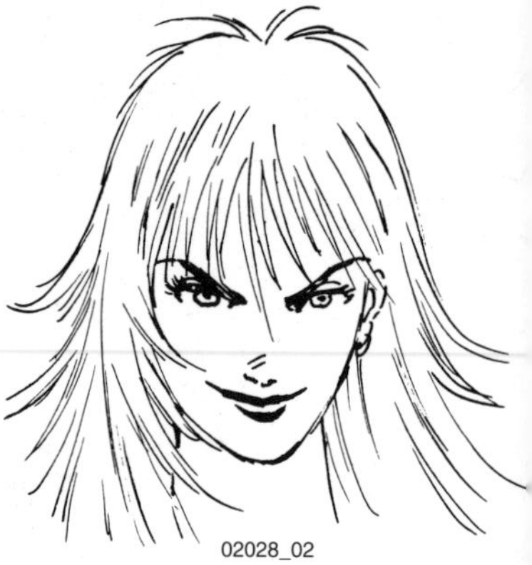

02028_02

2 two

コスチュームを考えてみよう。マントは欲しいところだ。

Let's think about her costume. A mantle is needed.

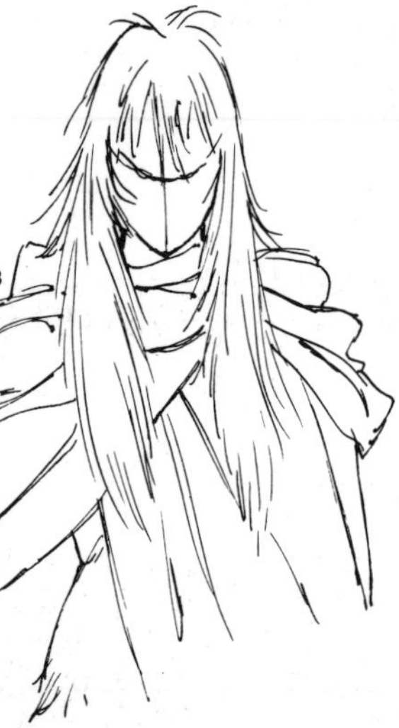

02028_03

シャープなマントだ。
It is a cool mantle.

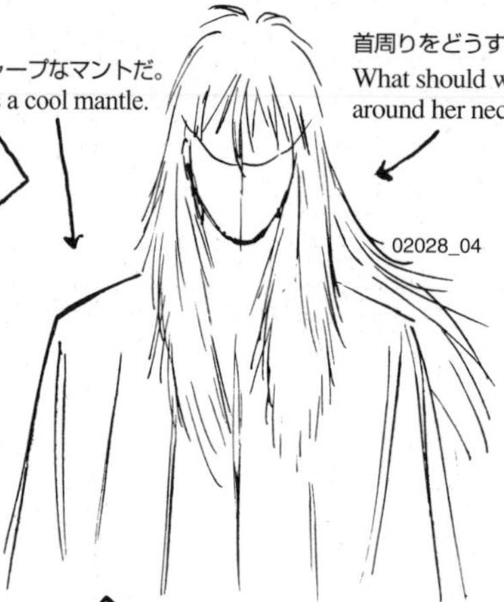

02028_04

首周りをどうするか。
What should we do around her neck.

フードを着けてみる。OK。イメージ通りだ。
I tried a hood. Great! Just how I imagined her.

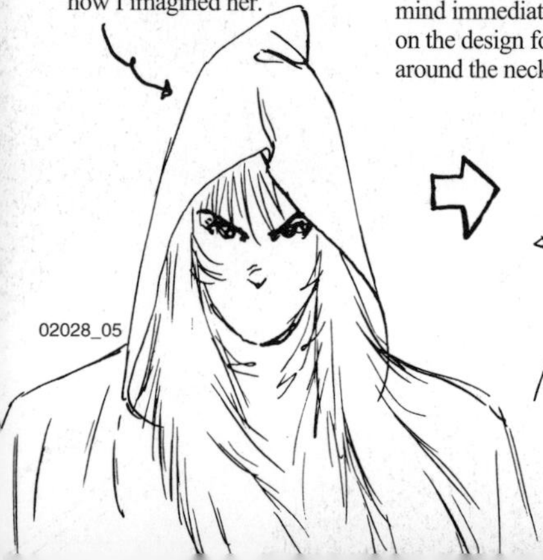

02028_05

すぐトレンチコートが頭に浮かび、肩の部分のデザインが決まった。
The trench coat came into my mind immediately, and I decided on the design for the portion around the neck.

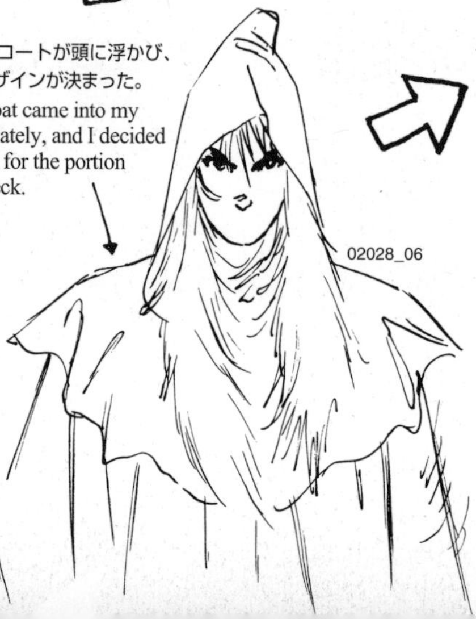

02028_06

3 three

完成。
Complete.

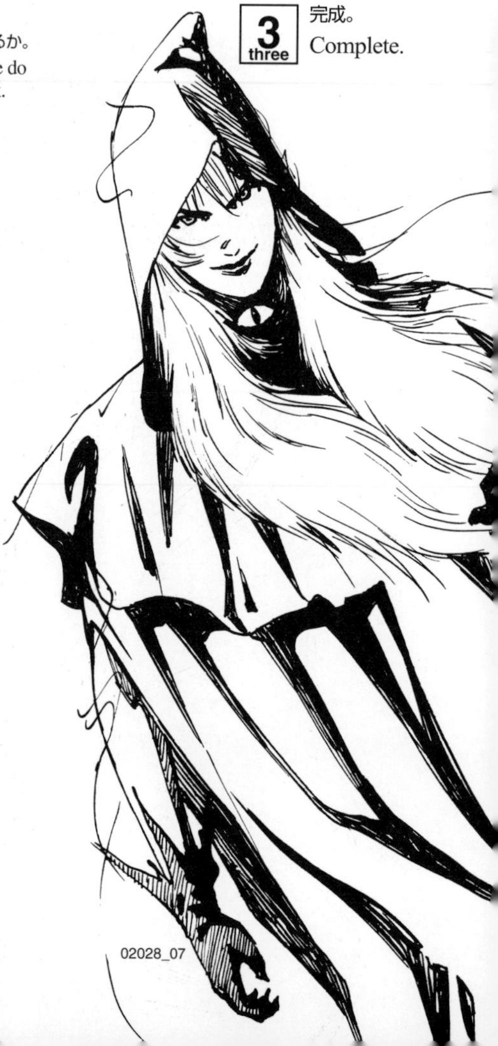

02028_07

SEALA THE WITCH

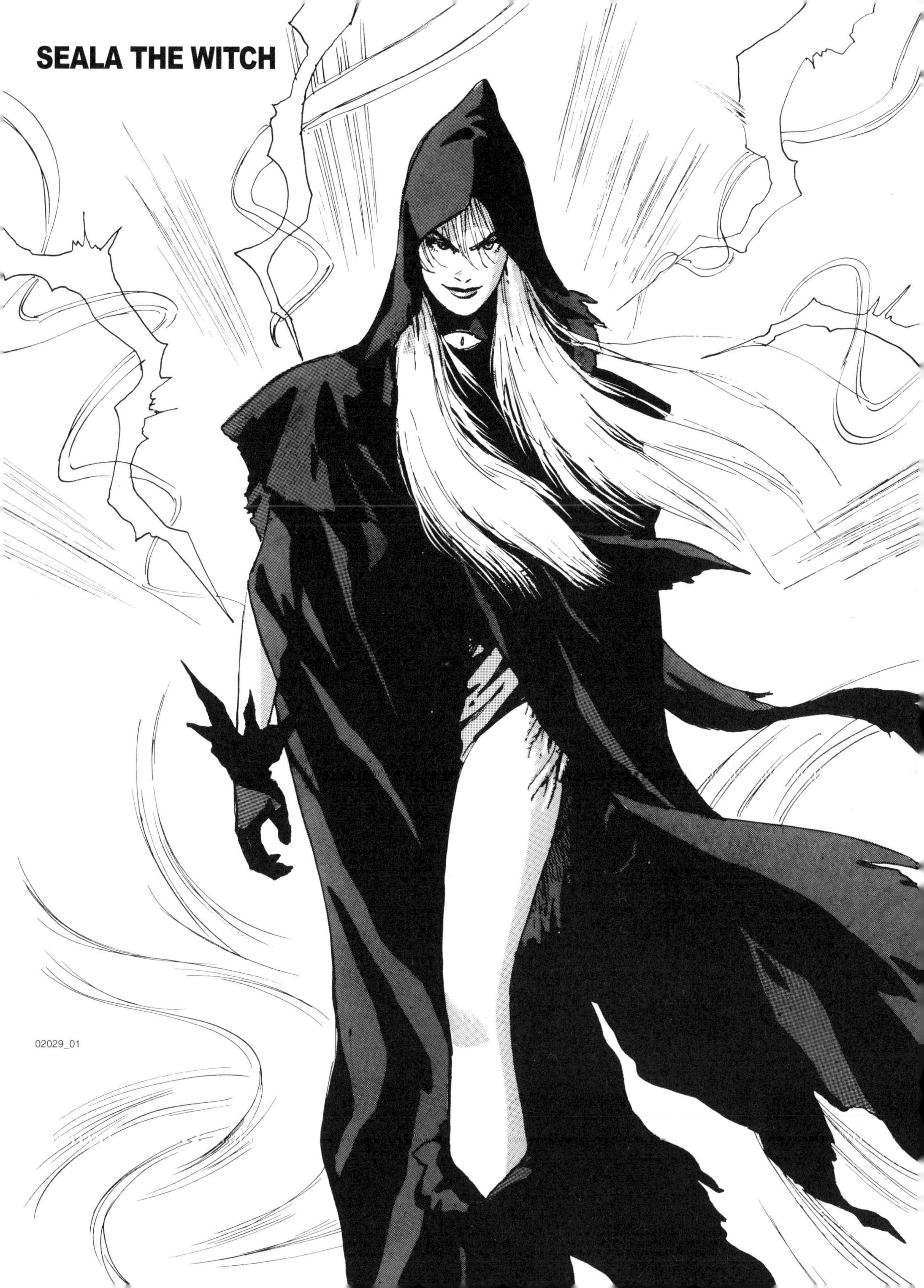

02029_01

ALIEN WOMAN
エイリアン・ウーマン

今回唯一のモンスターだ。ワイルドな女戦士のエイリアンを制作。あくまでもモンスターだが、女性的なイメージも必要。一言で言えば、美しくカッコイイ怪物を制作するということだ。

She is the only monstar in this book. I made a wild alien female fighter. Although she is a monstar, she still needs a feminine image so I have created a beautiful but cool monstar.

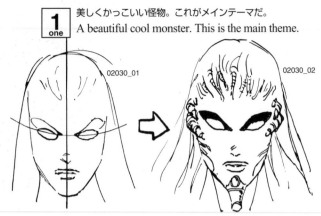

1 one 美しくかっこいい怪物。これがメインテーマだ。
A beautiful cool monster. This is the main theme.

02030_01

02030_02

怪物であるが美しく、そしてセクシーに。
Although she is a monster, she is beautiful and sexy .

不気味さを創造するにもセンスを必要とされる。
You will also need to keep an eeriness to her.

2 two 身体は、全体がカニのような甲羅で覆われている。不気味さの度合いが大切。
Her whole body is covered with a shell like a crab. A degree of eeriness is important.

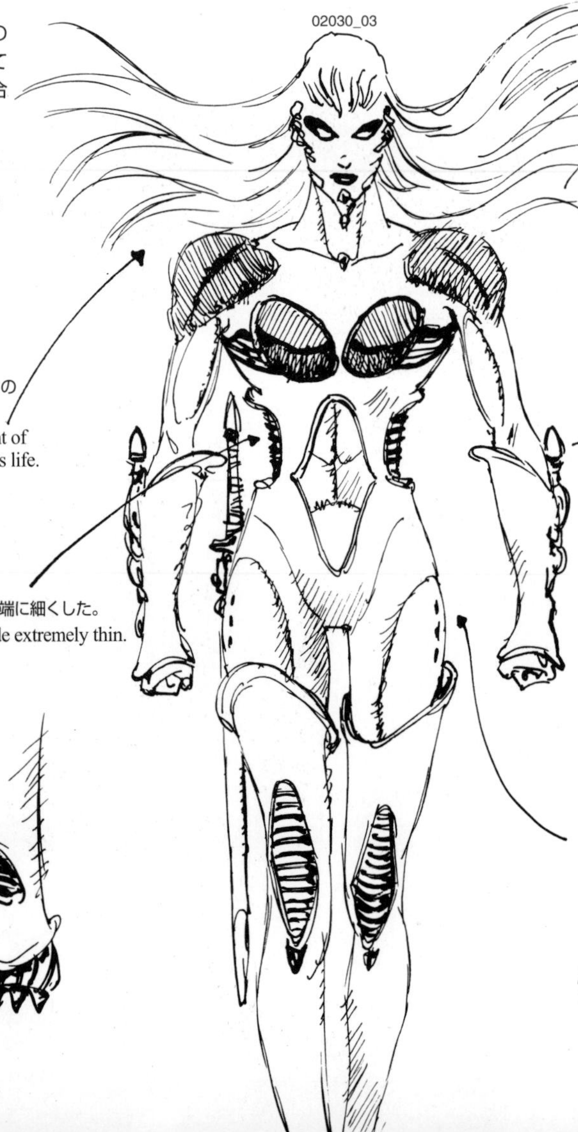

02030_03

このような肩のデザインも考えた。
I considered this design for her shoulders.

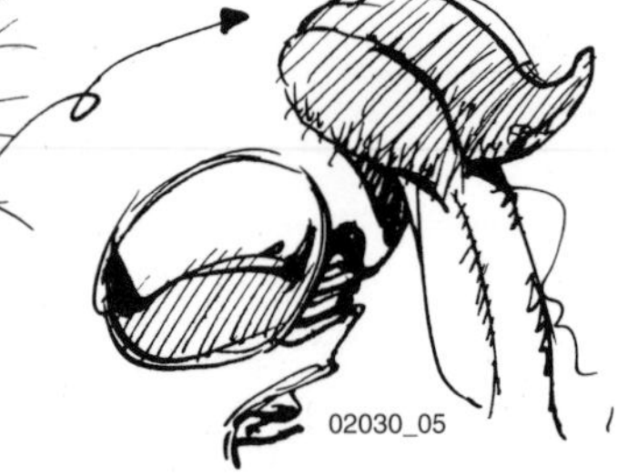

02030_05

長いブロンドの髪が美しさのポイント。髪は女の命？
Long blond hair is a point of beauty. Hair is a woman's life.

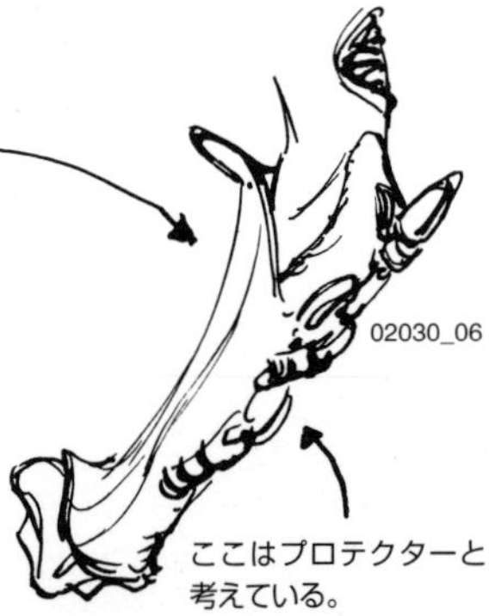

ウエストはあえて極端に細くした。
Her waist was made extremely thin.

02030_06

ここはプロテクターと考えている。
I designed these for her protectors.

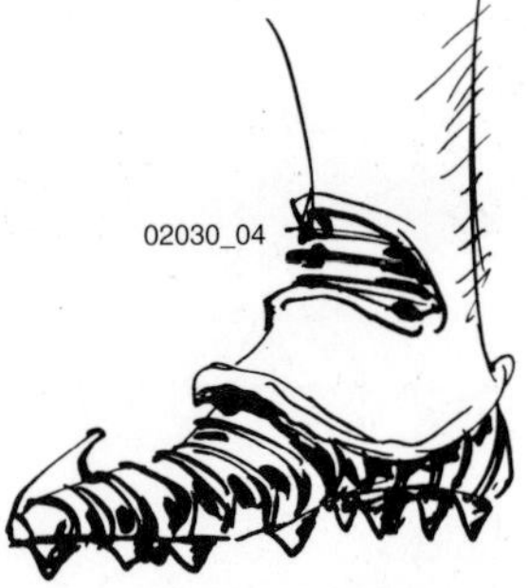

お尻に尻尾をつけて動物のようにした。
I added a tail to her bottom to create the feeling of an animal.

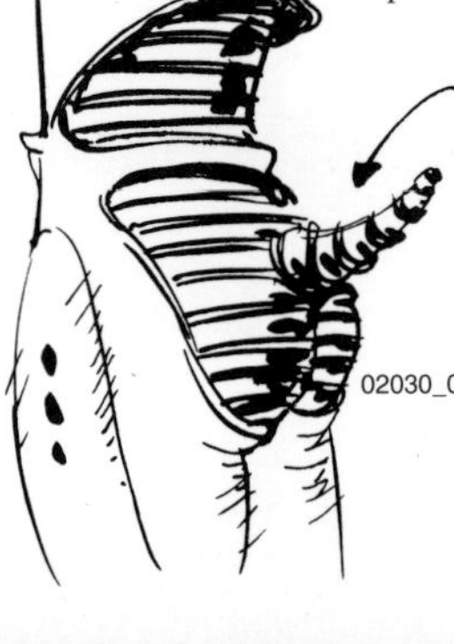

02030_04

02030_07

ALIEN WOMAN

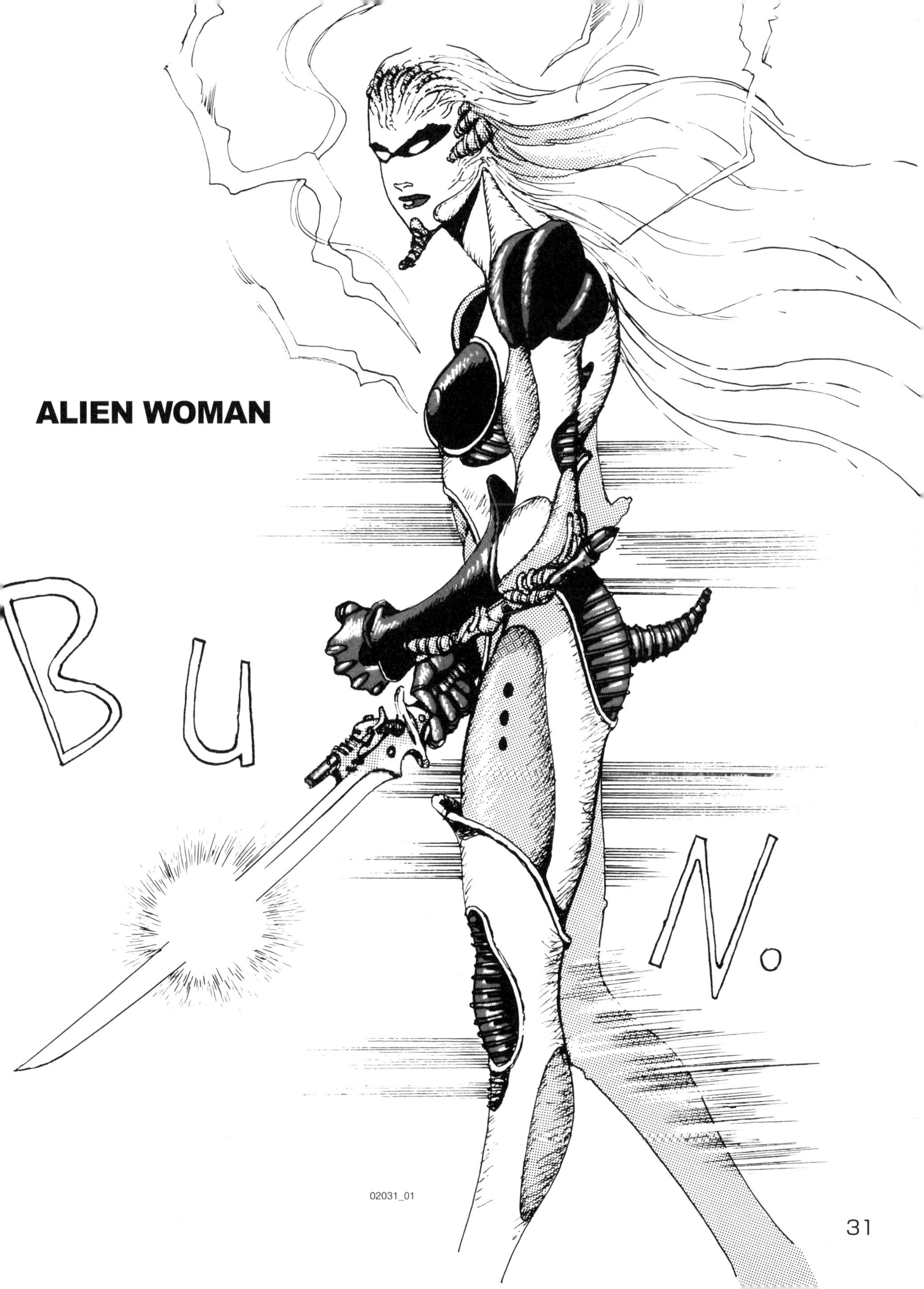
Bu
N.

02031_01

■制作テーマ■

MARIA THE SUPER HEROINE

スーパーヒロイン・マリア

このキャラクターも定番の一つだ。女性版スーパーマンだ。超能力を持ち空を飛ぶSFの主人公である。特にコスチュームは無限に考えられて面白い。マントもつけよう。

This character is one of the stereotype heroines. She is the female version of Superman. she is a SF heroine who flies through the air with supernatural powers. You can have fun designing her costume because there are so many different options. Let's give her a mantle.

1 one 顔はやはり美人でかわいいキャラクターがいい。
She has a cute character and beautiful face.

もうこの一点で決定。健康的で知的な雰囲気が欲しかった。
This was already decided. I wanted a healthy and intellectual feeling to her.

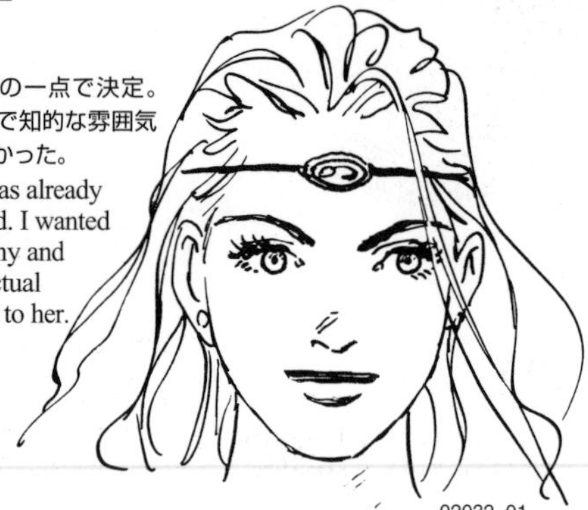

02032_01

2 two 次はコスチュームデザインだ。
Next it is costume design.

ボディスーツというよりもプロテクターの方がいいようだ。
It seems that a protector is better than a body suit.

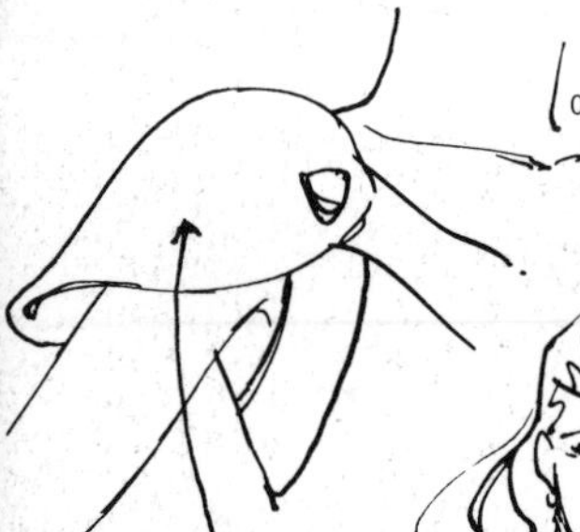

02032_02

肩にプロテクターを着けてみた。
The protector was attached on her shoulders.

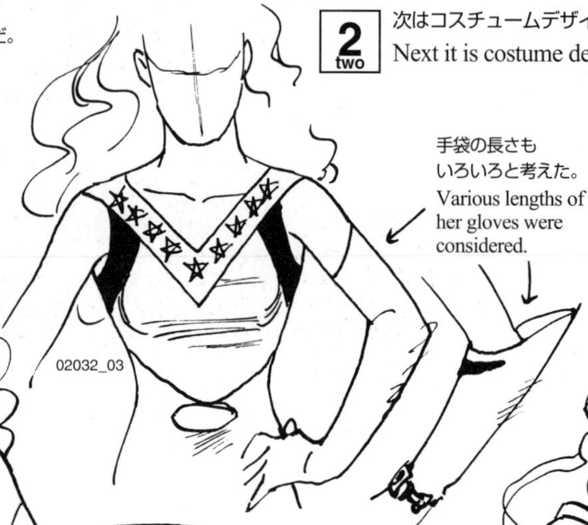

02032_03

手袋の長さもいろいろと考えた。
Various lengths of her gloves were considered.

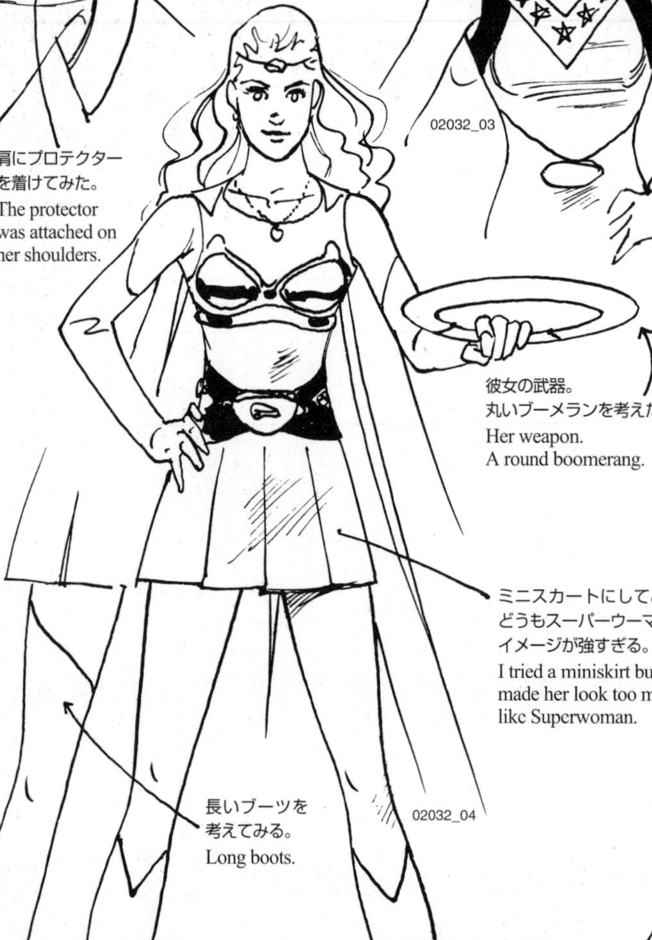

彼女の武器。丸いブーメランを考えた。
Her weapon.
A round boomerang.

ミニスカートにしてみるが、どうもスーパーウーマンのイメージが強すぎる。
I tried a miniskirt but it made her look too much likc Superwoman.

長いブーツを考えてみる。
Long boots.

02032_04

3 three 完成。
Completion.

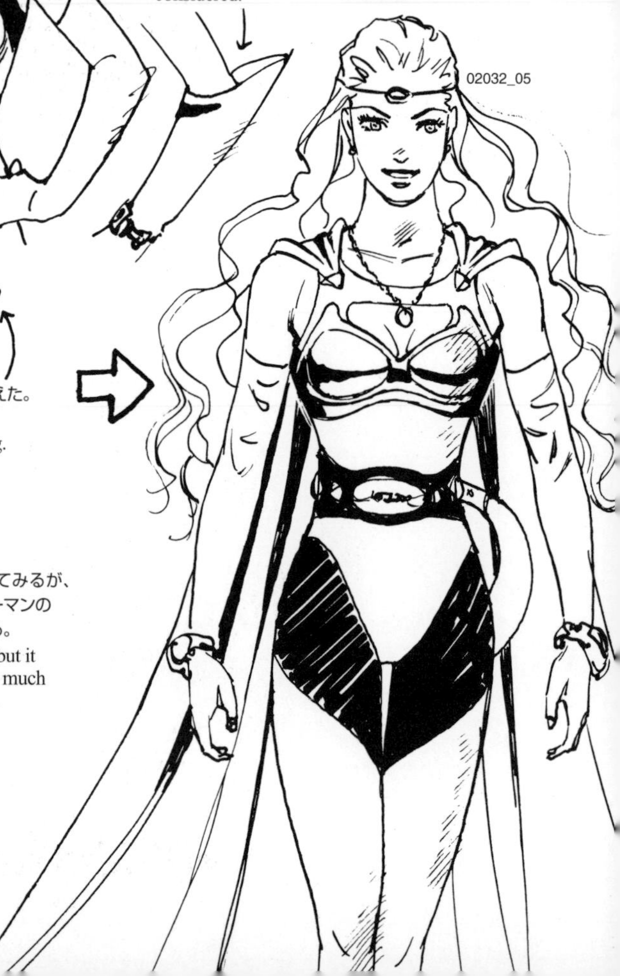

02032_05

MARIA
THE SUPER HEROINE

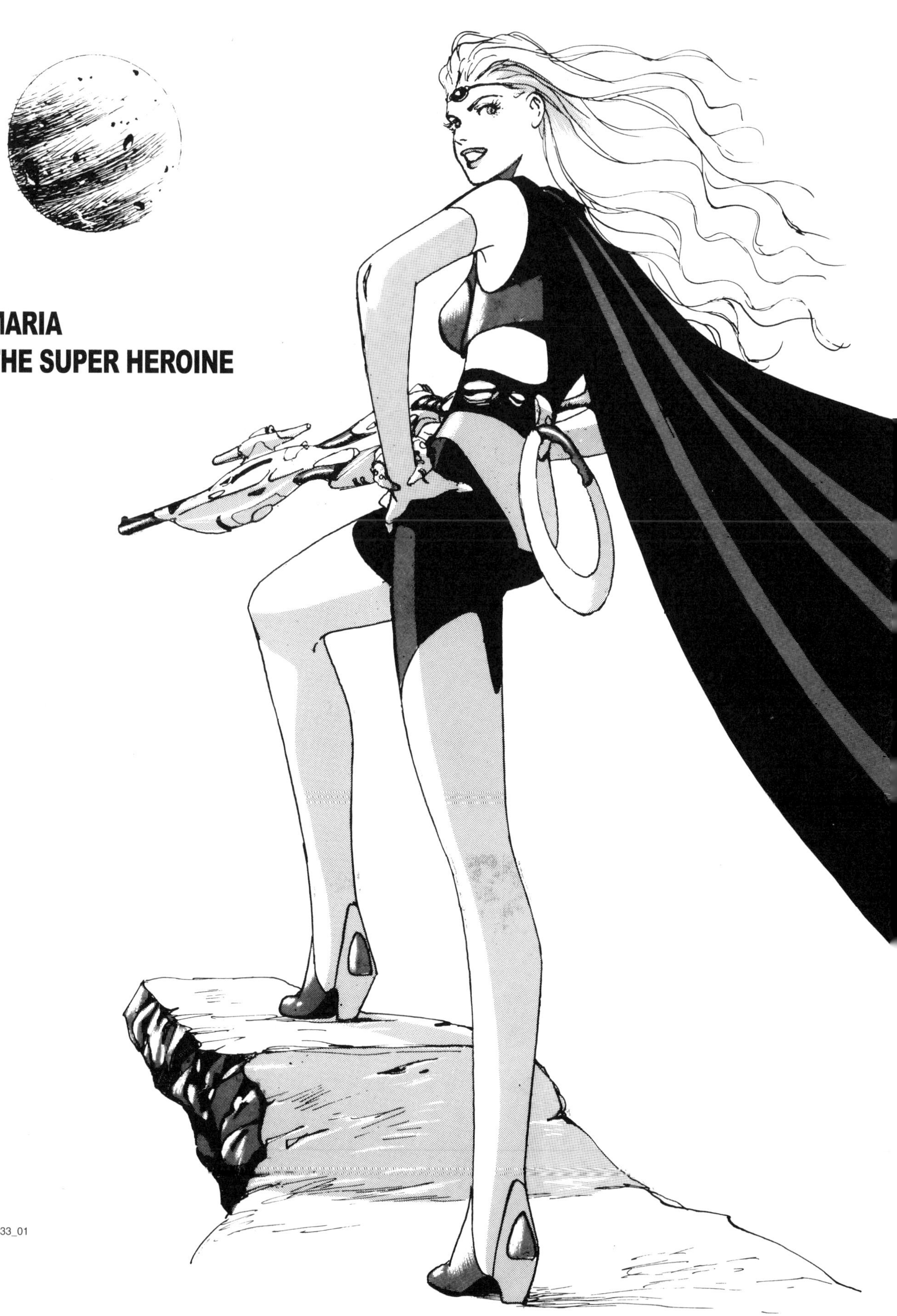

02033_01

02034_01

ハードキャラクターを創るための

BODY

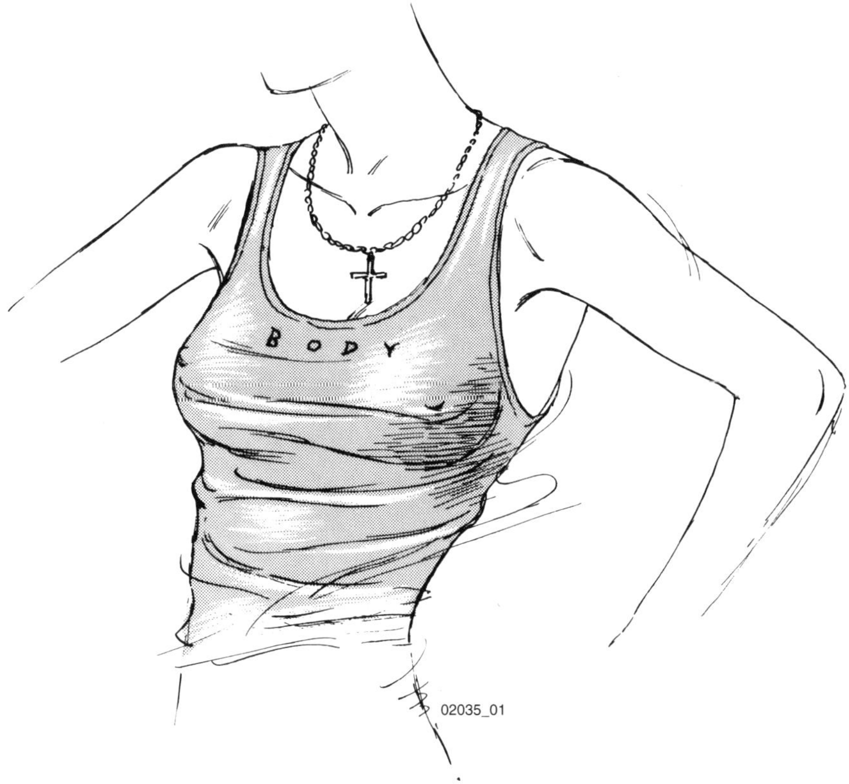
BODY
02035_01

■BODY■

SUPER BODY
スーパーボディを知る

女性の身体をかっこよく
描くのはなかなか難しい。
しかし、右図の図解を覚
えてしまうとかなり簡単
に描けるようになる。

It is rather difficult to draw a
smart female body. However,
if you menorize the
illustration on the right, you
will be able to draw it easily.

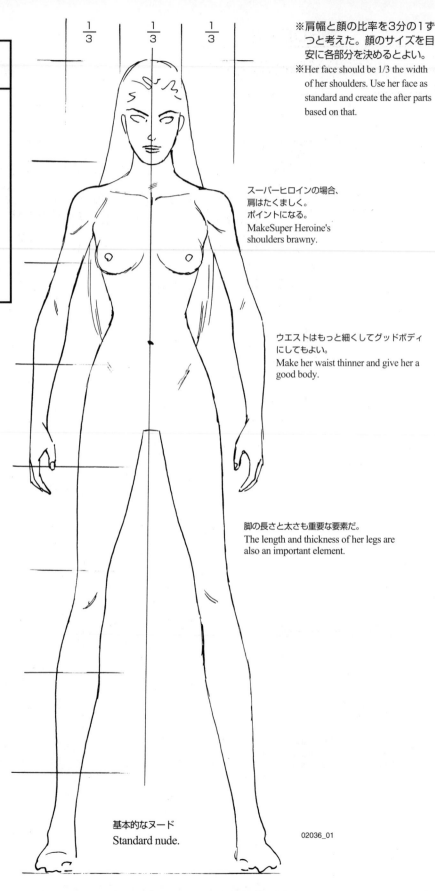

※肩幅と顔の比率を3分の1ず
　つと考えた。顔のサイズを目
　安に各部分を決めるとよい。
※Her face should be 1/3 the width
　of her shoulders. Use her face as
　standard and create the after parts
　based on that.

スーパーヒロインの場合、
肩はたくましく、
ポイントになる。
MakeSuper Heroine's
shoulders brawny.

ウエストはもっと細くしてグッドボディ
にしてもよい。
Make her waist thinner and give her a
good body.

※あまり筋肉をつけすぎ
　ない方がセクシーだ。
　女性誌などを見て研究
　しよう。
※It is sexier not to draw too
　much muscle. Look at and
　study women's magazines
　etc.

脚の長さと太さも重要な要素だ。
The length and thickness of her legs are
also an important element.

基本的なヌード
Standard nude.

02036_01

36

SIDE&BACK
横から見た身体&後ろから見た身体

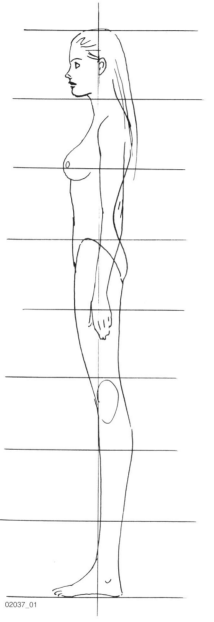

02037_01

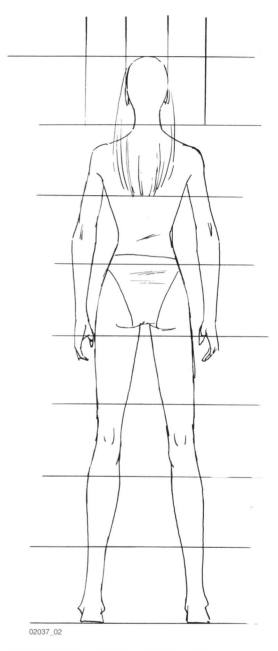

02037_02

女性の場合は、男性と違って胸を張って立つと美しい。
Unlike a male, when a female stands stretching
her breast out, she is beautiful.

※横から見た姿も、後ろ姿も、前から見た姿と同じように肩幅や
　足の太さに気をつけて美しいボディを創り上げよう。
※Let's make a beautiful body by making sure the width of her shoulders
　and thickness of legs are the same seen from the front, back and side.

BODIES
体格の比較

※36ページに比べてよりマッチョなボディ。
Compared with P36, it is a more macho body.

※36ページに比べてより女性的なボディ。
Compared with P36, it is a more feminine body.

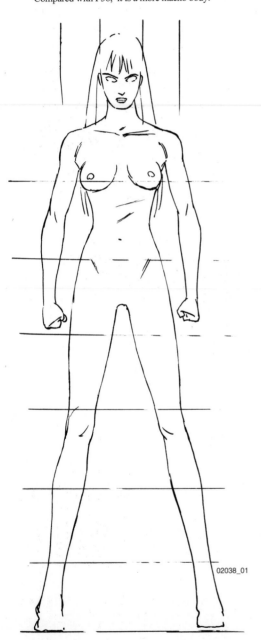

02038_01

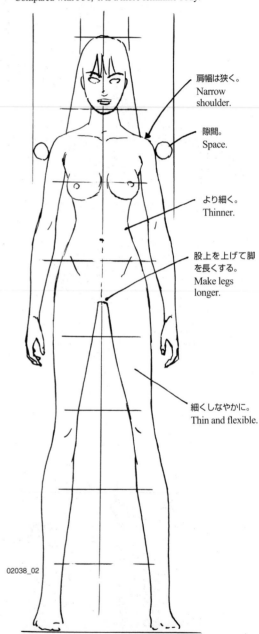

肩幅は狭く。
Narrow shoulder.

隙間。
Space.

より細く。
Thinner.

股上を上げて脚を長くする。
Make legs longer.

細くしなやかに。
Thin and flexible.

02038_02

肩幅に尽きる。36ページの基本的な身体より広めの肩幅でたくましさを強調して欲しい。
I want you to emphasize brawniness and increase the breadth of her shoulders more than on the standard body on P36.

左と比べるとわかるように、肩は丸く優しい印象だ。各部分も細めに描かれている。
Compared to the left, her shoulders are round and gentle. Other portions of her body are much finger.

※よりマッチョ。
More macho.

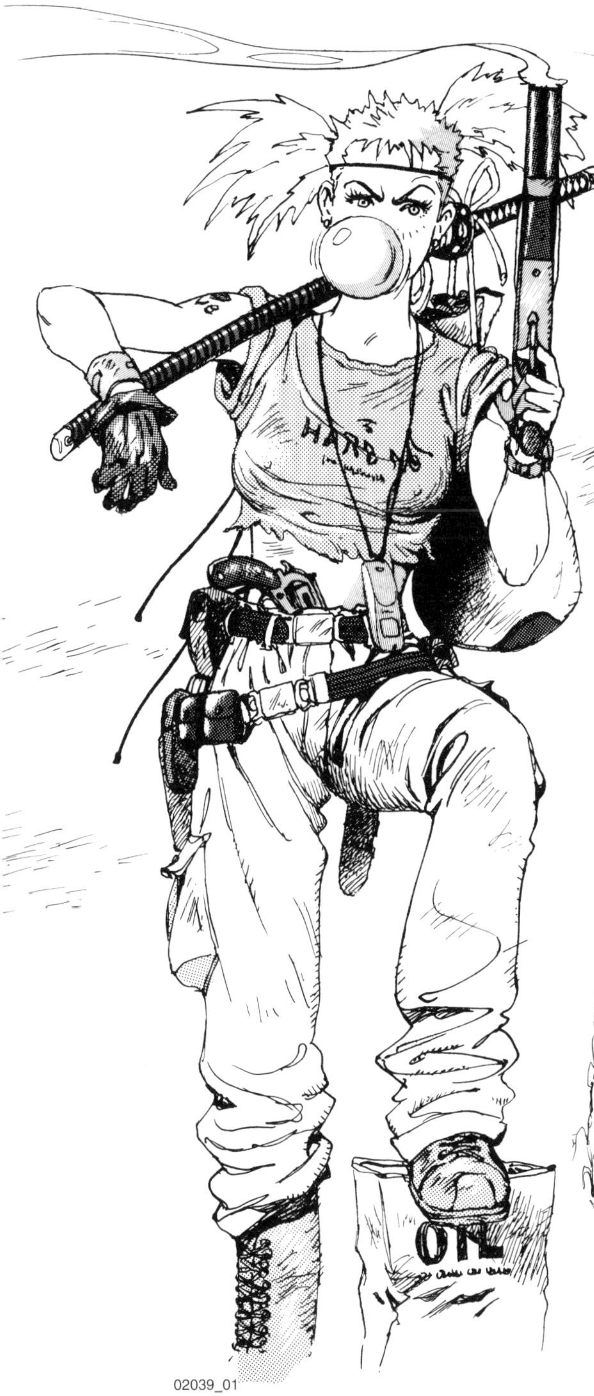
OIL

02039_01

※より女性的。
More feminine.

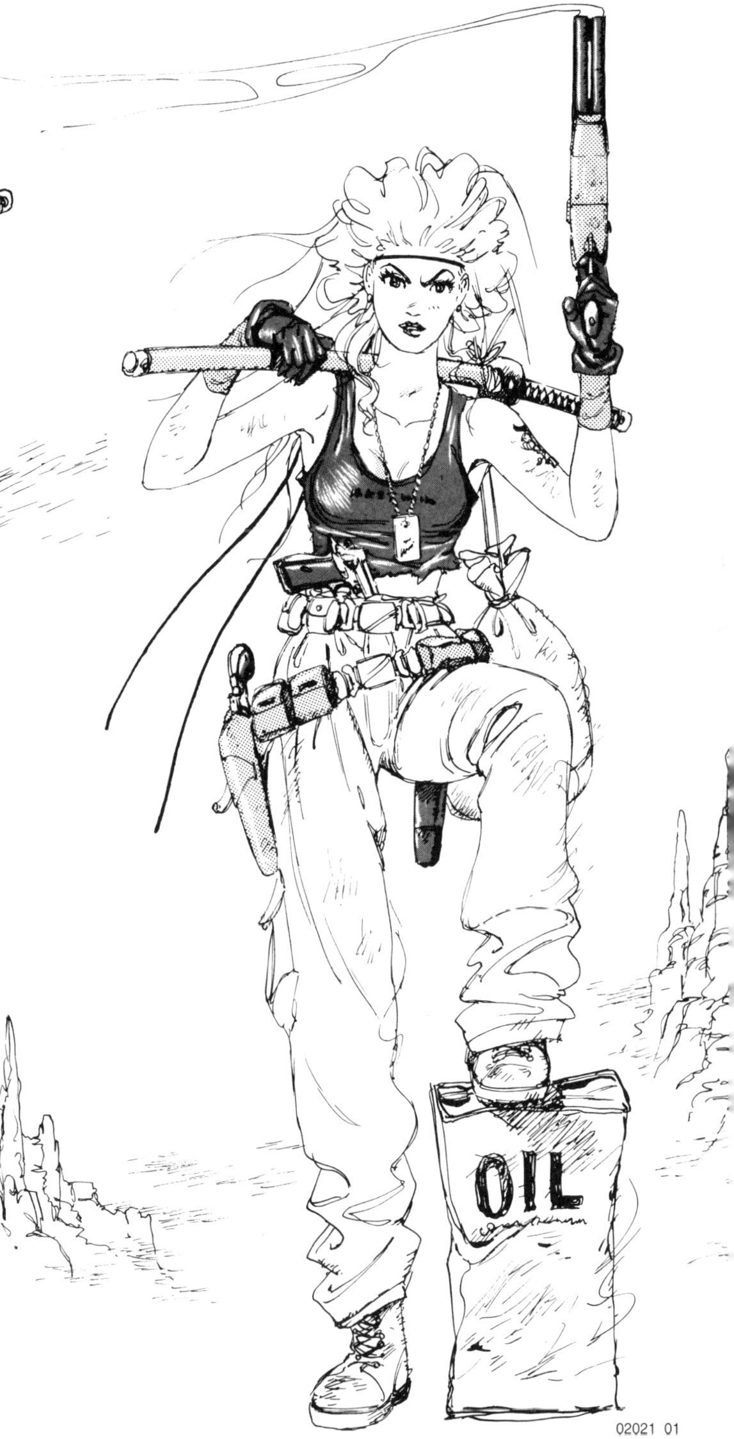
OIL

02021 01

上の2作品を比較してみよう。ワイルドなイメージと女性的なイメージの表現の違いに気がつくはずだ。

Let's compare the two upper fingers. The difference between a wild image and a feminine image should be noticed.

UNDERSTANDING BODY
スーパーボディを知る

ファッション雑誌やヌード雑誌を資料にして、
Sexyで女性らしい動きを理解しよう。

Use fashion and nude magazines as a reference, and you will understand the sexy motion.

A 女性らしい動き。
A lady-like motion.

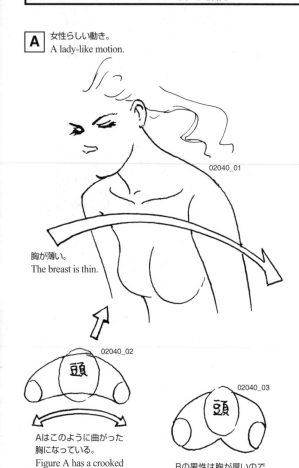

02040_01

胸が薄い。
The breast is thin.

02040_02

Aはこのように曲がった
胸になっている。
Figure A has a crooked breast.

02040_03

Bの男性は胸が厚いので
女性ほど曲がらない。
The male in figure B has a thick breast so it does not bend.

B 男性らしい動き。
A manly motion.

胸が厚い。
A thick breast.

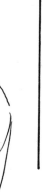

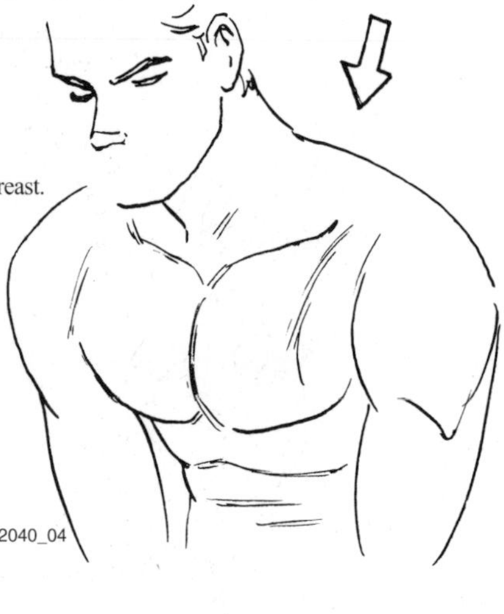

02040_04

A 02040_05　**B** 02040_06

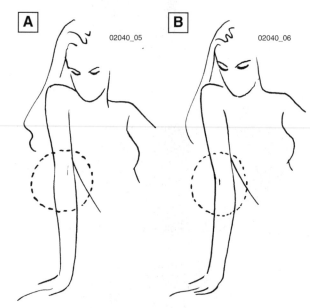

AよりBの方が肘が曲がっている。女性はBのような人が多い。
細かいことだが、女性らしさを表現するのに大切なコツだ。

The lady's arm in figure B is bent more than figure A. Most women look like this. Although this seems trivial it is an important element in expressing a women's feminity.

A 02040_07　**B** 02040_08

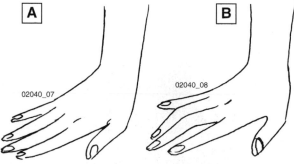

手も女性らしさを表現するのに大切な要素だ。AよりもBのように指を少し
曲げると、より女性的な仕草になって美しい。しかし、やりすぎるとわざ
とらしくなるので注意しよう。

It's also important to show feminity in hands as well. You can capture a lady's beauty by bending the fingers a little as in figere B. However, be careful not to overdo it as it then becomes unnatural.

●女性の身体の動き●

The movement of a women's body.

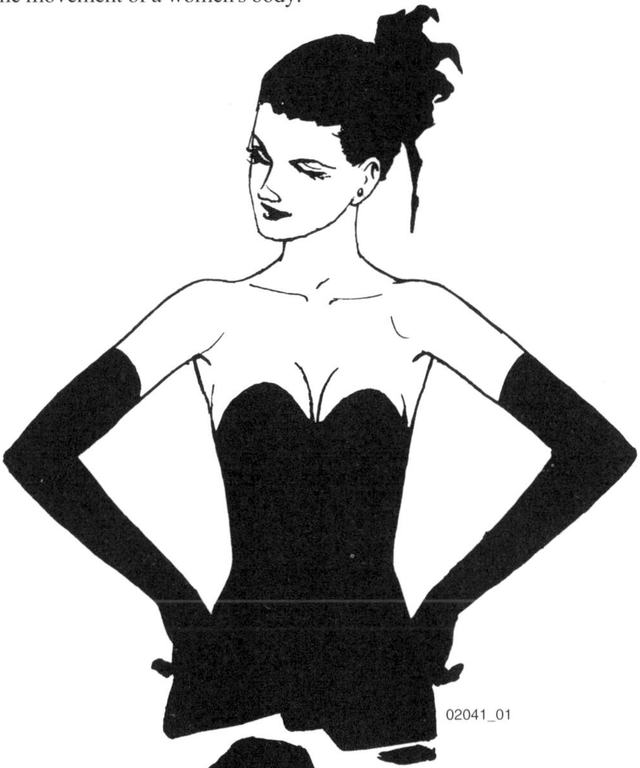

02041_01

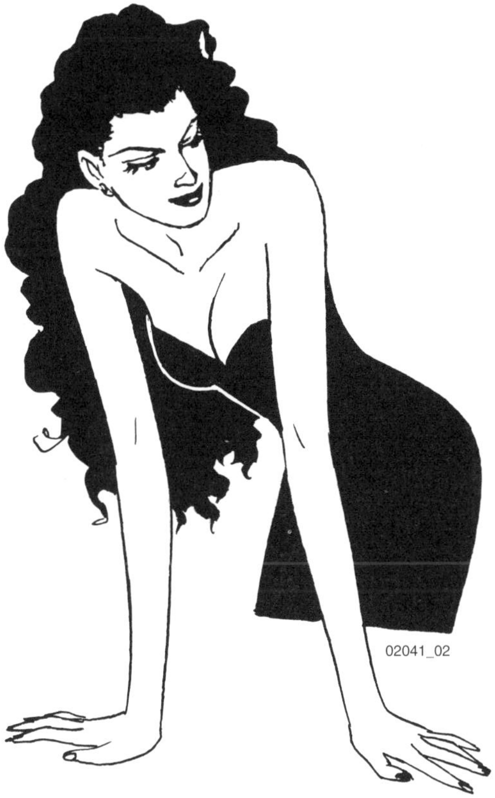

02041_02

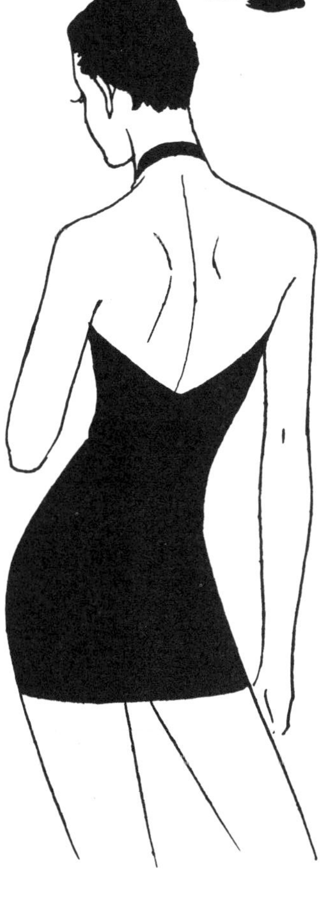

02041_03

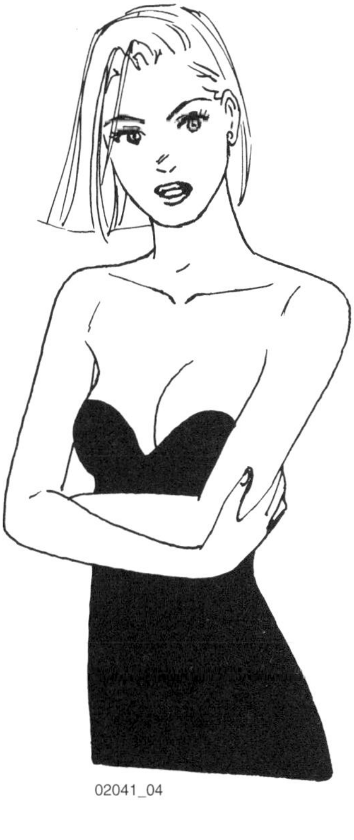

02041_04

BREAST
バスト

女性の身体を描くのに、バストを表現しないわけにはいかないだろう。大切なポイントだ。

To draw a female body realistically, it is important to include her breasts.

A 正しい。
Correct.

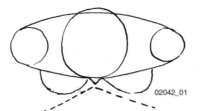

02042_01

上から見ると横に広がっている。
When seen from above, it spreads horizontally.

B 間違い。
Incorrect.

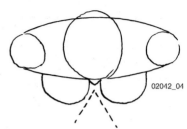

02042_04

よほどバストを誇張するとき以外は使わない表現だ。
Do not use this except when you want to exaggerate her breasts.

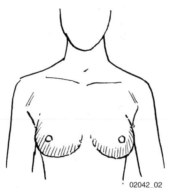

02042_02

Aは自然なバストだ。
A is a natural bust.

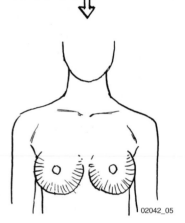

02042_05

正面から見るとBは不自然だ。
If seen from the front her breasts look unnatural.

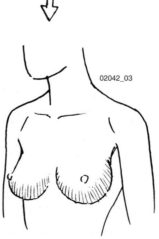

02042_03

斜めから見てもAは自然なバストだ。
A is a natural bust even when seen diagonally.

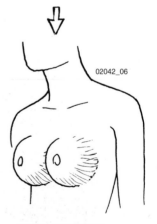

02042_06

腫れ物のようで不自然だ。
It is unnatural and looks swollen.

■BODY■
BREAST
バスト

身体にぴったりとした服や、ゆったりとしたシャツを着たときのバストの表現について解説しておこう。

Let's see how to show her bust in tight fitting clothes and loose shirts.

1 one 身体にフィットしたシャツを着る。
バストの両側の膨らみに引っ張られて横向きのしわができる。
When she wears a fight fitting shirt it is pulled by the bulging on both sides of the bust therefore wrincles appar sideways.

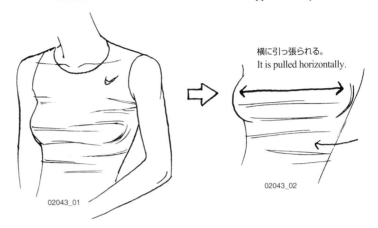

横に引っ張られる。
It is pulled horizontally.

02043_02

02043_01

2 two 少しゆるめのシャツを着る。
バストの先端にリードされて少したるみのあるしわができる。
She has a somewhat looser shirt on. It starts from the tip of a bust and creates slack wrinkles.

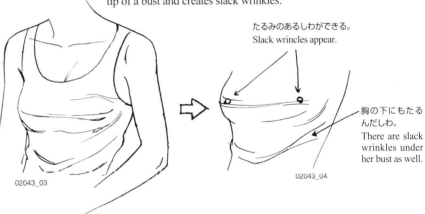

たるみのあるしわができる。
Slack wrincles appear.

胸の下にもたるんだしわ。
There are slack wrinkles under her bust as well.

02043_03

02043_04

3 three ブラウスを着る。
バストの先端を中心に縦のしわができる。
She has a blouse on. Vertical wrinkles appear around the tip of a bust.

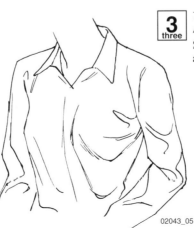

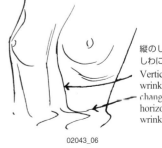

縦のしわが横のしわに変わる。
Vertical wrinkles change to horizontal wrinkles.

02043_05

02043_06

43

HIP
ヒップ

チャーミングなお尻も重要な要素だ。ジーンズをはいた時や、スカートをはいた時、ヒップの基本的な形を知っていれば、簡単そうで意外と難しいヒップラインも格段に描きやすくなる。

Charming hips are an important element. Whether she's wearing jeans or a skirt it you understand the basic shape of the hip, it will make it easier to draw difficult hiplines.

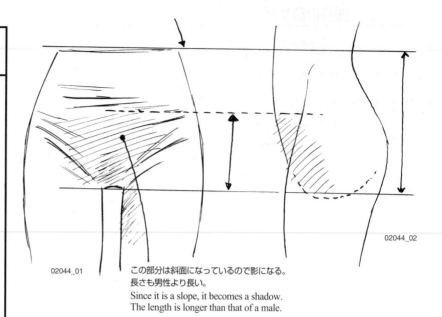

02044_01

02044_02

この部分は斜面になっているので影になる。
長さも男性より長い。
Since it is a slope, it becomes a shadow.
The length is longer than that of a male.

02044_03

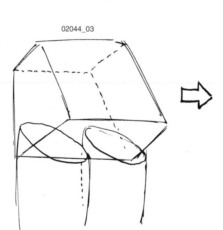

右図のお尻を図形で表現すると
左図のようになる。
If the figure on the right is shown diagrammatically, it will look like the figure on the left.

02044_04

男
Man.

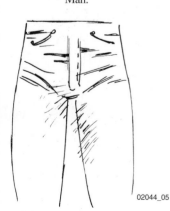

02044_05

女
Woman.

02044_06

スカートをはいているとき（下図）。
When wearing a skirt.

02044_07

44

■BODY■

ARM
腕

腕の構造を理解しよう。
Let's understand the structure of the arm.

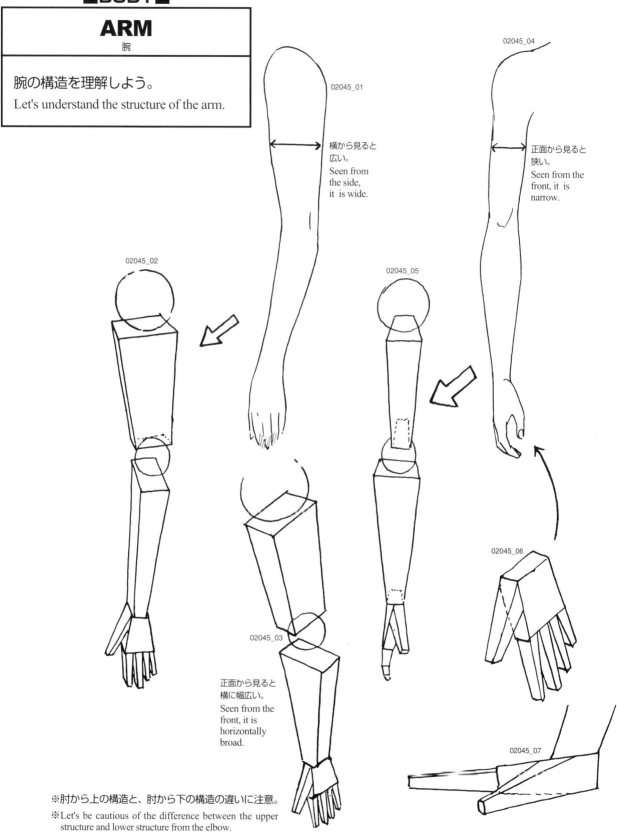

02045_01

横から見ると
広い。
Seen from
the side,
it is wide.

02045_04

正面から見ると
狭い。
Seen from the
front, it is
narrow.

02045_02

02045_05

02045_03

正面から見ると
横に幅広い。
Seen from the
front, it is
horizontally
broad.

02045_06

02045_07

※肘から上の構造と、肘から下の構造の違いに注意。
※Let's be cautious of the difference between the upper
　structure and lower structure from the elbow.

LEG
脚

脚の構造を理解しよう。

Let's understand the structure of legs.

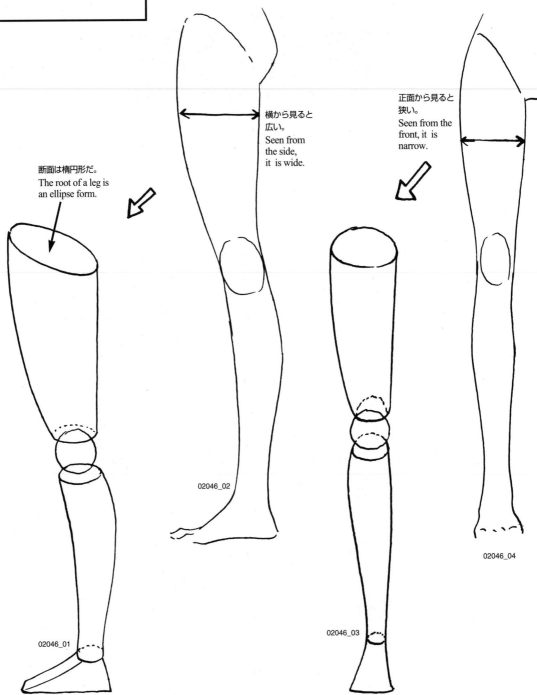

断面は楕円形だ。
The root of a leg is
an ellipse form.

横から見ると
広い。
Seen from
the side,
it is wide.

正面から見ると
狭い。
Seen from the
front, it is
narrow.

02046_02

02046_04

02046_01

02046_03

顔
FACE

02047_01

ANGLE
いろいろな角度から見た顔

卵を使っていろいろな角度から見た顔を研究しよう。右の図のように卵の表面に線を引いて、目、鼻、口を描いてみる。上や横、斜めから見て、顔の変化を研究しよう。

Let's study the face seen from various angles using an egg. As shown in a right figure, a line is drawn on the surface of an egg, and an eye, a nose, and a mouth are drawn. Let's study how the face changes when seen from above, the side and diagonally.

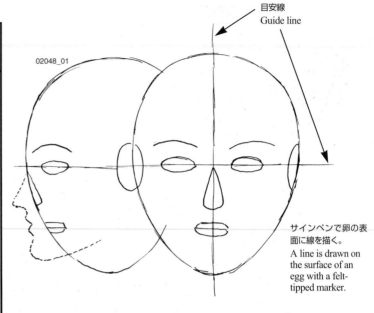

目安線
Guide line

02048_01

サインペンで卵の表面に線を描く。
A line is drawn on the surface of an egg with a felt-tipped marker.

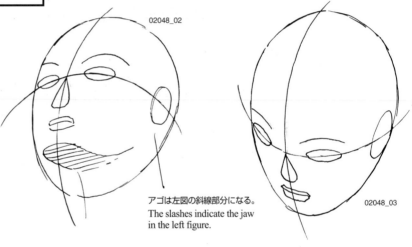

02048_02

アゴは左図の斜線部分になる。
The slashes indicate the jaw in the left figure.

02048_03

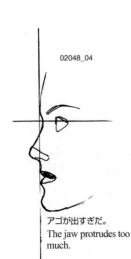

02048_04

アゴが出すぎだ。
The jaw protrudes too much.

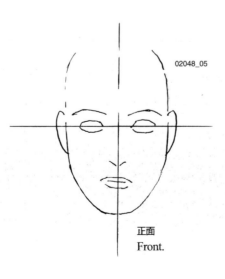

02048_05

正面
Front.

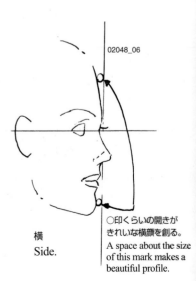

02048_06

横
Side.

○印くらいの開きがきれいな横顔を創る。
A space about the size of this mark makes a beautiful profile.

48

EYE
目

女性を描く上で最も大切なのが目だ。目で顔のすべてが決まるといってもいいだろう。魅力的な目を描くコツを紹介しよう。

The eyes are the most important features when drawing a woman. It can be said that all the features of a face are decided by the eyes. I will show you some tips for creating beautiful eyes.

目と目の間隔は目一つ分がちょうどよい。もちろん微調整は必要。

The space between the eyes should be the width of one eyes. Of course, fine tuning is required.

横顔の目の位置は下図くらいがよい。

The position of the eye for a profile should be similar to the figure below.

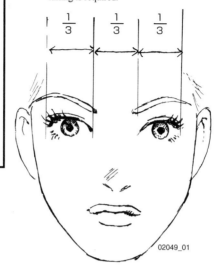

02049_01

02049_02

●目の位置●
The position of eyes

02049_03

目が寄りすぎ
The eyes are too close.

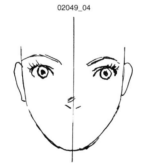

02049_04

離れすぎ
The eyes are too far apart.

02049_05

へこみすぎ
Too sunken.

02049_06

出過ぎ
Too far forward.

02049_07

彫りの深い欧米人の目。
Well defined eyes typical of Caucasians.

02049_08

アジア人の目。
Eyes typical of Asian people.

●目の大きさ●
The size of eyes

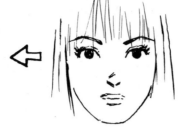

02050_01 02050_02 02050_03

少し大きい目
Somewhat large eyes.

普通の目の大きさ
The size of ordinary eyes.

とても大きい目
Very large eyes.

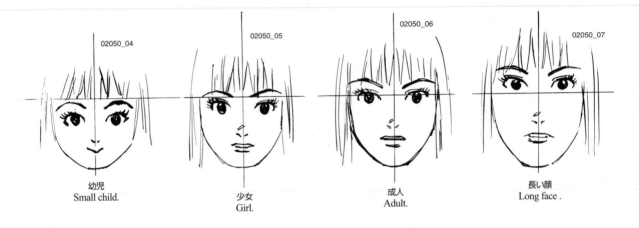

02050_04 02050_05 02050_06 02050_07

幼児
Small child.

少女
Girl.

成人
Adult.

長い顔
Long face .

●目の種類●
Various eyes

02050_08 02050_09 02050_10 02050_11

つり上がった目
Slanted eye.

鋭い目
Sharp eyes.

彫りの深い目
Clear-cut eyes.

普通の目
Ordinary eyes.

02050_12 02050_13 02050_14 02050_15

アニメ風の目
Eyes often used for
animation.

マンガ風の目
Eyes often used for comics.

少女コミック風の目
Little girl's eyes
often used for comics.

キャラクター風の目
Eyes often used for cartoons.

NOSE
鼻

鼻を描くのが苦手な人は多いだろう。特に正面から鼻を描くのは難しい。あまりリアルに描くと可愛くないし、あまり簡単に描くと他のパーツとのバランスがとれない。

I'm sure there are lots of people who are not good at drawing noses. It is difficult to draw a nose especially from the front. If it's not cute and if you draw it to simple its hard to balance the other parts.

●鼻の位置●
The position of noses

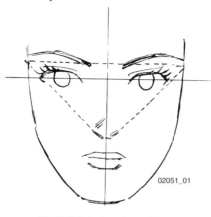

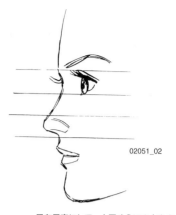

正三角形を目安にしてバランスをとろう。
Maintain balance with an equilateral triangle.

02051_01

目を目安にして、上図くらいの大きさと位置がちょうどよい。
Use the eyes as a guideline, the size and positioning is just right in the picture above.

02051_02

●鼻の長さ●
The length of noses

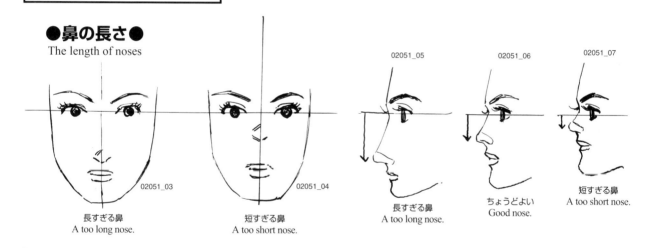

長すぎる鼻
A too long nose.

02051_03

短すぎる鼻
A too short nose.

02051_04

02051_05

長すぎる鼻
A too long nose.

02051_06

ちょうどよい
Good nose.

02051_07

短すぎる鼻
A too short nose.

鼻を意図的に長くしたり、短くしたりすることによって個性的なキャラクターを制作することができる。右にいくつか作例を紹介したい。

You can create an distinctive character by intentionally shortening or lengthening the nose. I want to introduce some examples in the right figures.

短く大きい鼻
A short large nose.

02051_08

長い鼻
A long nose.

02051_09

ペチャンコな鼻
A short nose

02051_10

■FACE■

NOSE

鼻

●鼻の表現法●

The variation of noses

いろいろな表現法で鼻を描いてみよう。

Let's try drawing noses using various methods.

02052_01

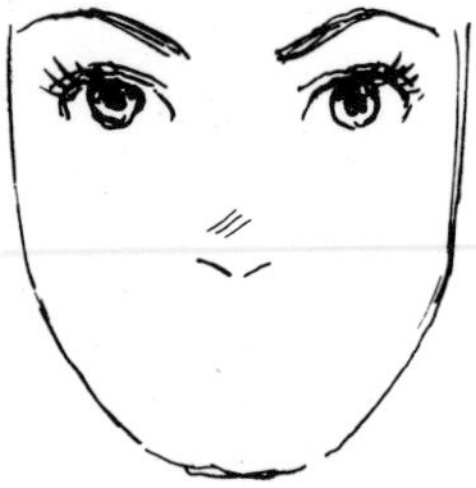

鼻の頭だけで表現。

Only draw the head of the nose.

02052_02

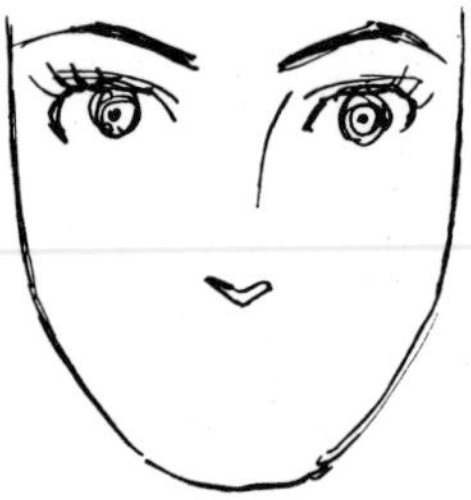

鼻筋と鼻の下の影で表現。

The nose is shown by shadowing the bridge and under the nose.

02052_03

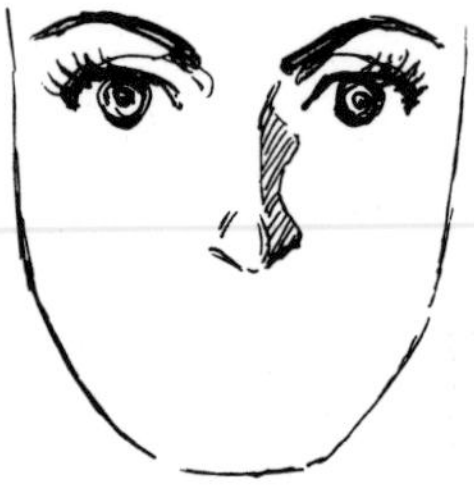

陰影を使った表現。

Shown by shading.

02052_04

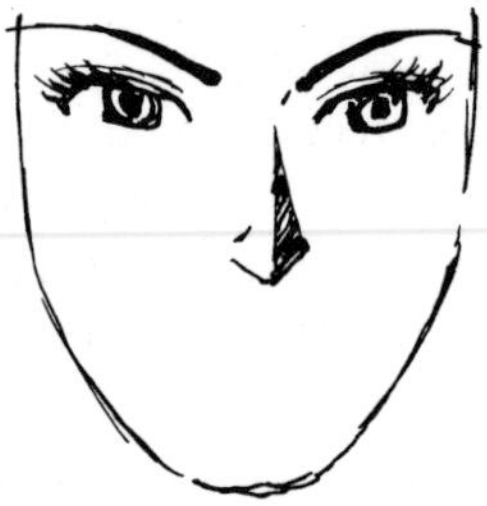

簡略化した陰影を使った表現。

Shown by simplified shading.

●鼻の種類●

Various noses

02052_05

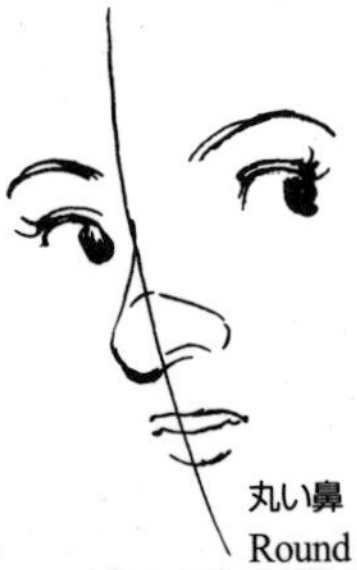

丸い鼻

Round nose.

02052_06

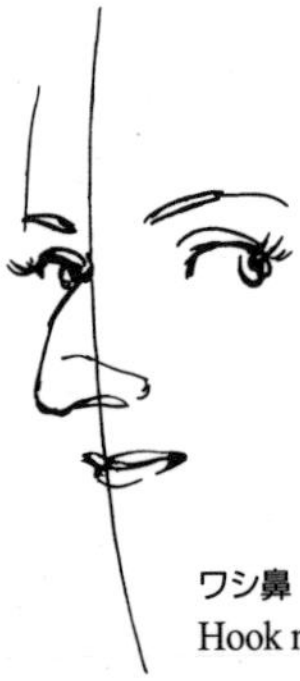

ワシ鼻

Hook nose.

02052_07

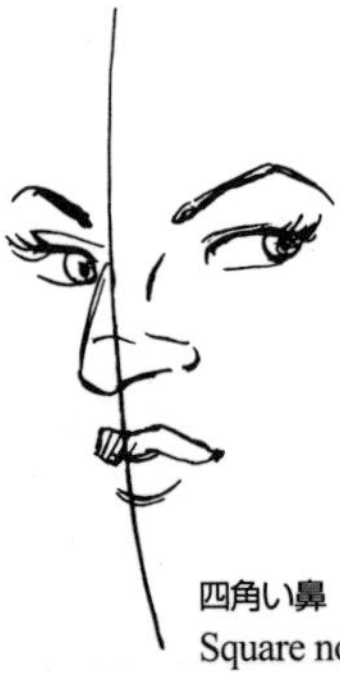

四角い鼻

Square nose.

02052_08

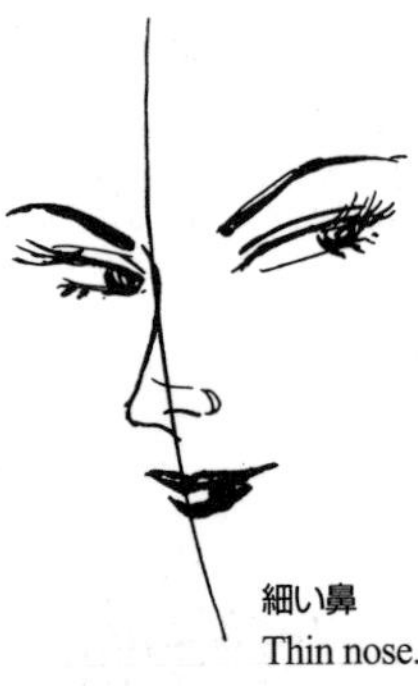

細い鼻

Thin nose.

02052_09

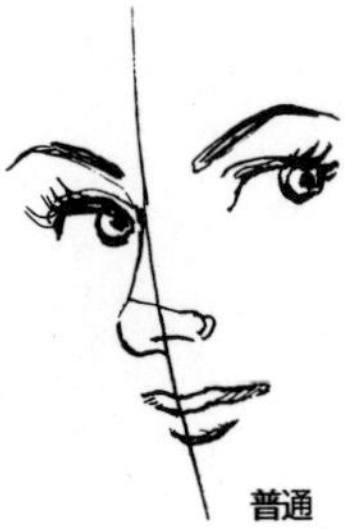

普通

Standard nose.

02052_10

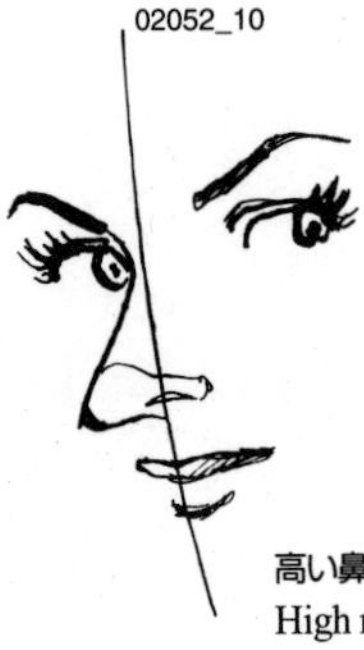

高い鼻

High nose.

02052_11

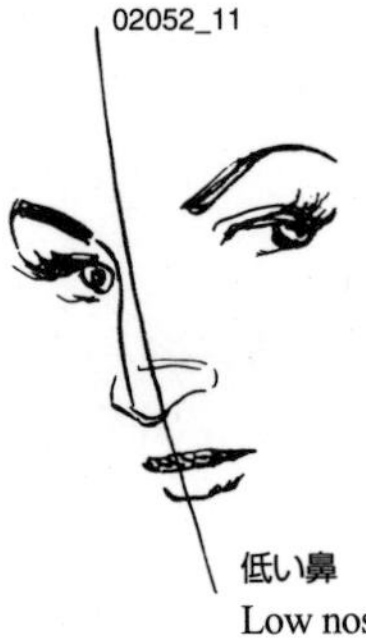

低い鼻

Low nose.

02052_12

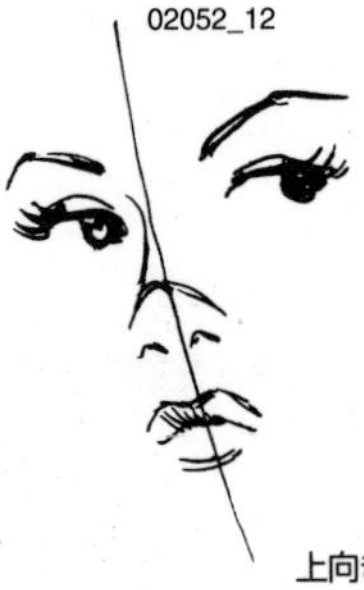

上向きの鼻

A upward nose.

MOUTH
口

口は目に次ぐ大切なパー
ツだ。魅力的でセクシー
な表情や、可愛らしい表
情など口の役割は大きい。

The mouth is the 2nd most
important part after the eyes.
The role of the mouth is
important in expressing
sensuality cuteness etc.

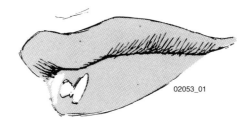

02053_01

顔の中心線
The central line of a face.

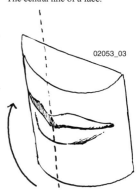

02053_03

右の口角は隠れて見えない。
The right edge of the
mouth is hidden.

※口は右の図のような台に付いていると考えると
　理解しやすい。円い筒の上に描くようにして、
　平坦にならないようにしたい。

※It is easy to understand if you imagine the mouth is
　attached to a stand as shown in the right figure. Draw it
　on a round cylinder and be careful it doedn't turn out
　flat.

02053_02

正面から見た笑っている口。右の図はそれを少し横から見たもの。
A smiling mouth seen from the front. The right figure shows
the same smiling mouth from the side.

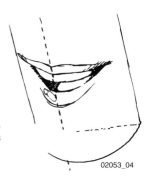

02053_04

●正面から見た口の作例●
Various mouths seen from front

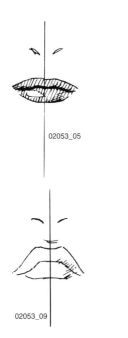

02053_05

02053_09

02053_06

02053_10

02053_07

02053_11

02053_08

02053_12

53

■FACE■

MOUTH
口

●口のバリエーション●
The variation of mouths

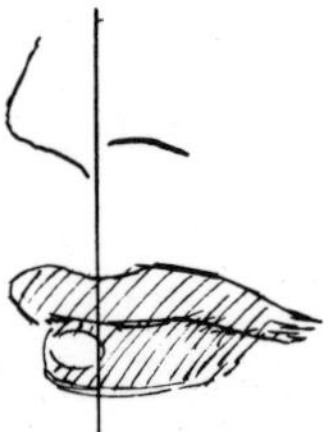
02054_01

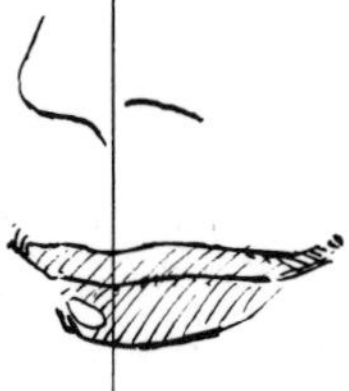
02054_02

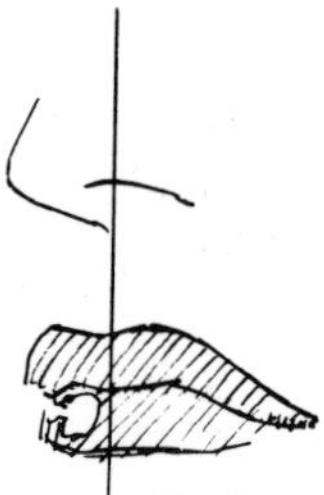
02054_03

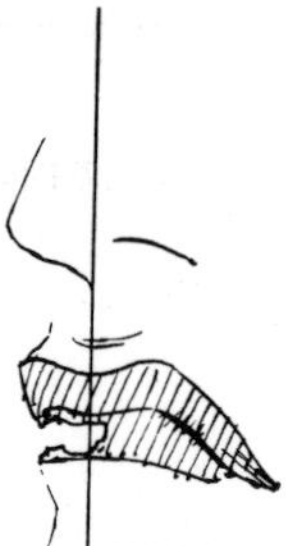
02054_04

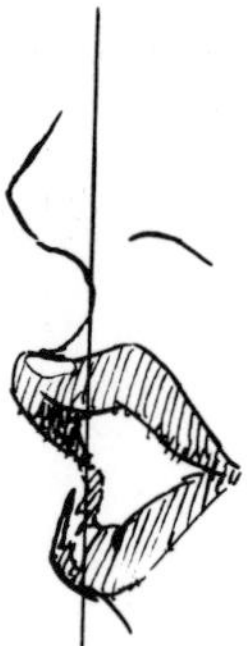
02054_05

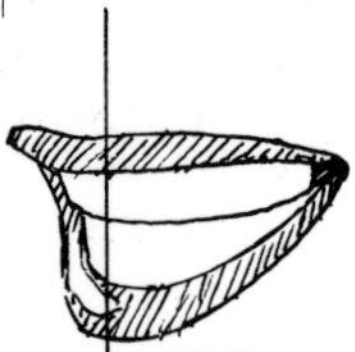
02054_06

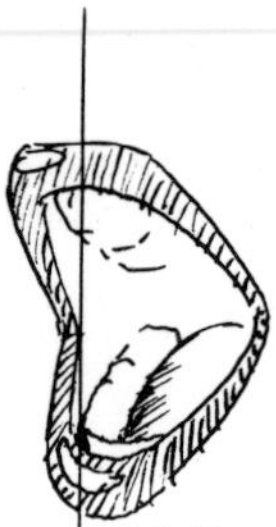
02054_07

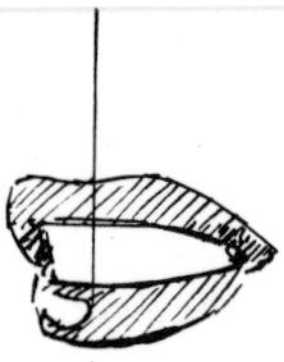
02054_08

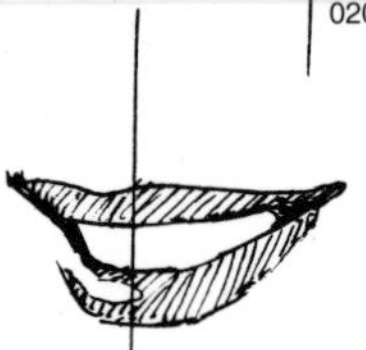
02054_09

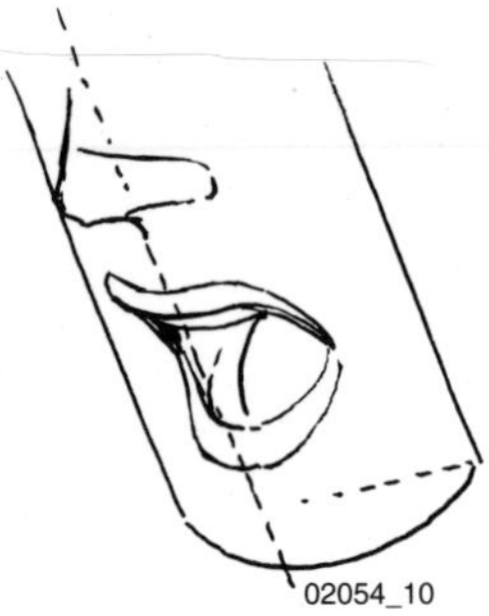
02054_10

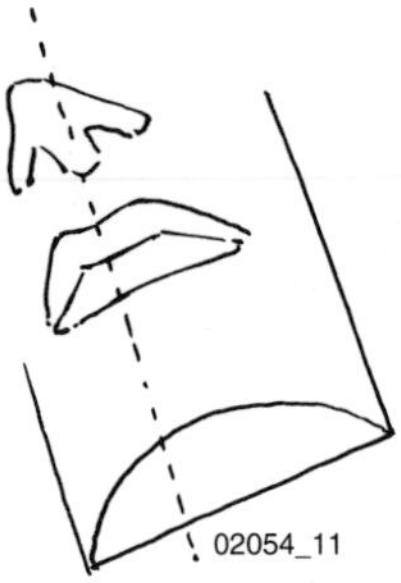
02054_11

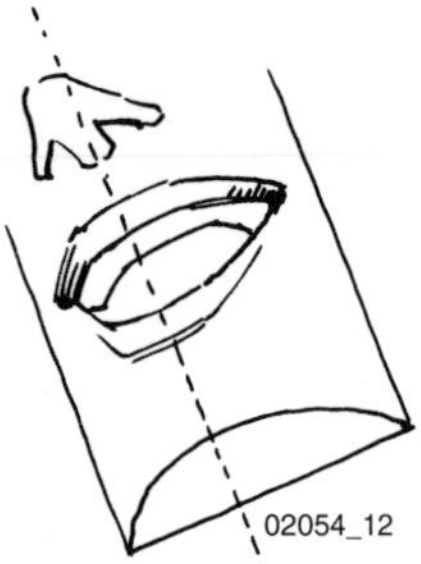
02054_12

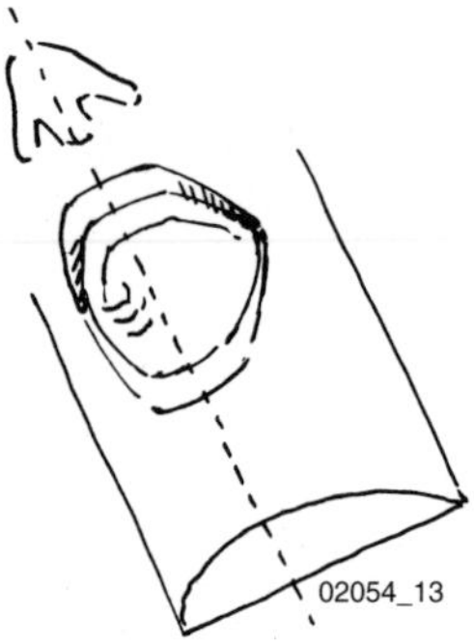
02054_13

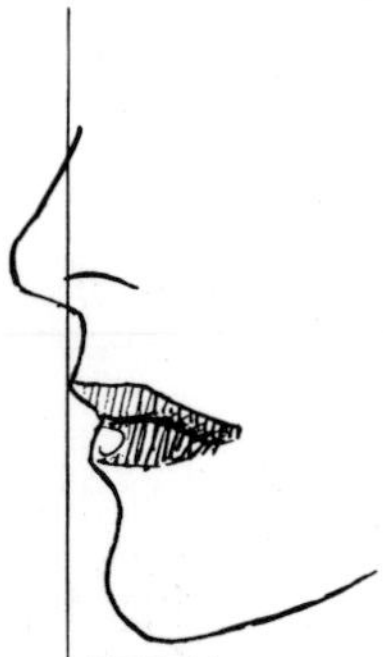
02054_14

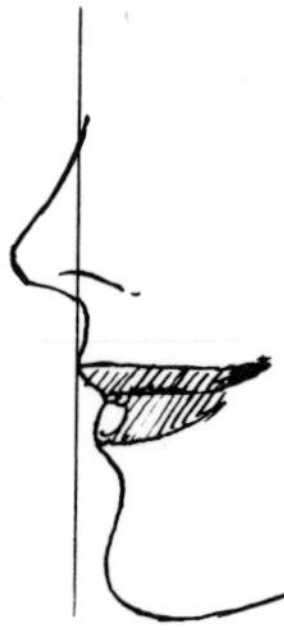
02054_15

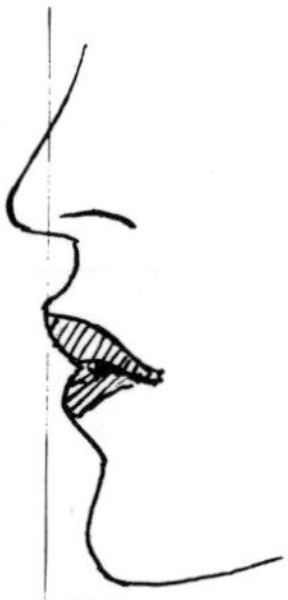
02054_16

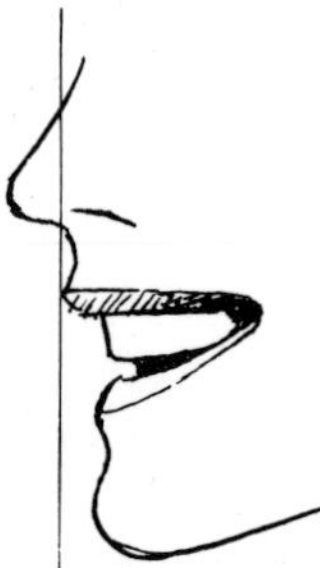
02054_17

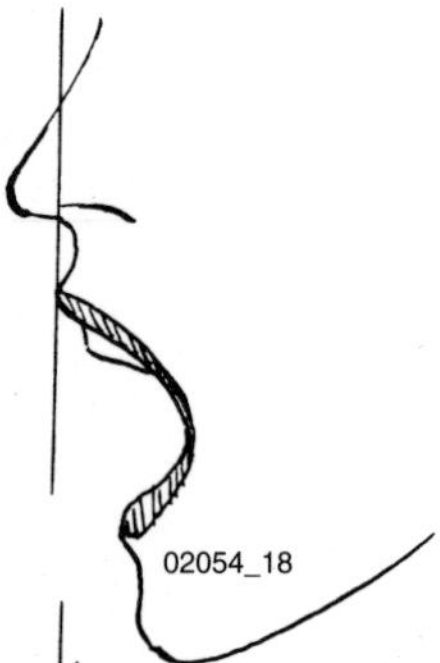
02054_18

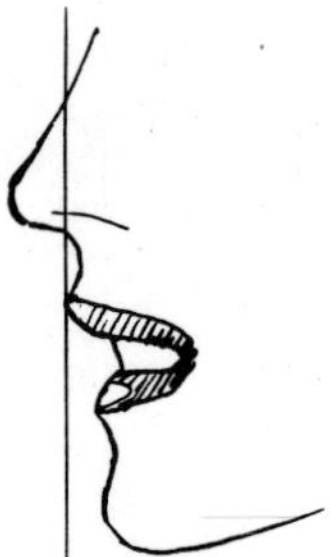
02054_19

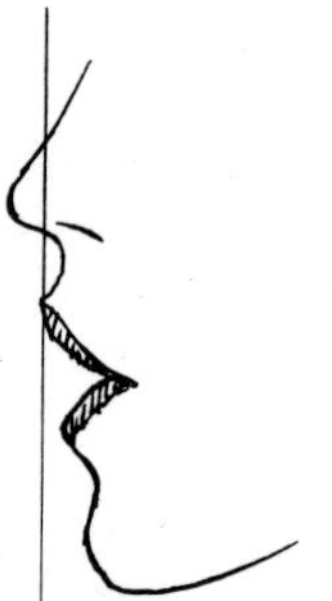
02054_20

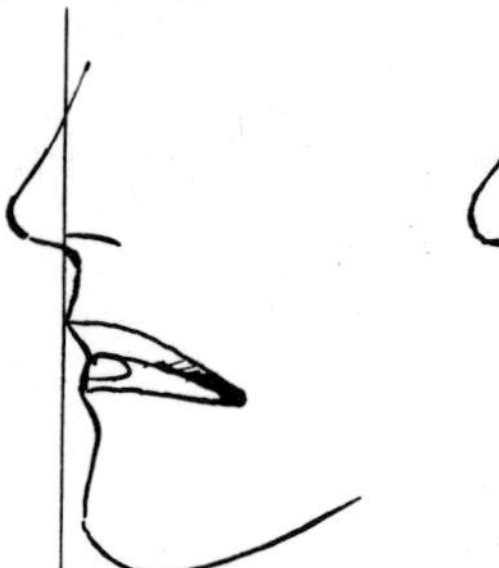
02054_21

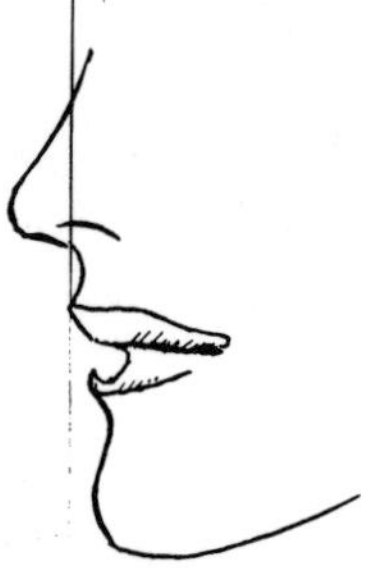
02054_22

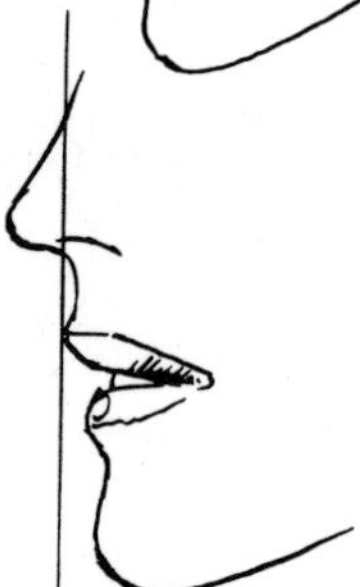
02054_23

THE SHAPE OF FACE

顔の形と人相

●顔の形●
The shape of face

同じ目でも顔の形が違うと人相が変わるところに注目。
Even with the exact same eyes, her look totally changes with different shape of the face.

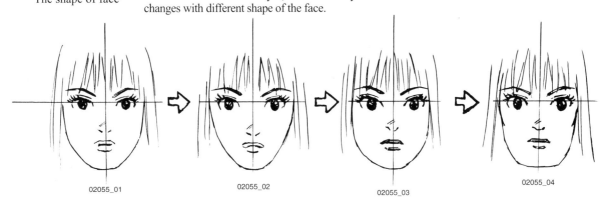

02055_01   02055_02   02055_03   02055_04

●顔の種類●
Various faces

02055_05

02055_06

02055_07

02055_08

02055_09

02055_10

55

UNDERSTANDING FACE
顔を知る

●上から見た顔●
Faces from above

02056_01

02056_02

02056_03

●下から見た顔●
Faces from below

02056_04

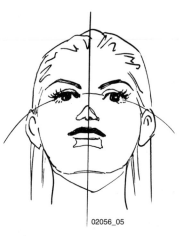

02056_05

02056_06

●後ろから見た顔●
Faces from back

02056_07

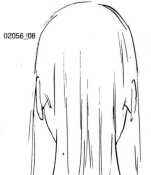

02056_08

02056_09

HAIR STYLE
髪型

女性の場合男性よりもヘアスタイルが重要だ。ところで君たちは、髪を描くということを、線を引くことだと思いこんでいないだろうか？ 髪の毛を描くことは確かに難しい。髪の流れを掴み表現しなければならないからだ。ここでは髪の毛の表現を研究しよう。

Hairstyles are more imoprtant on females than males. You probably think that drawing hair is just drawing lines. But actually it is quite difficult because you need to capture the flow of the hair. Let's study different ways of expressing hair.

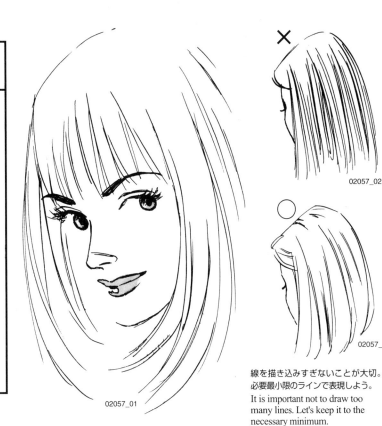

02057_01

02057_02

02057_03

線を描き込みすぎないことが大切。
必要最小限のラインで表現しよう。

It is important not to draw too many lines. Let's keep it to the necessary minimum.

●線を整理する●
Arrange Hair lines

02057_04

線が多くうるさい。
There are too many lines.

OK

02057_05

02057_06

線が多くうるさい。
There are too many lines.

OK

02057_07

02058_01

設定
CHARACTERIZATION

SMALL BUT STRONG

小柄でも迫力のあるキャラクター

ハードさは外見によるところが多いが、キャラクターの設定により、よりパワーアップしたハードさを表現できる。

Although toughness is mostly shown through appearance, you can also enhance this toughness by how you position the character.

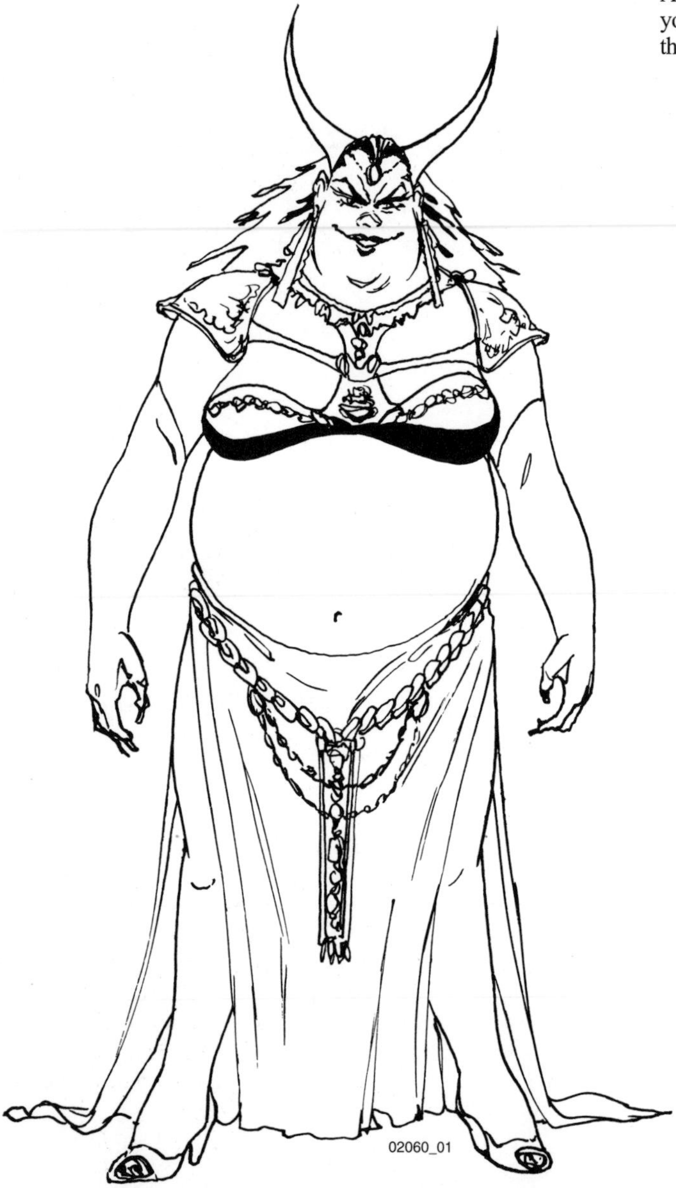
02060_01

A 一般的なキャラクター。身体が大きく力強さを全面に押し出している。
A ordinary big character. The body is big and power is expressed throughout the whole body.

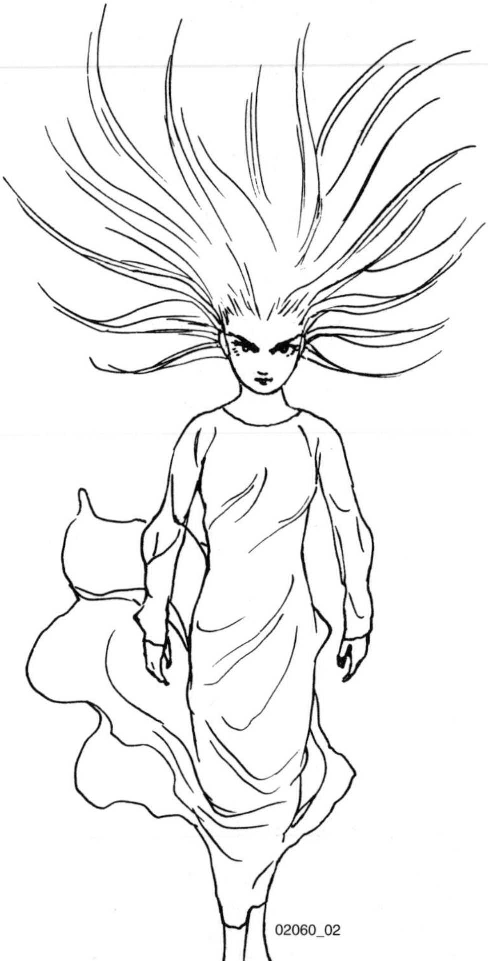
02060_02

B 少女であるにもかかわらず、なにか得体の知れない能力を秘めているような迫力を醸し出している。
Although she is a girl she has a mysterious hidden ability which produces fierceness.

■設定■

POWER INSIDE

内面から来るハードさ

一見した感じはおとなしそうなキャラクターが、内に秘めた激情を露わにするとより過激になる。

A character may seem genyle but becomes violent when inner emotions are revealed.

■ベース■
Original

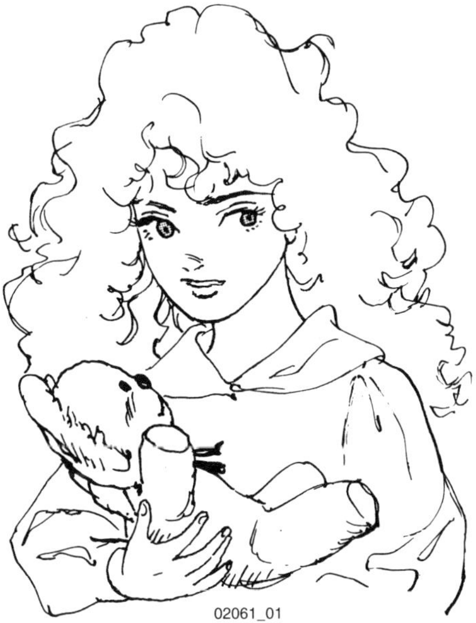

02061_01

■ハード■
Hard

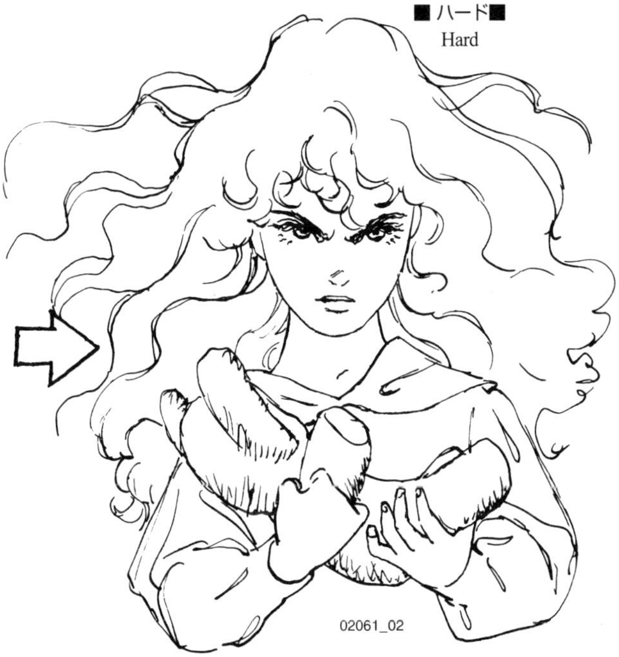

02061_02

■ベース■
Original

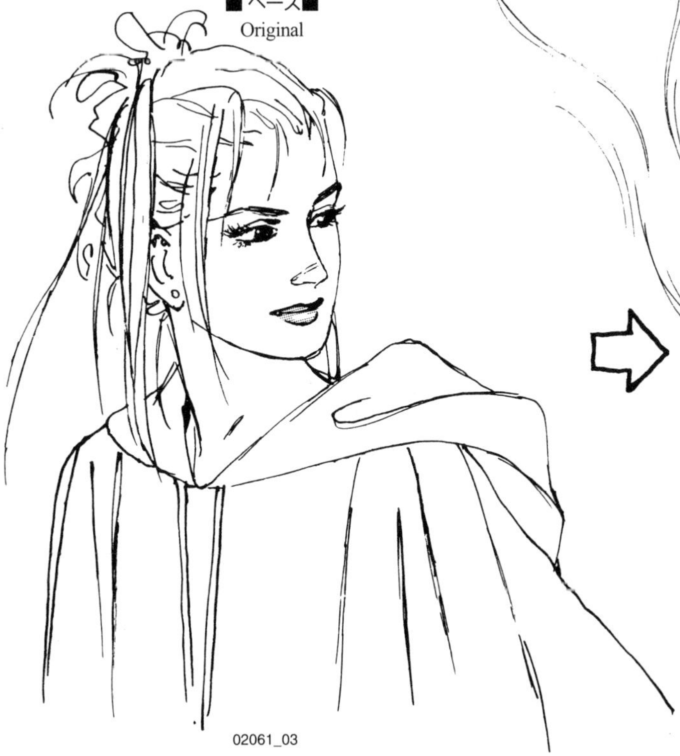

02061_03

■ハード■
Hard

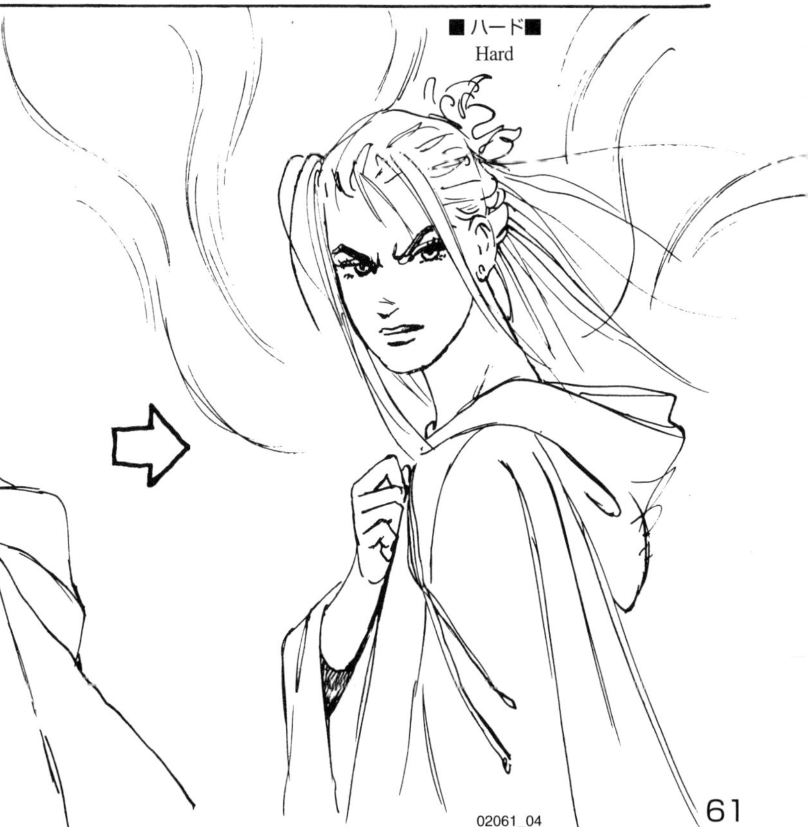

02061_04

■設定■

COSTUME

コスチューム

コスチュームのデザイン次第で斬新にもなりキャラクターを力強く魅力的にもする。とても重要な要素だ。

Depending on the design of costume, it becomes a novelty and it can make the character very attractive. It is a very important technique.

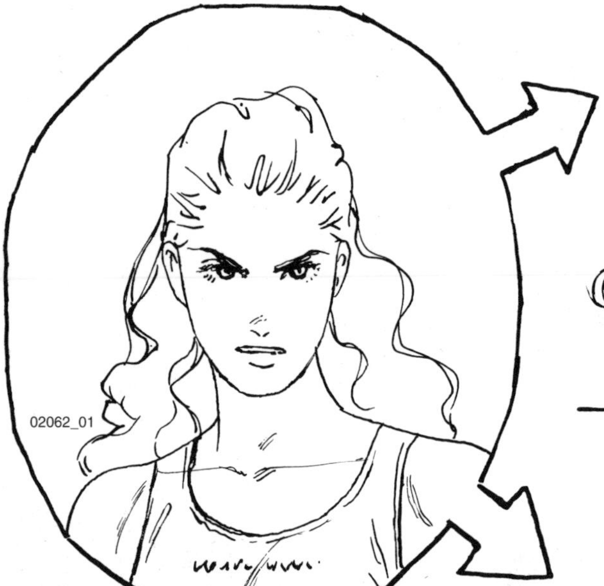

02062_01

■ベース■
Original

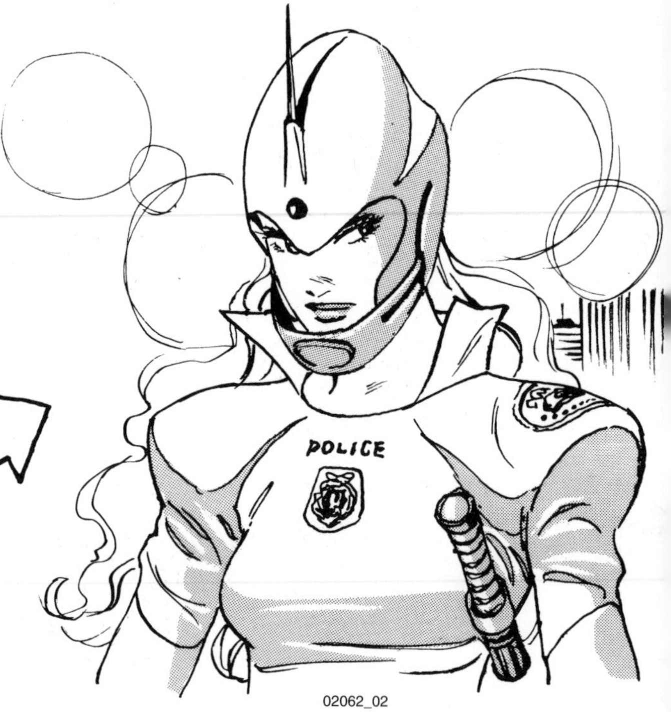
POLICE

02062_02

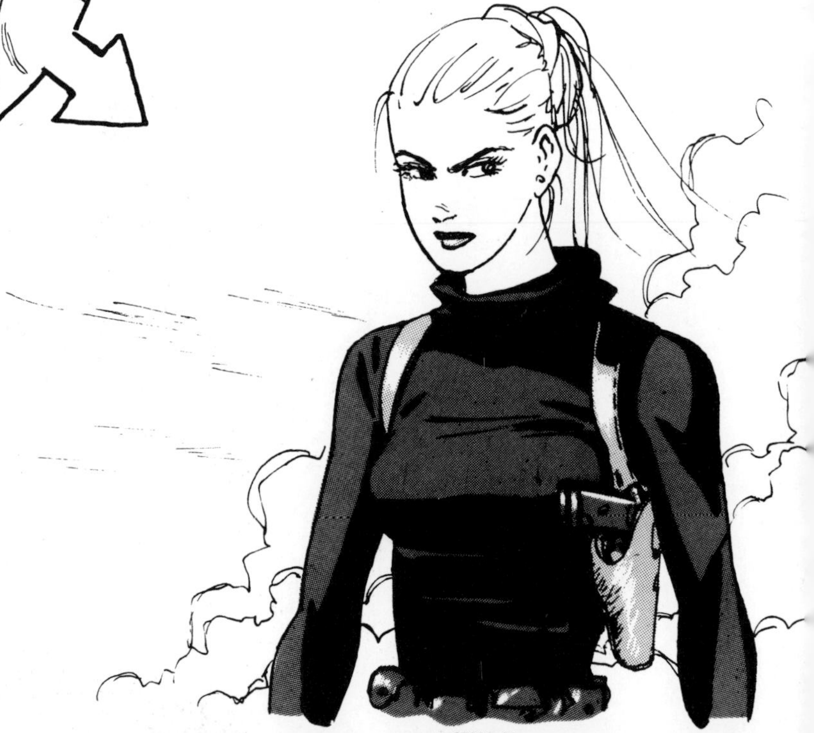

02062_03

■設定■

SPECIAL EFFECT

特殊効果

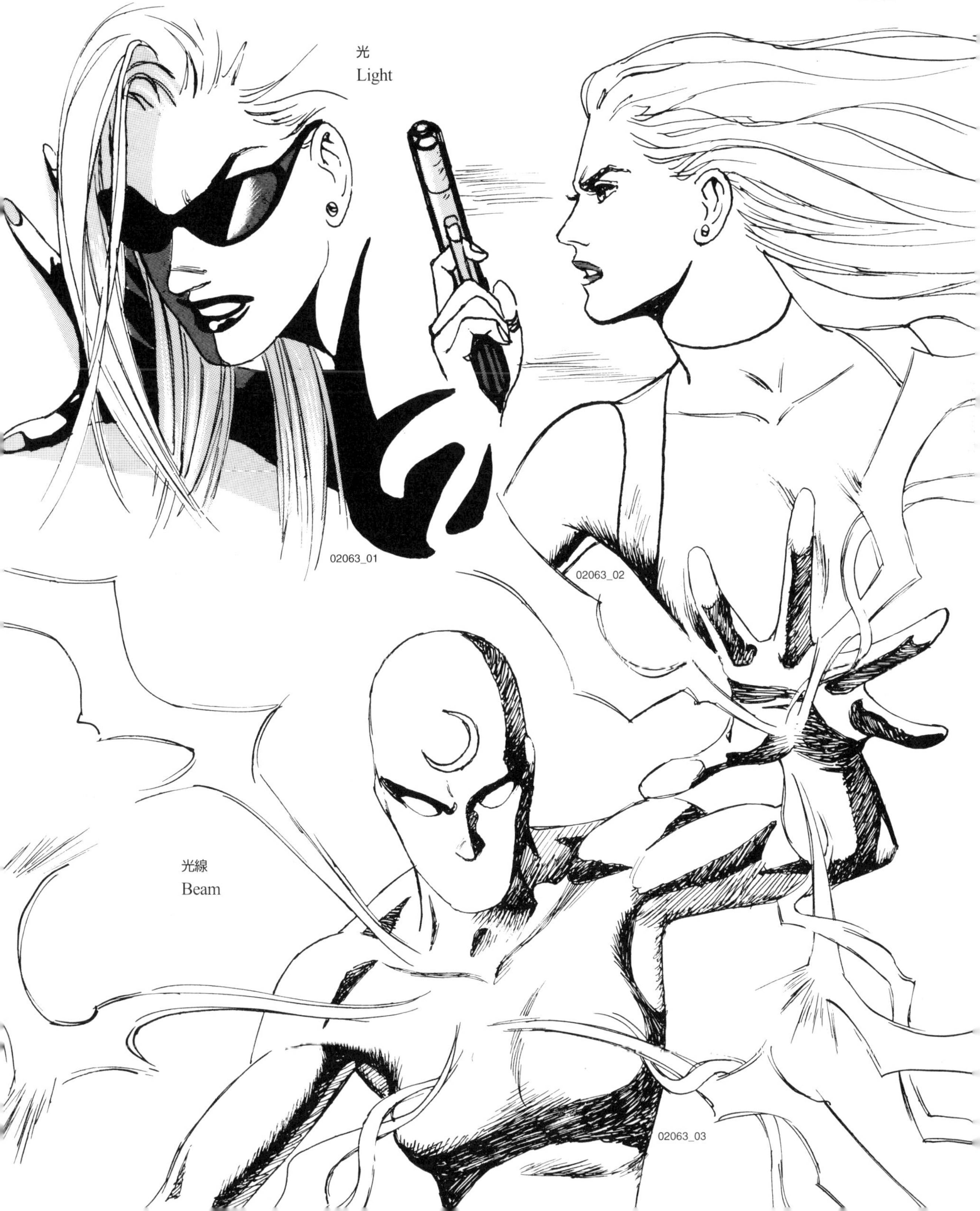
風
Wind
光
Light
02063_01
02063_02
光線
Beam
02063_03

■設定■

FEATURE

表情

●表情のバリエーション●

The variation of expression

キャラクターを描くためには、いろいろな表情や性格を使い分けなければならない。セクシーさや可愛さを表現できればもう最高だ。

In order to draw a character, you have to be able to use various characters and expressions properly. If sexiness and loveliness can be expressed, that is fine.

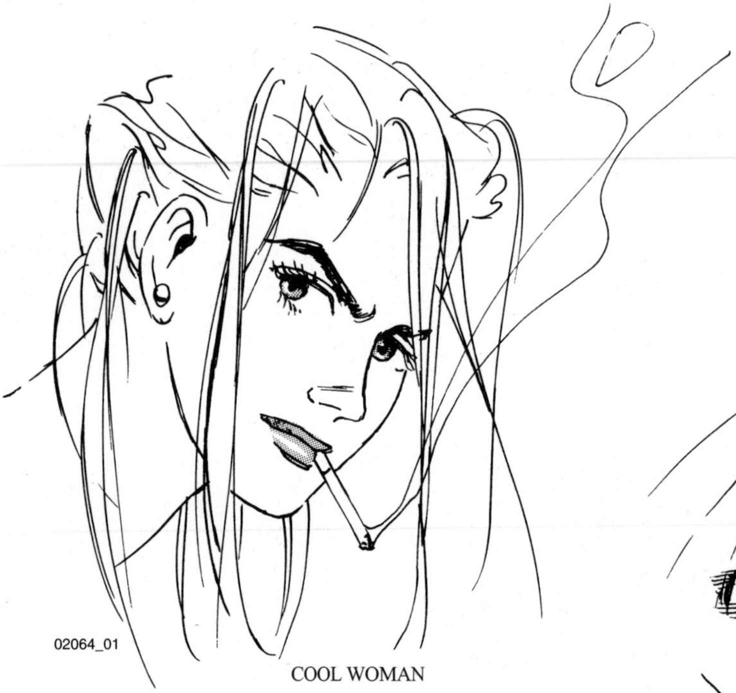

02064_01

COOL WOMAN

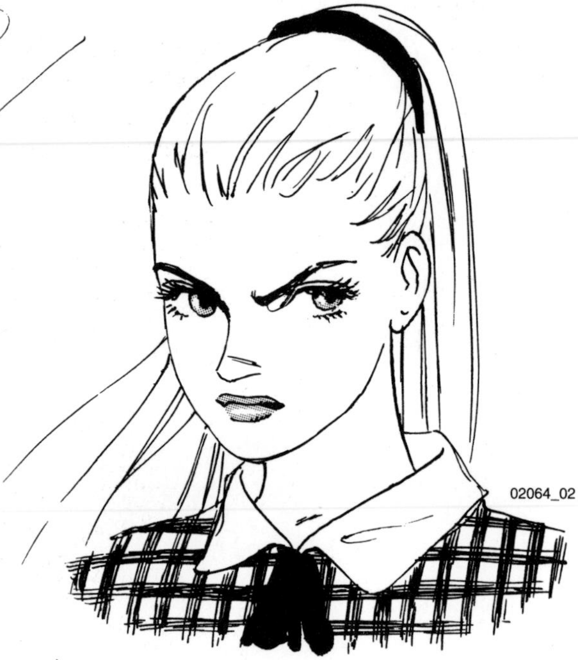

02064_02

PRETTY GIRL

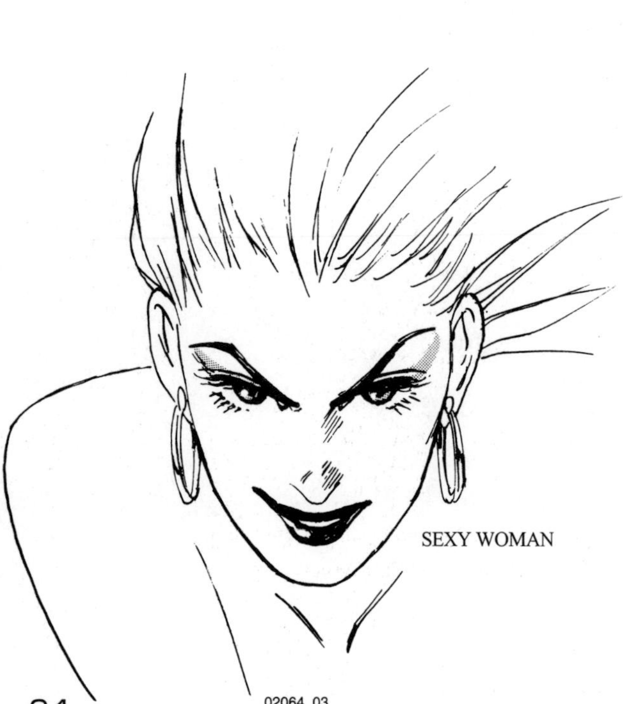

SEXY WOMAN

02064_03

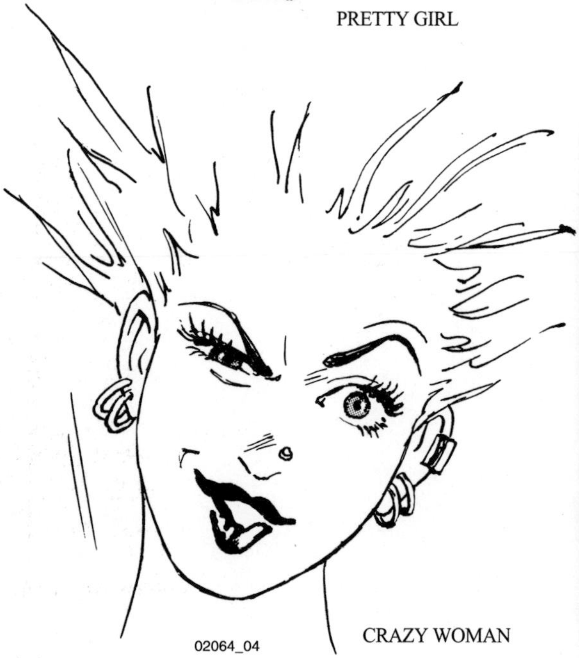

02064_04

CRAZY WOMAN

■設定■

THE WORK

まとめ作品

体格、性格、コスチューム、効果、表情をすべて統合して作例を創ってみた。参考にして欲しい。

I made examples of physique, character, costume, effects and expressions. I hope you are able to use this as a reference.

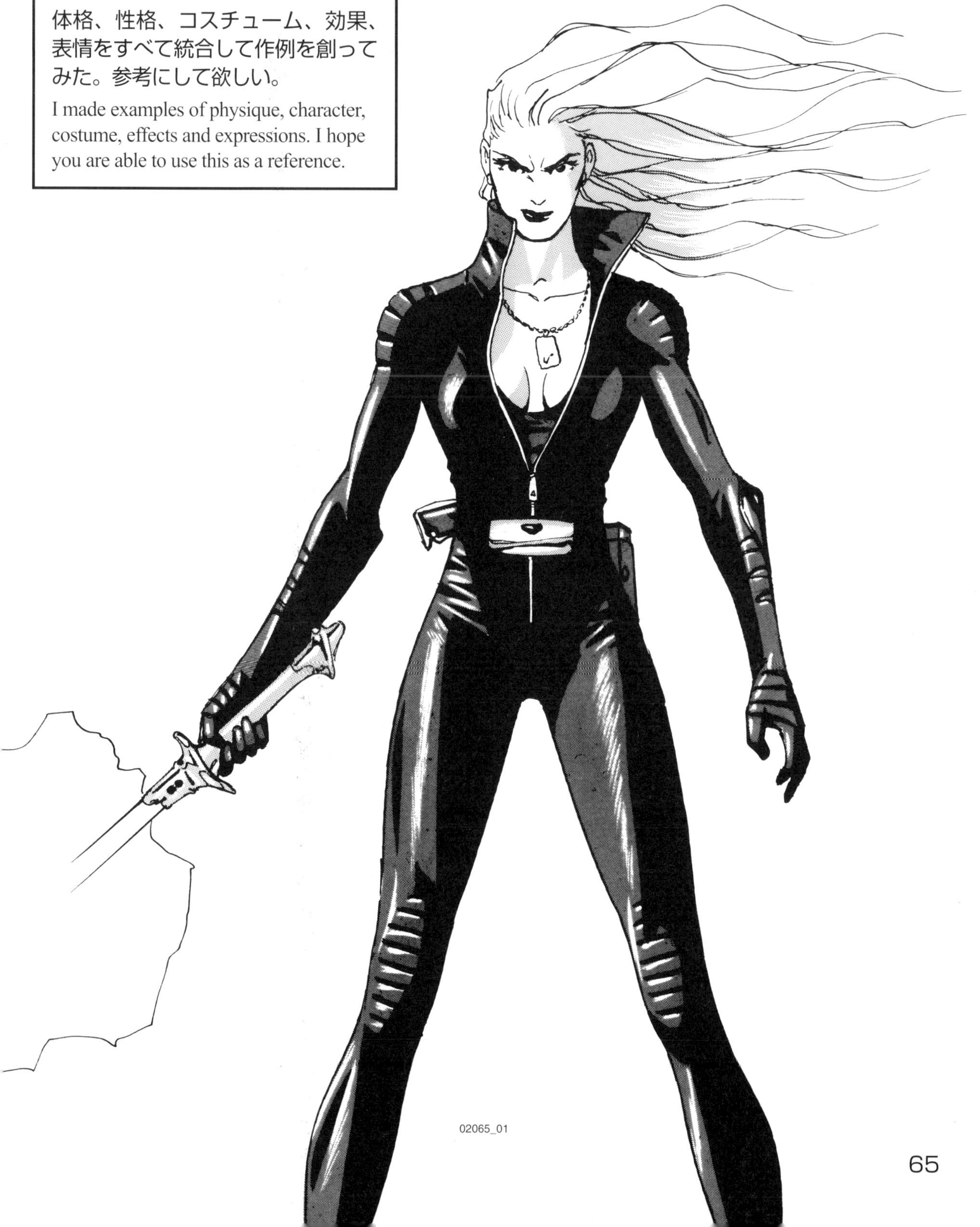

02065_01

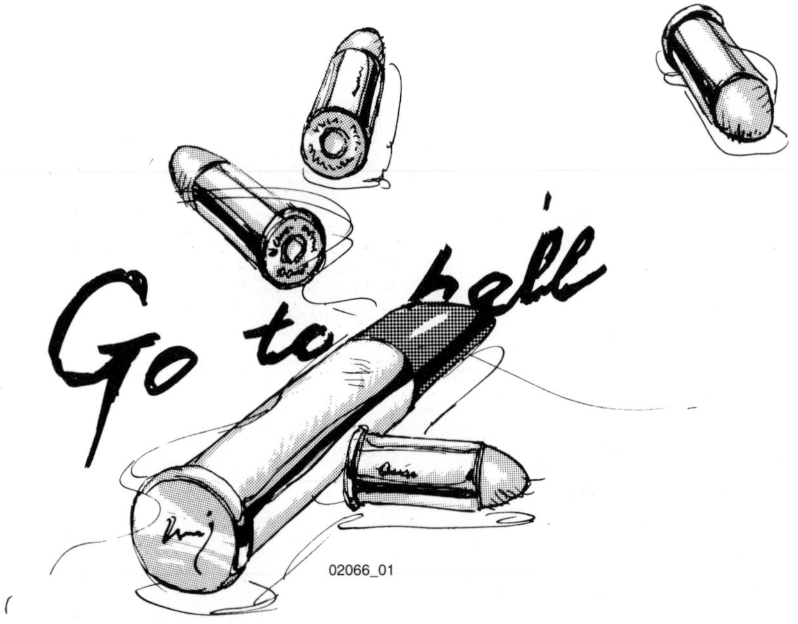
Go to hell

02066_01

ペンとワンポイント
PEN&TECHNIQUE

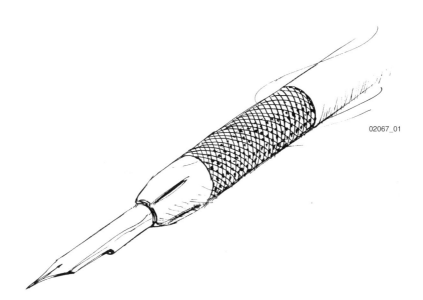

02067_01

PEN
ペン

作品を描くとき、私は主に製図用の
丸ペンを使っている。丸ペンは固く
てロットリングの0.1mmに負けな
いくらい細い線から、太い線まで描
ける。更に砥石で軽く先を研げば、
また新しい状態で細い線が引ける。
合理的で経済的なペンだ。

I mainly use a circle pen for drafting.
The circle pen is hard and can draw very
thin lines and very thick lines. If you
sharpen it on a whetstone, it draws line
new again. It is practical and economical
pen.

●ペンの種類●
The variation of pens

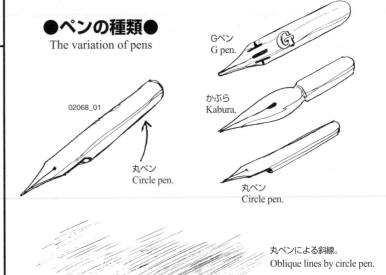

Gペン
G pen.

かぶら
Kabura.

02068_01

丸ペン
Circle pen.

丸ペン
Circle pen.

丸ペンによる斜線。
Oblique lines by circle pen.

●丸ペンで描いた線。
The line drawn with the circle pen.

02068_02

細い線
Thin line.

やや細い線
Comparatively thin line.

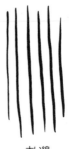

太い線
Thick line

とても太い線
Very thick line

02068_03

KMKケント
150kg

KMT kent
150kg

マンガ用
ケント紙

Kent for
comics

●紙
丸ペンは硬質なので、描いたときにひっかかったりしない紙を選ぶこ
とが大切。いろいろテストして、自分にあった紙を選ぼう。ちなみに
私はKMKケントの150kgを使用している。
●Paper
It is important to choose the right paper so that the pen
doesn't catch on the paper. Test various types and choose the
one that suits you. I use 150kg KMK Kent.

●インク
耐水性がよい。ホワイトで修正するときに溶けてにじまない
からだ。私はホルベインの耐水性カラーインクの黒を使用し
ている。
●Ink
Water resistant ink is better because it does melt and
run when using white correction fluid. I use black
from Holbein waterproof color inks.

PEN
ペン

丸ペンを使いこなすには、少し練習をしたほうがよい。他のペンに比べるとやや手強いペンだ。しかし、一度慣れたら手放せなくなる最高のペンだ。

In order to master the circle pen you will need to practice. Compared to other pens it is quite strong. However, once you get used to it, it is an exellent pen and you won't be able to part with it.

●丸ペンによる表現バリエーション●
The variation of expression by circle pen

A 細い線で描いたイラスト。
An illustration drawn with a thin line.

02069_01

B 細い線と太い線を組み合わせたイラスト。
An illustration combining thin and thick lines.

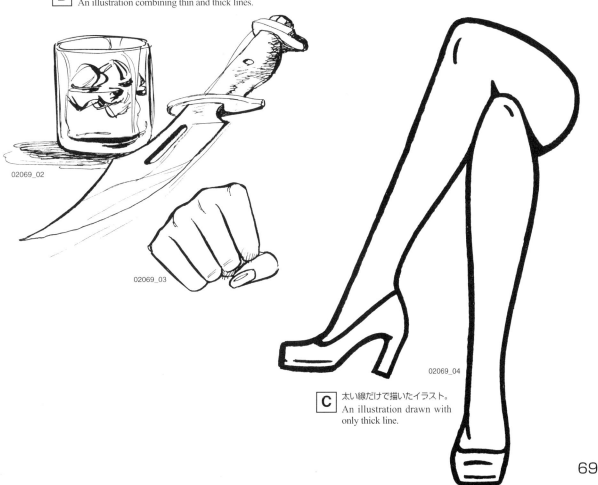

02069_02

02069_03

02069_04

C 太い線だけで描いたイラスト。
An illustration drawn with only thick line.

69

OBLIQUE STROKES
斜線

斜線は主に立体感や質感を表現するのに使う。

Use the oblique strokes mainly to achieve a cubic effect and the feeling of quality.

斜線の角度で柔らかさが変わる。
Softness changes by the angle of oblique strokes.

A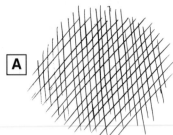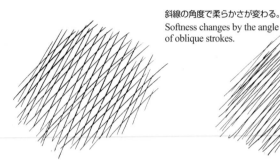

Aは、ペンを軽くもってこするように描く。
Hold a pen lightly and draw softly.

B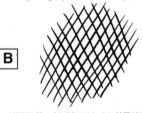

02070_01

Bは特別な使い方以外ではあまり効果がない。
B is almost ineffective except for special usage.

■質感表現例■
Texture example

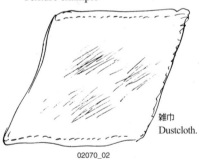

雑巾
Dustcloth.

02070_02

ジーパン
Jeans.

02070_04

鉄板を描くときは斜線の流れをそろえる。
The flow of a slash is arranged when drawing a griddle.

02070_05

上記Aのタッチでいろいろ表現してみた。
自分なりの表現を創り上げたい。
Many things were expressed by using touches in practice A.
Establish your own expression.

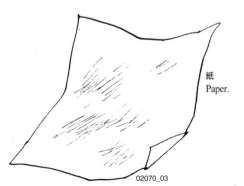

紙
Paper.

02070_03

02070_06

クロスしない斜線を上手に描こう。
Let's draw oblique lines well without crossing them.

■PEN&TECHNIQUE■

SOLIDITY
斜線による立体感の表現

02071_01

02071_02

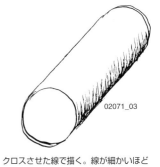

02071_03

A アメリカンコミックによくある表現。
This is often used in American comics.

B 細い一本の線で。
By one thin line.

C クロスさせた線で描く。線が細かいほど
リアルになるのがわかる。
It is drawn by crossing lines. You can
see that the thinner the lines the more
realistic it becomes.

■質感表現例■
Texture example

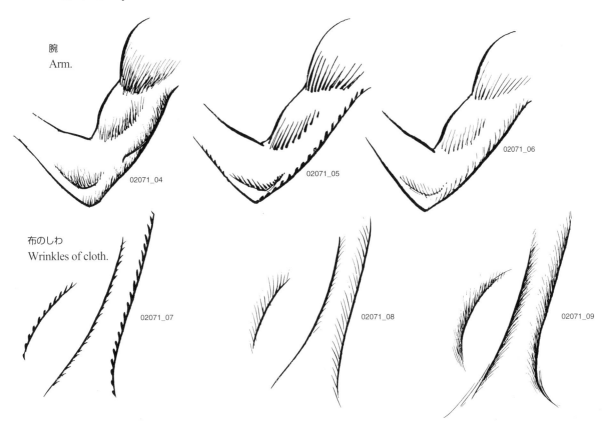

腕
Arm.

02071_04

02071_05

02071_06

布のしわ
Wrinkles of cloth.

02071_07

02071_08

02071_09

71

ONE POINT ADVICE
ワンポイント・アドバイス

1 one スーパーヒロインのフィギュアを1つ買おう！

スーパーウーマンやキャットウーマンのフィギュアを持っていれば、身体を描くときの参考になる。

Buy one Figure super heroine! If you have Superwoman or Catwoman, practice drawing a body by referring to this figure.

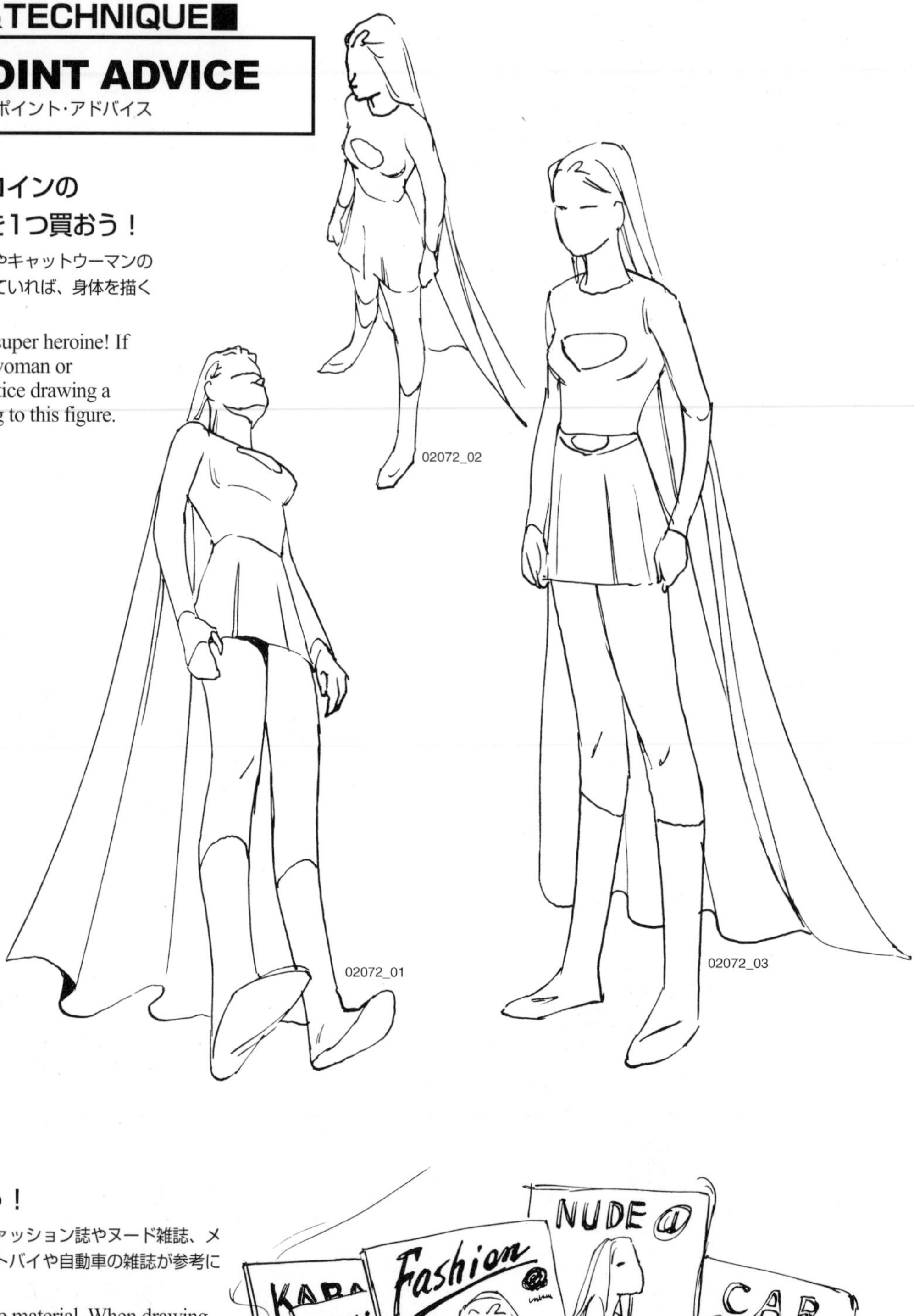

02072_01 02072_02 02072_03

2 two 資料を見よう！

身体を描くならファッション誌やヌード雑誌、メカを描くならオートバイや自動車の雑誌が参考になる。

Refer to reference material. When drawing bodies refer to fashion or nude magazines. When drawing machanics refer to motercycle or car magazines.

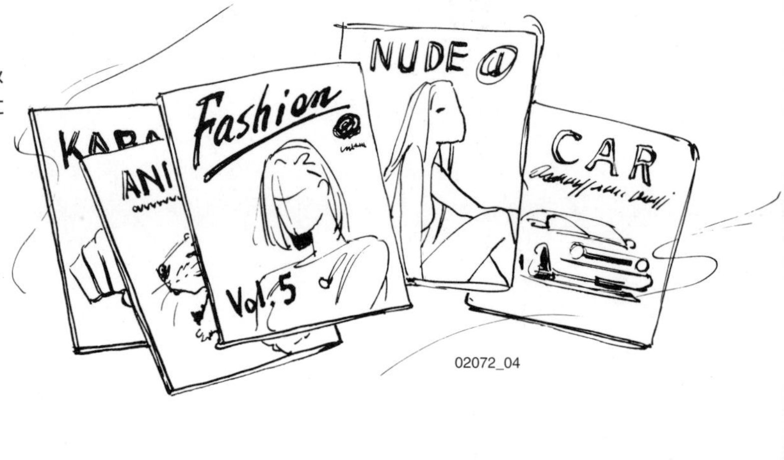
KARA
ANI
Fashion
Vol.5
NUDE
CAR

02072_04

3 three 鏡を利用しよう！

手鏡をいつも机の上に用意しておくととても便利だ。特に手を描くときに役立つ。コップを持った手などを鏡を見ながら描ける。

Use a mirror! It is very convenient if you always prepare a mirror on your desk. It is useful especially when drawing a hand. You can draw a hand holding a glass etc, while looking at it in the mirror.

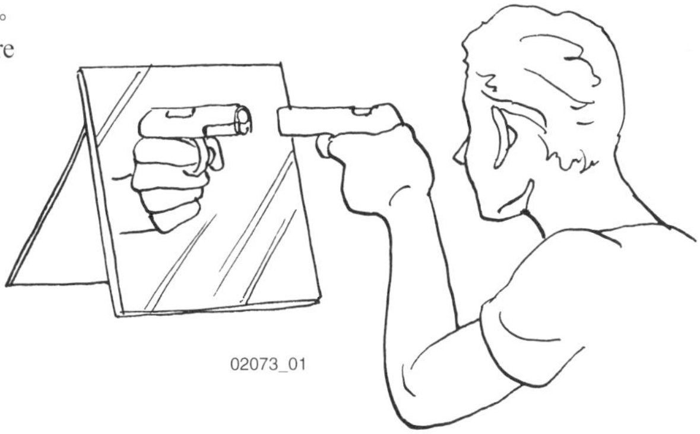

02073_01

4 four アップの効果を理解しよう！

同じポーズでも一部を誇張することによって迫力が出る。

You can make a character more powerful by exaggerating one portion of the same pose.

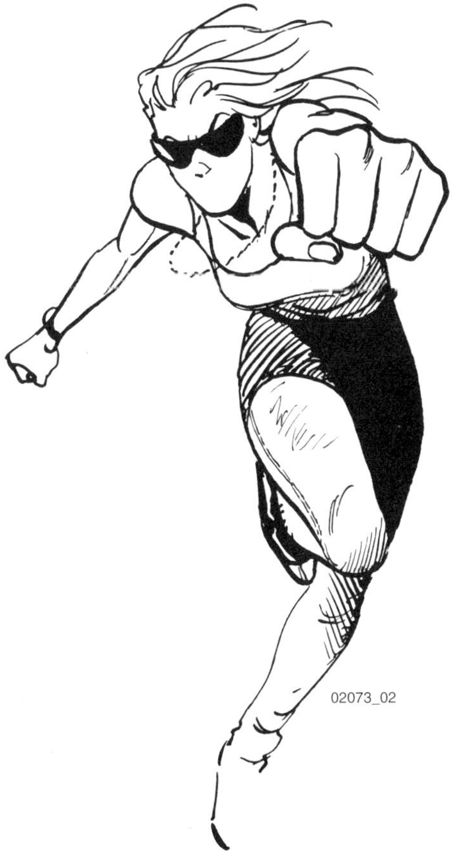

02073_02

拳を大きく誇張して描くと効果的だ。

It is effective if a fist is exaggerated.

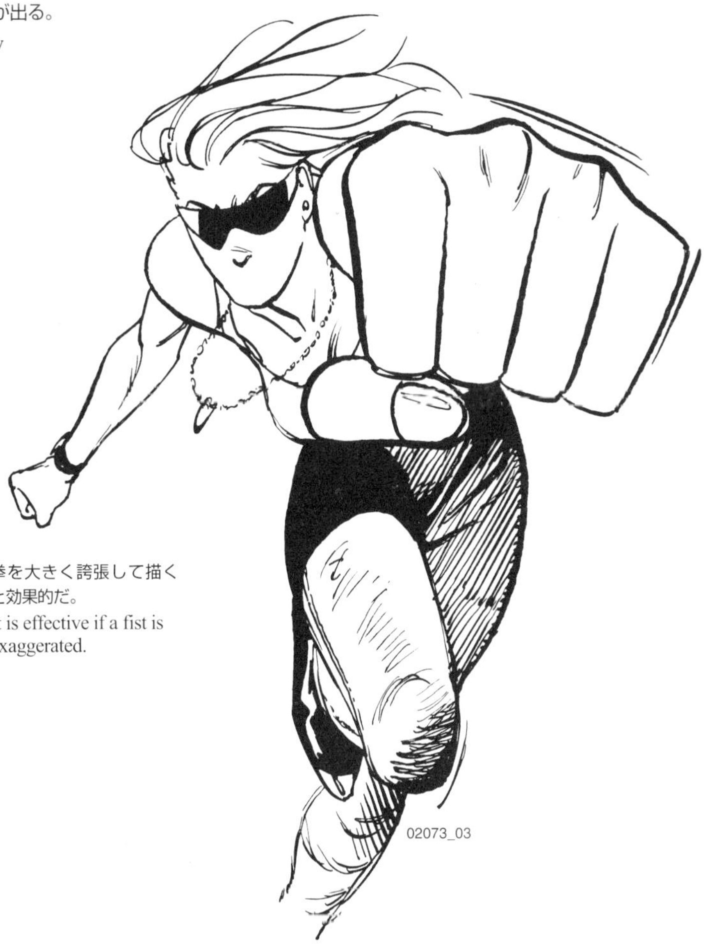

02073_03

■PEN&TECHNIQUE■

ZOOM

アップの効果

アップは誇張するほど効果がある。下の図で比較してみた。

The more exaggerated, the more effective. I compared the lower figures.

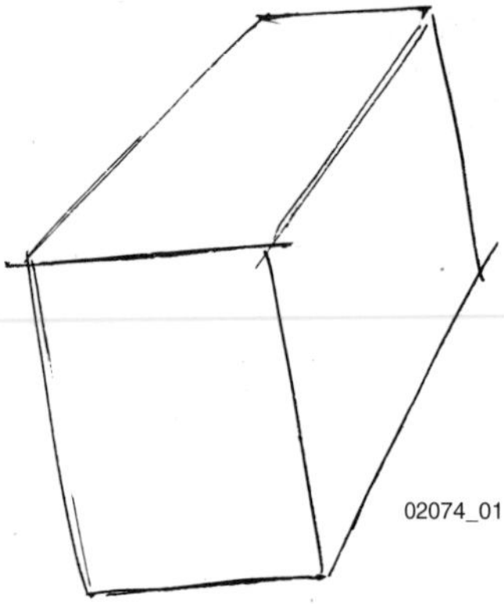

02074_01

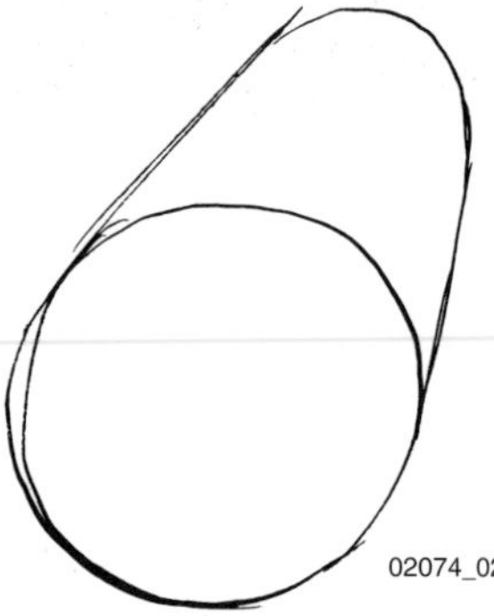

02074_02

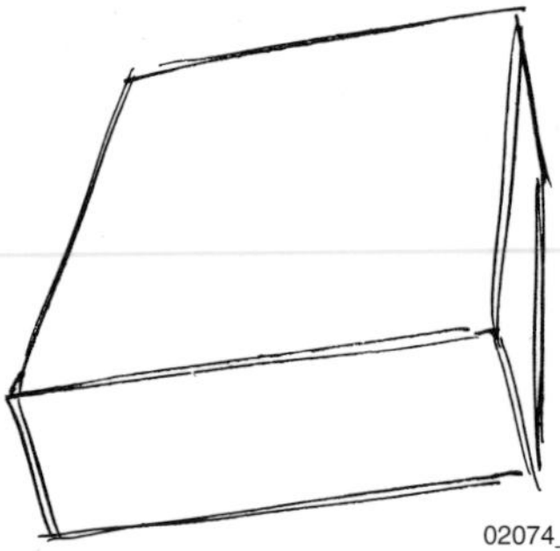

02074_03

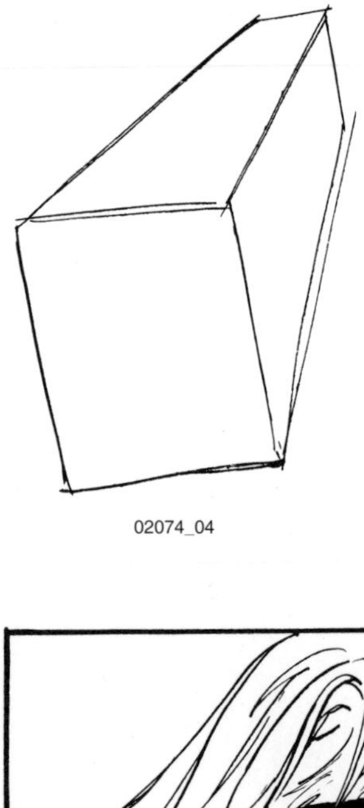

02074_04

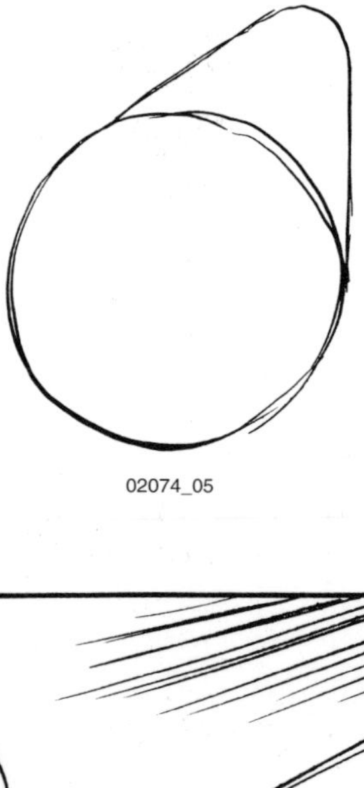

02074_05

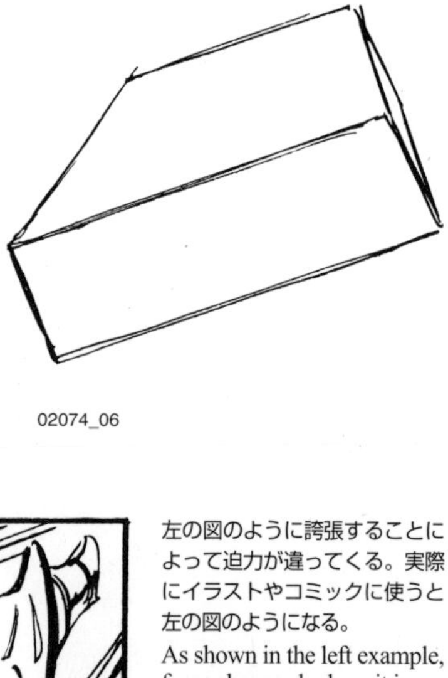

02074_06

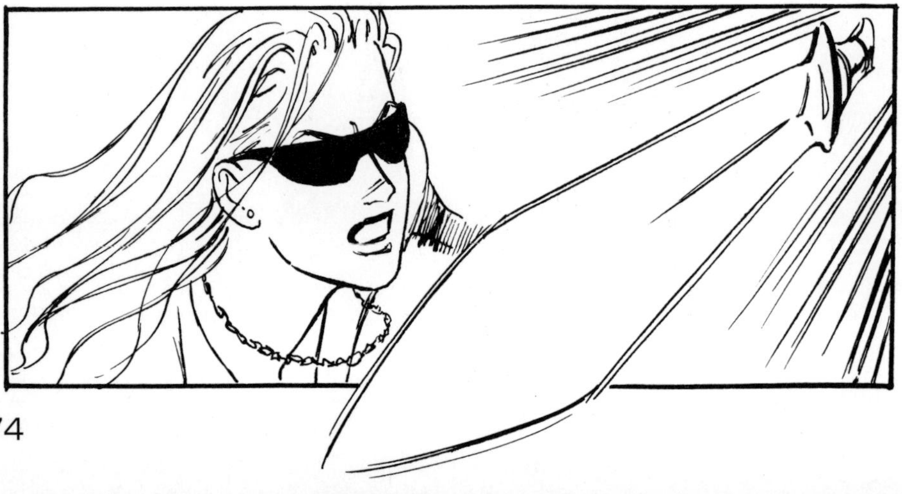

左の図のように誇張することによって迫力が違ってくる。実際にイラストやコミックに使うと左の図のようになる。

As shown in the left example, force changes by how it is exaggerated. If it is actually used in an illustration or comic it will turn out like the left example.

02074_07

POSES

ポーズ集

02101_04

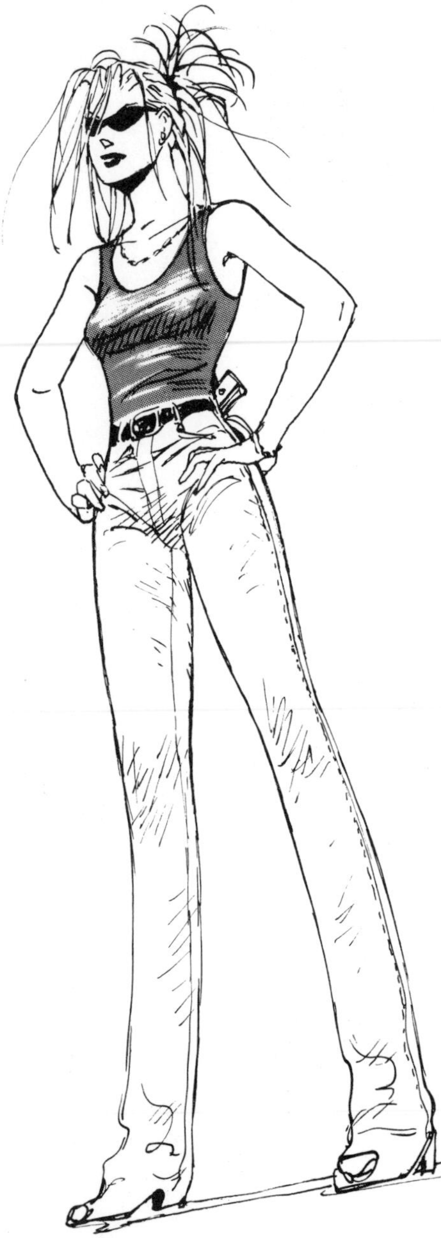

02076_01

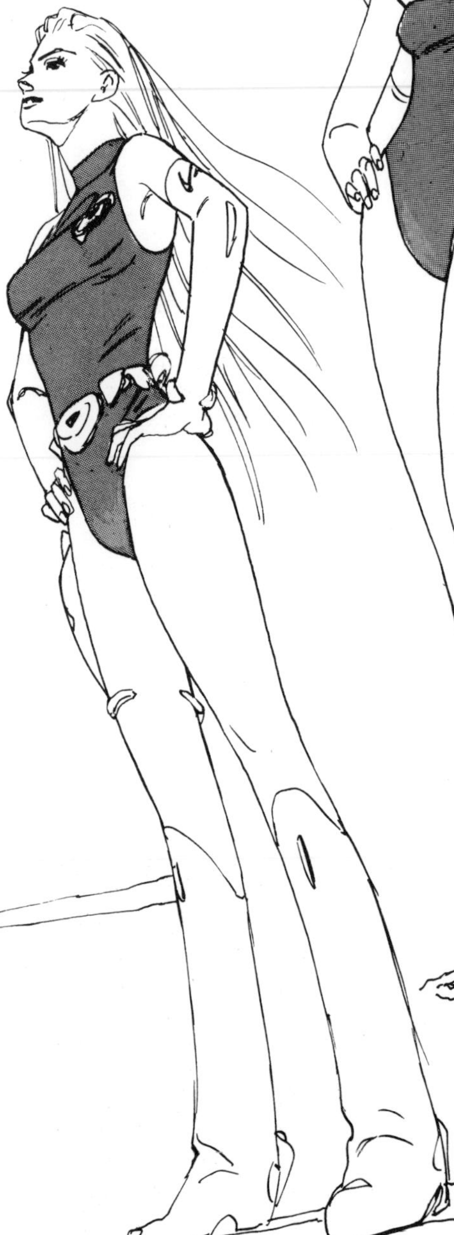

02076_02

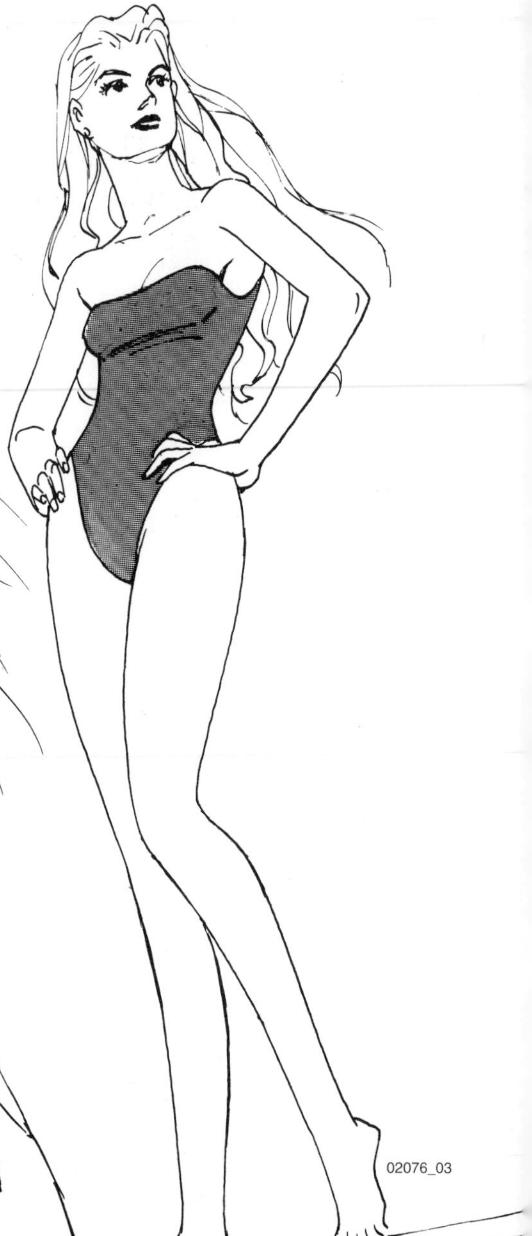

02076_03

WALK

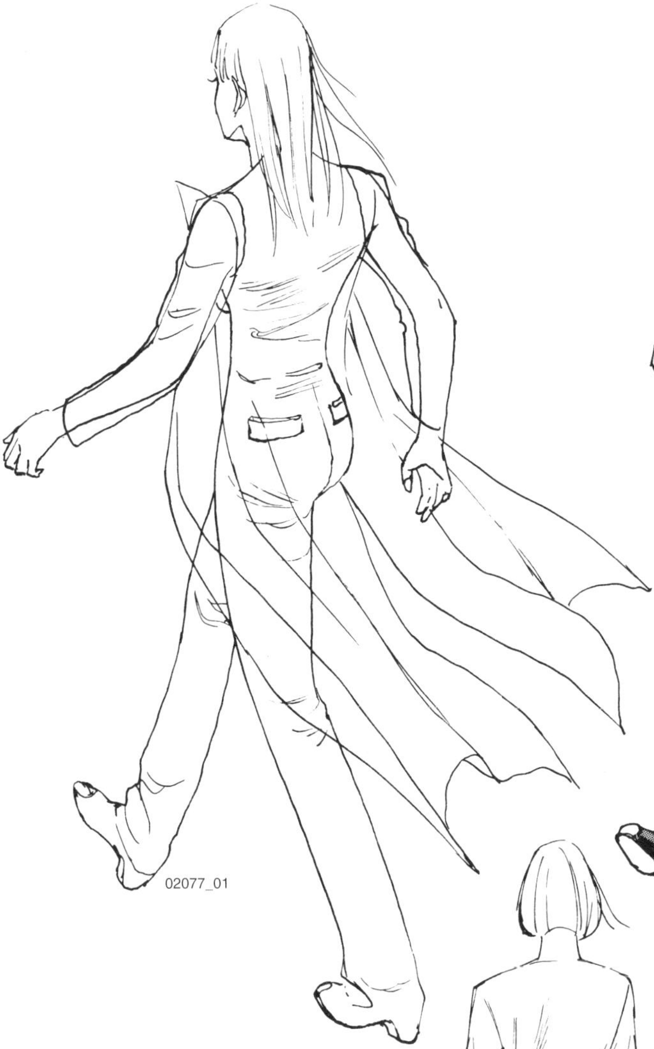

02077_01

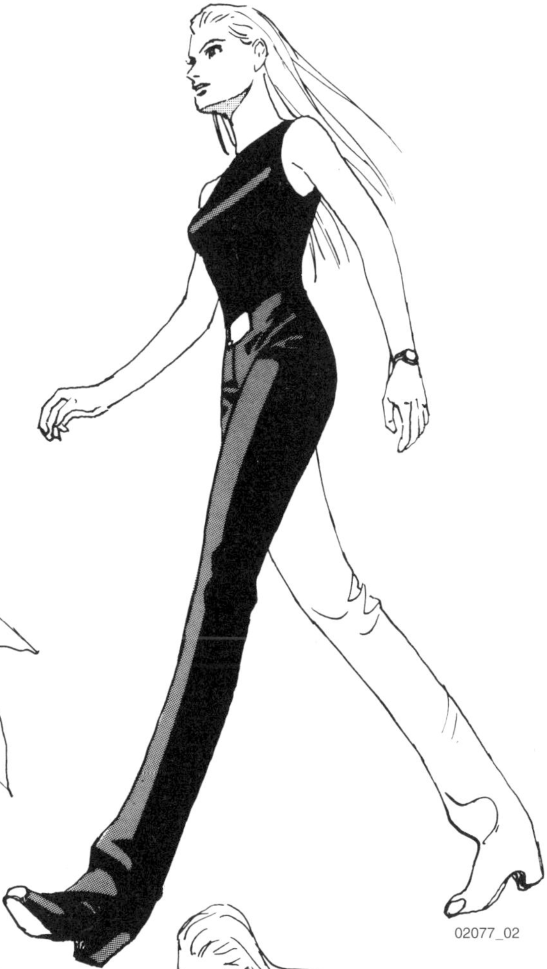

02077_02

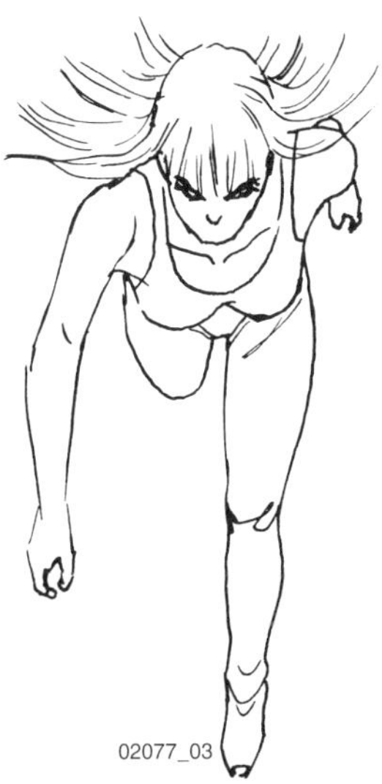

02077_03

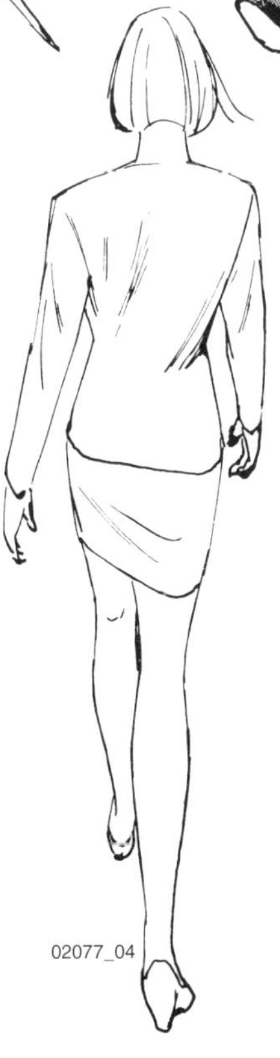

02077_04

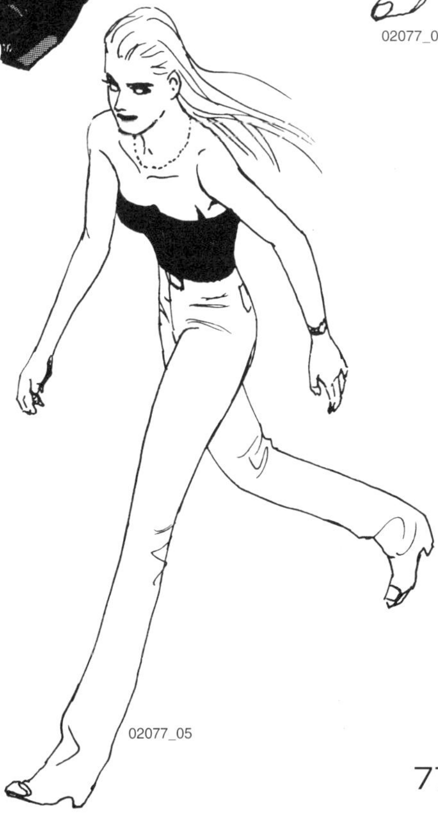

02077_05

WALK

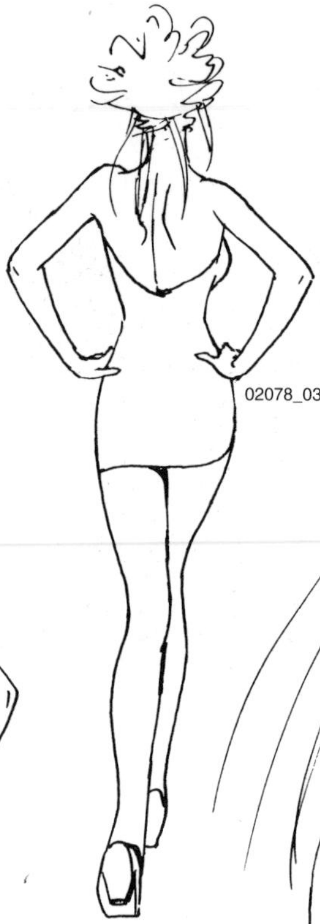

02078_03

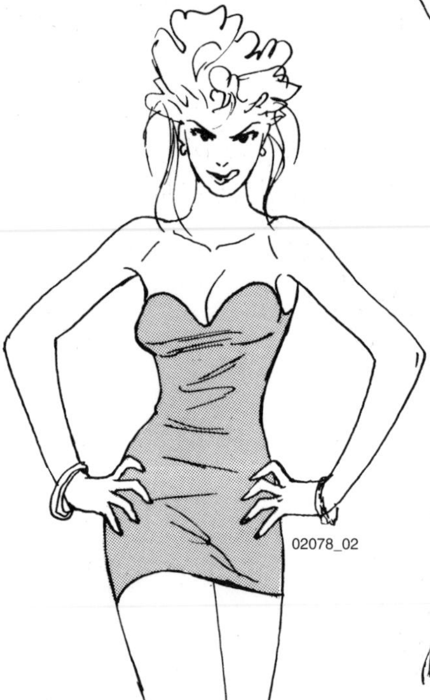

02078_02

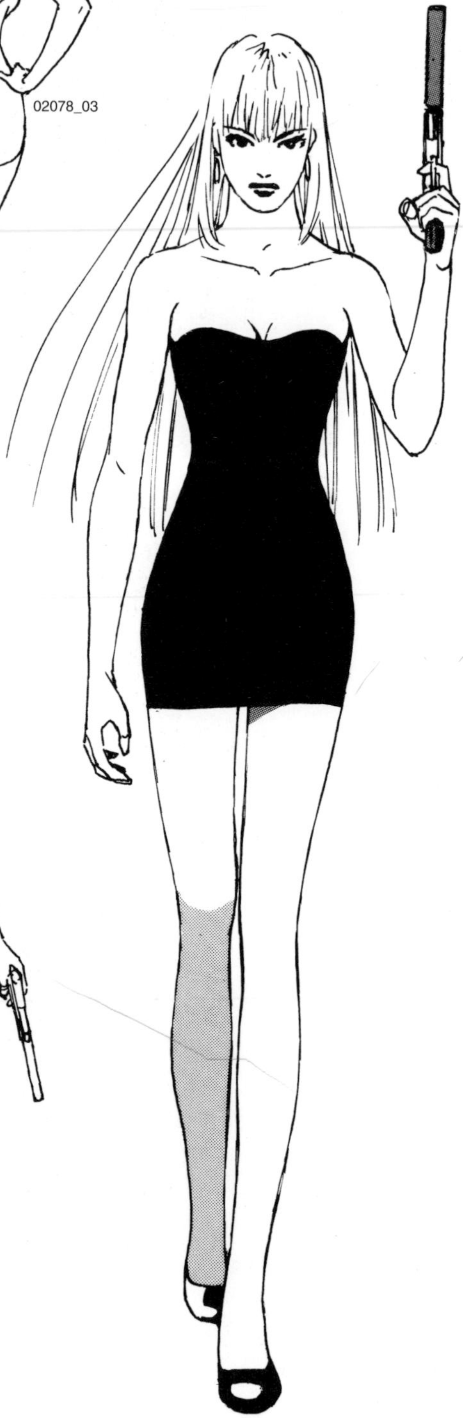

02078_05

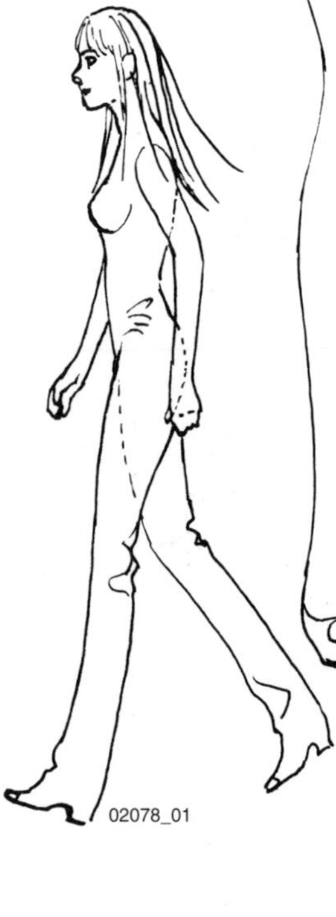

02078_01

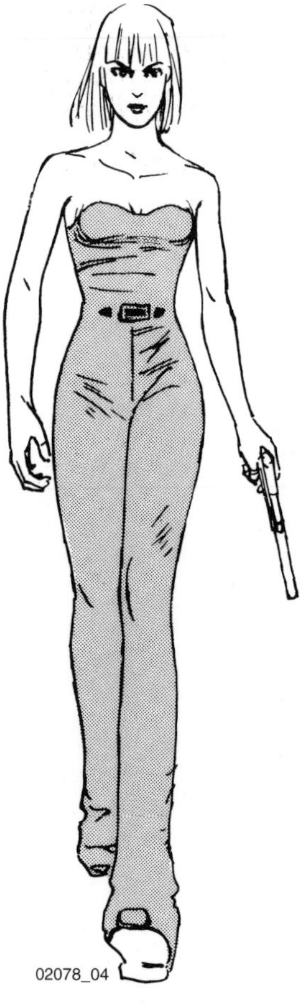

02078_04

RUN

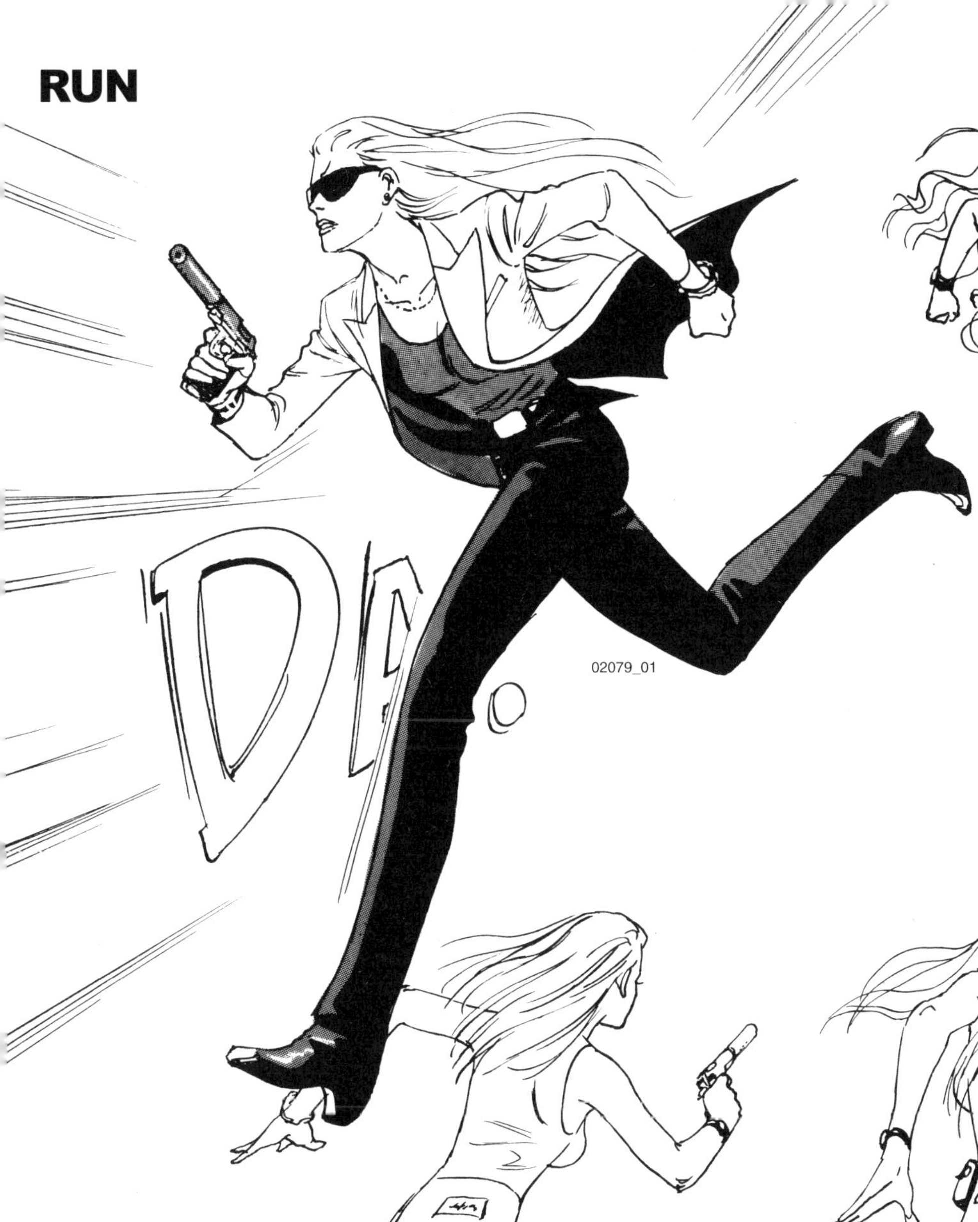

02079_01

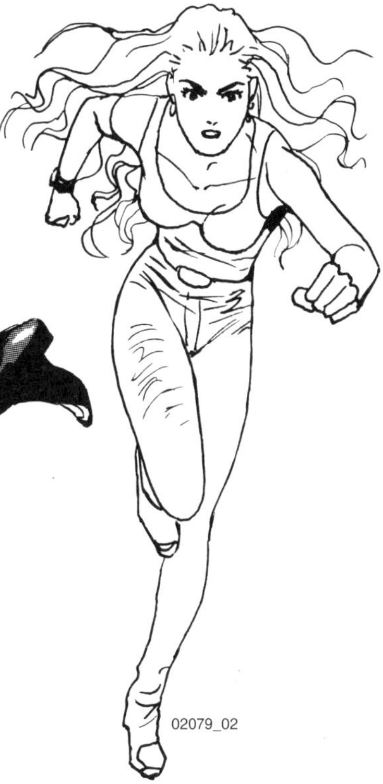

02079_02

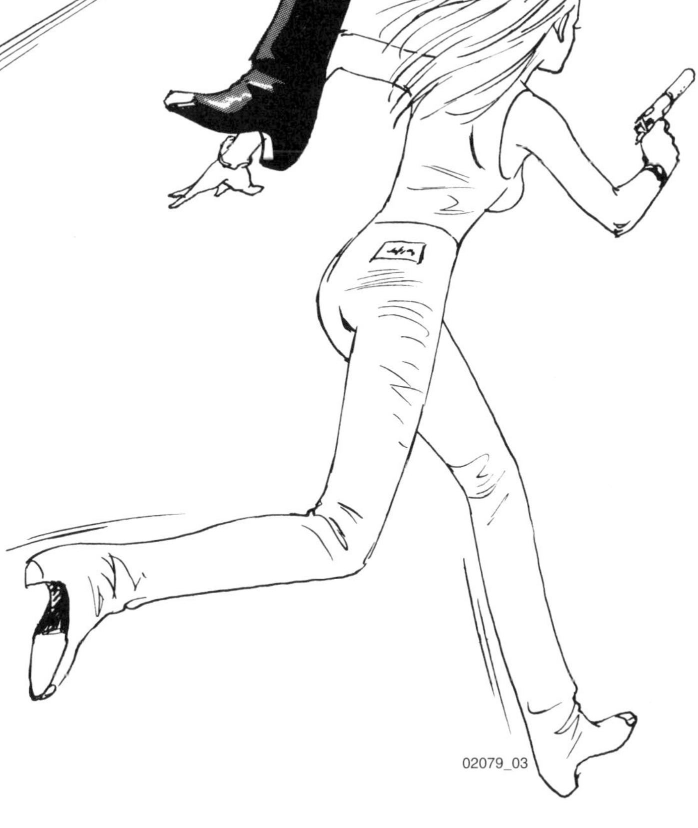

02079_03

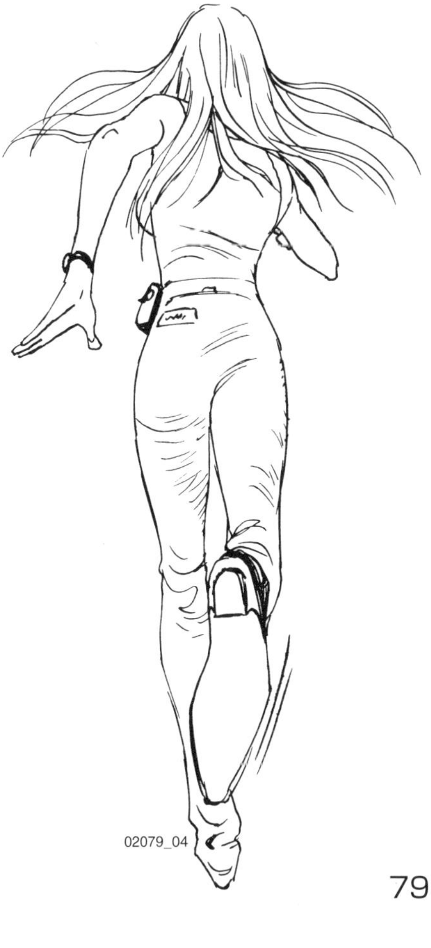

02079_04

RUN

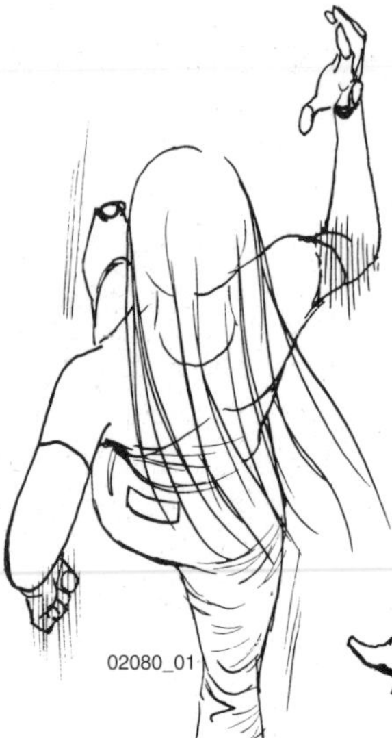

02080_01

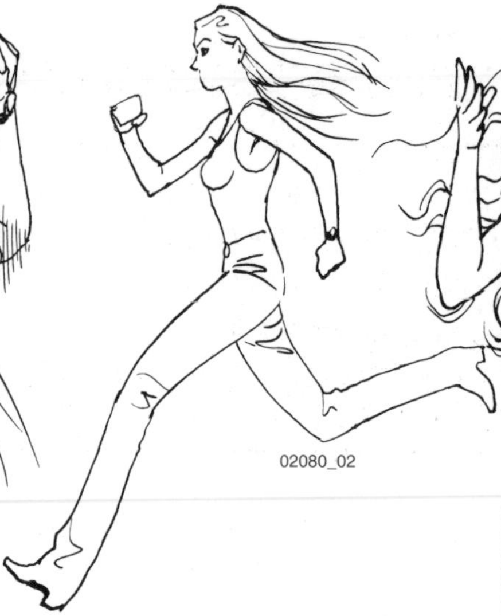

02080_02

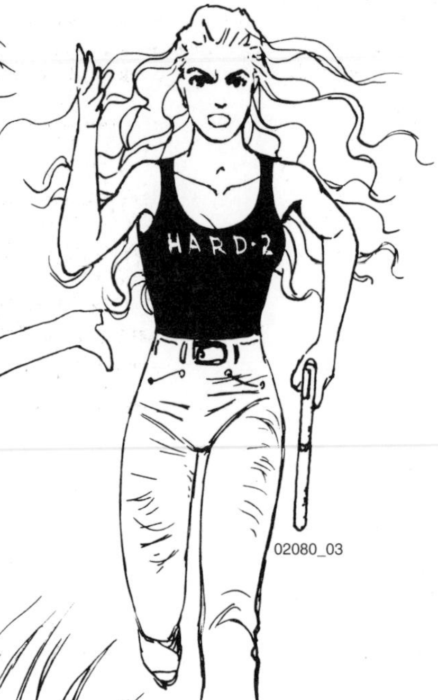
HARD-2

02080_03

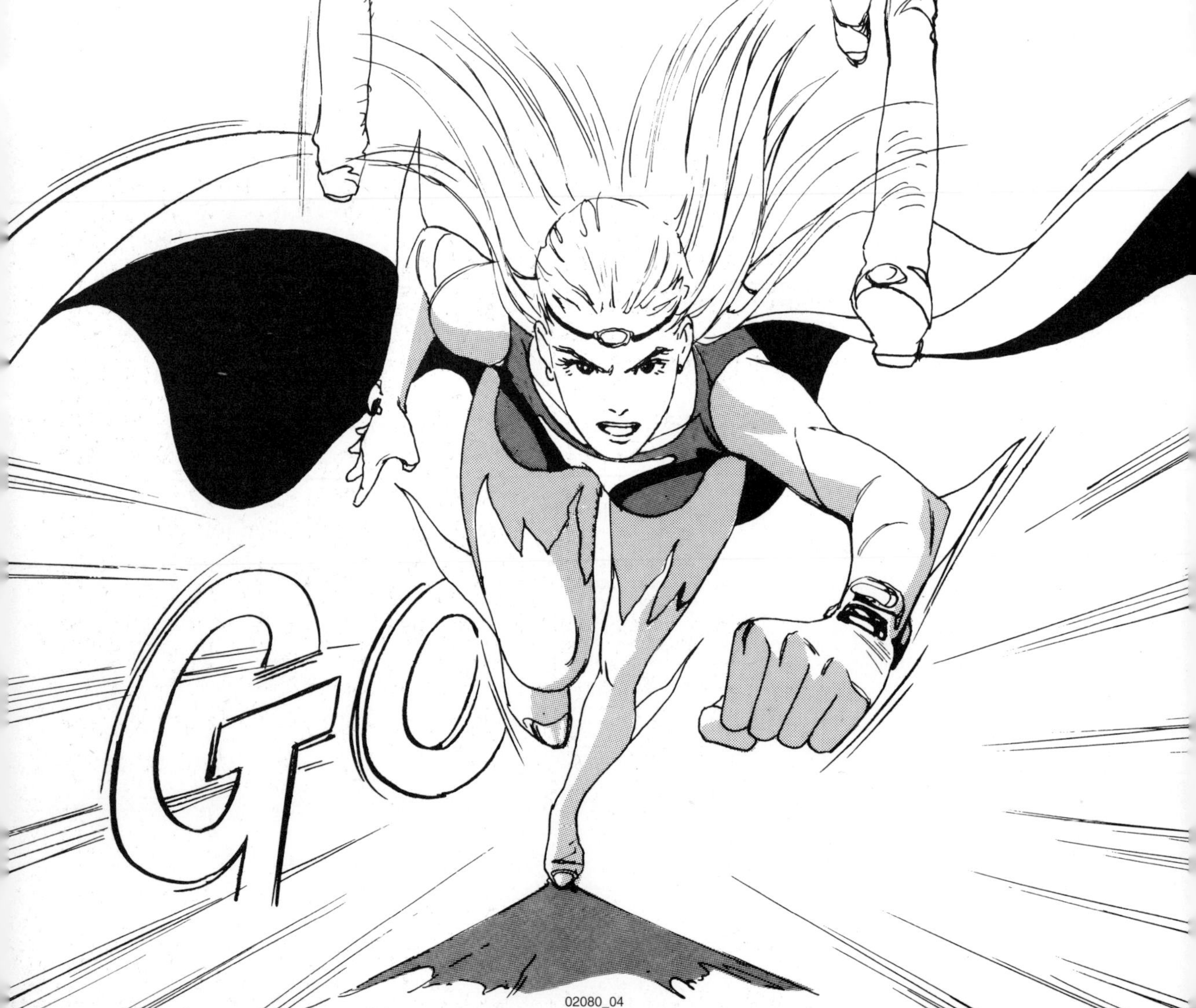
GO

02080_04

PUNCH

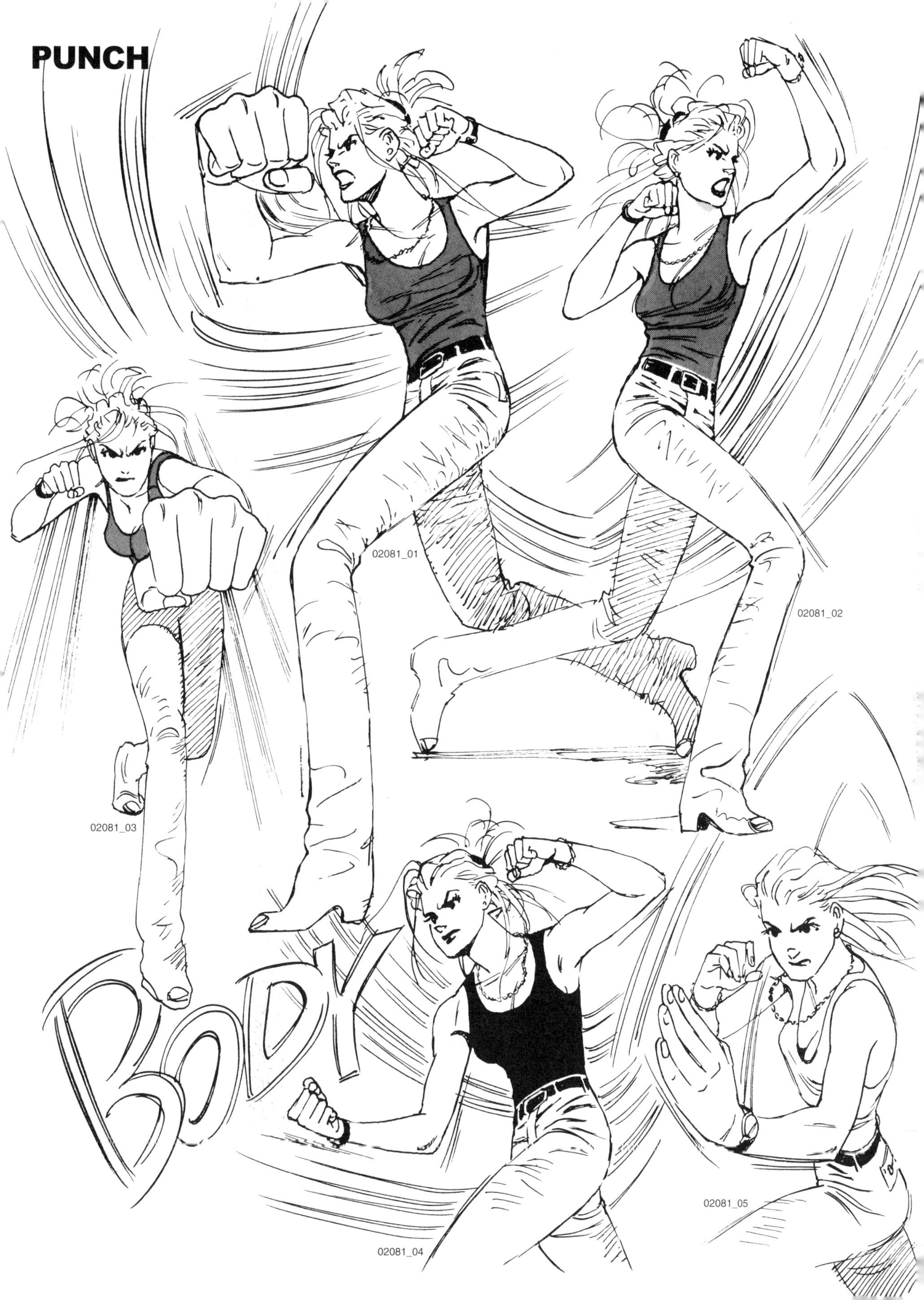

02081_01
02081_02
02081_03
BODY
02081_04
02081_05

PUNCH

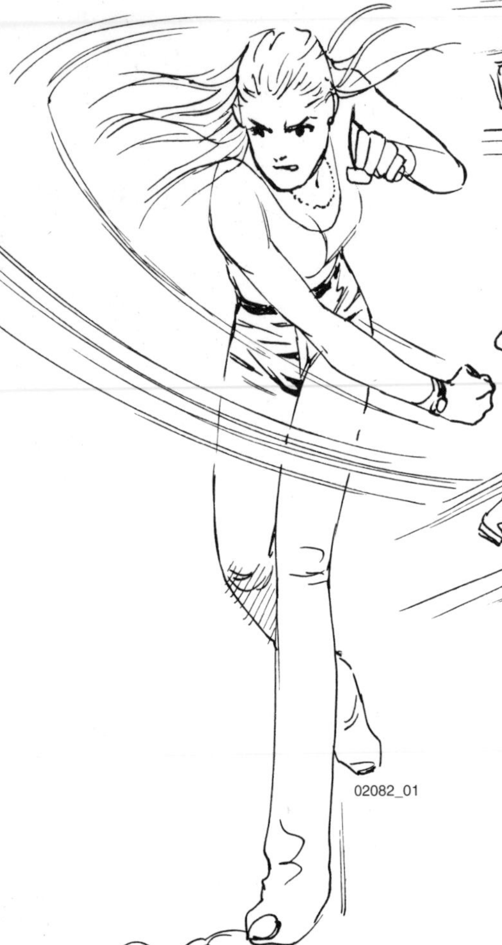

02082_01

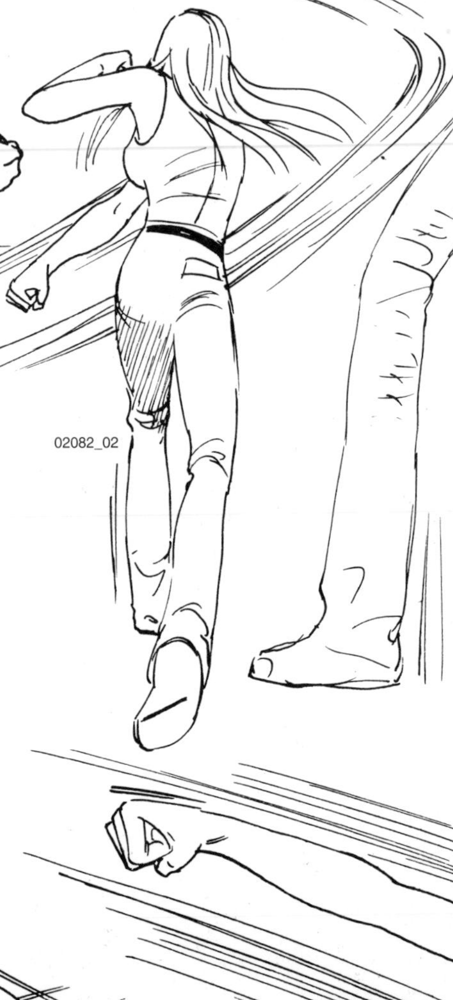

02082_02

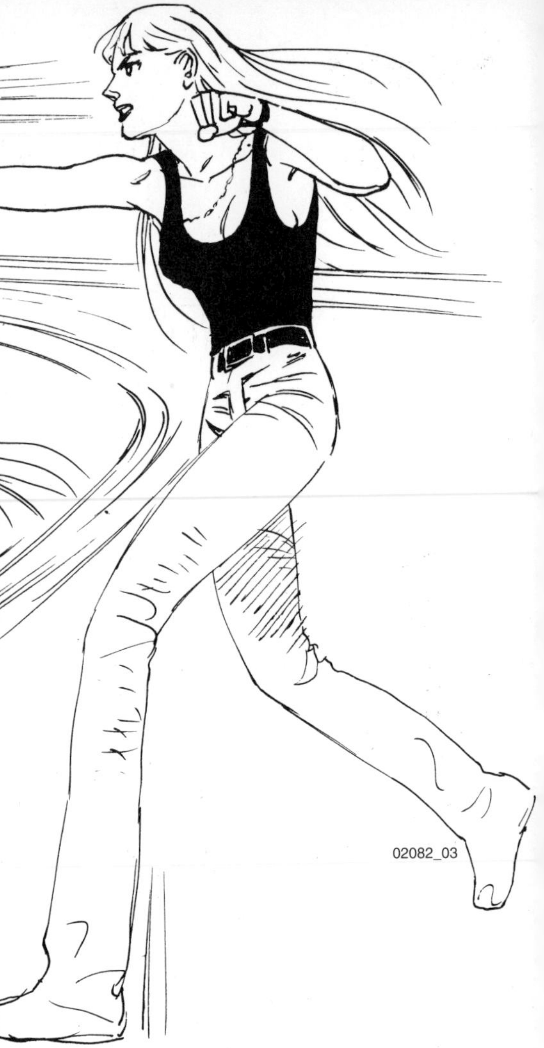

02082_03

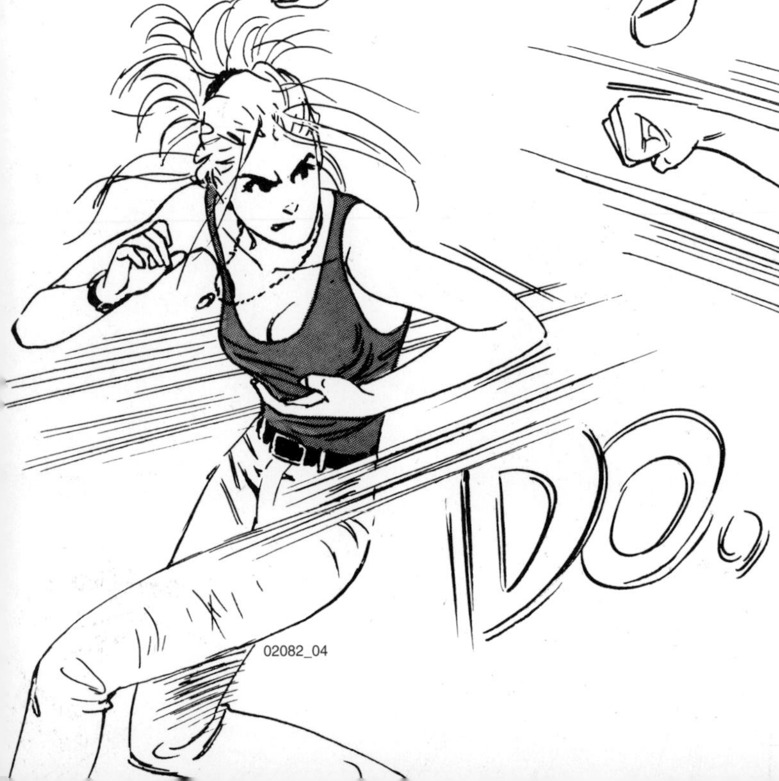
DO

02082_04

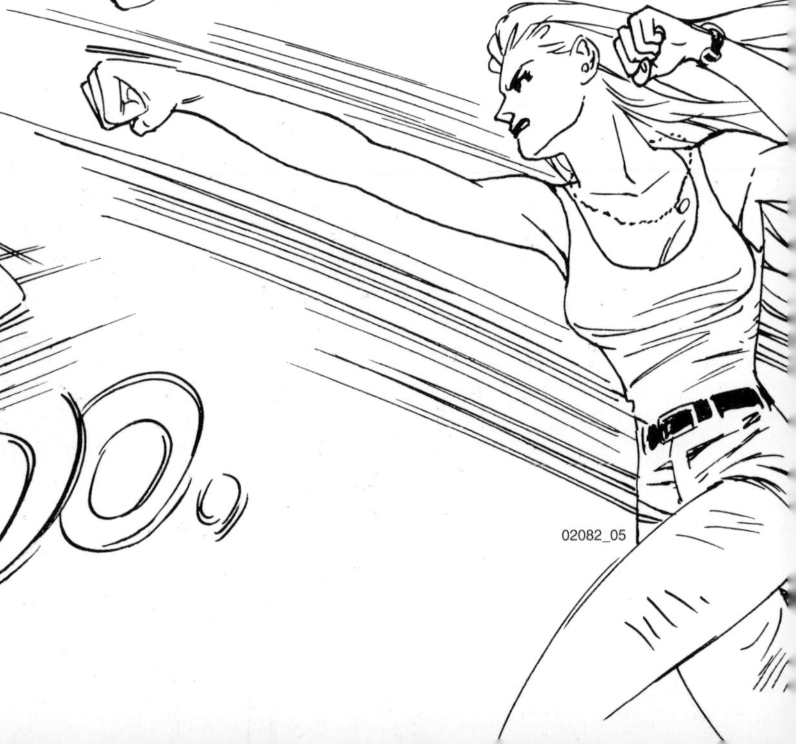

02082_05

KICK

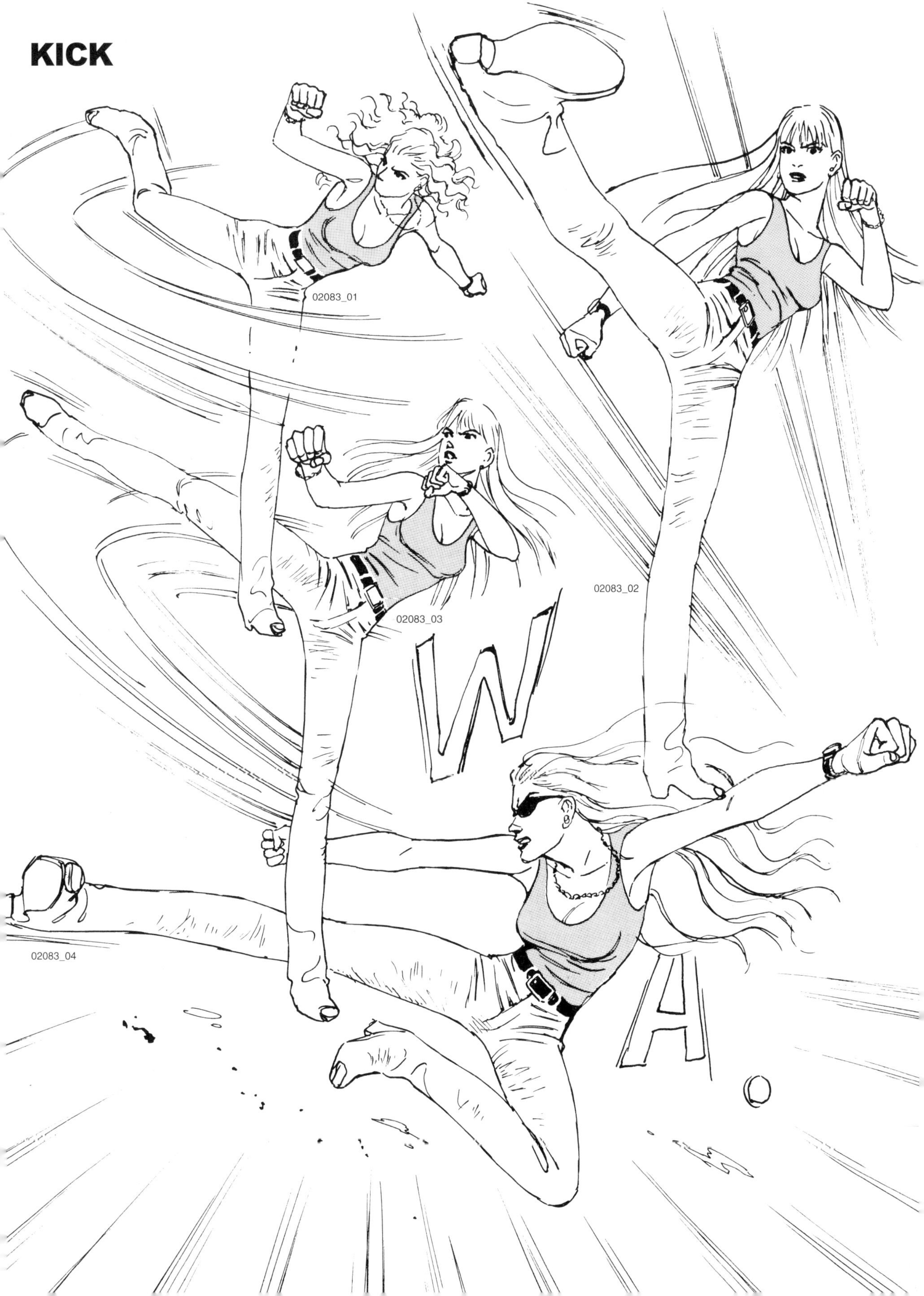
02083_01
02083_02
02083_03
W
A
02083_04

KICK

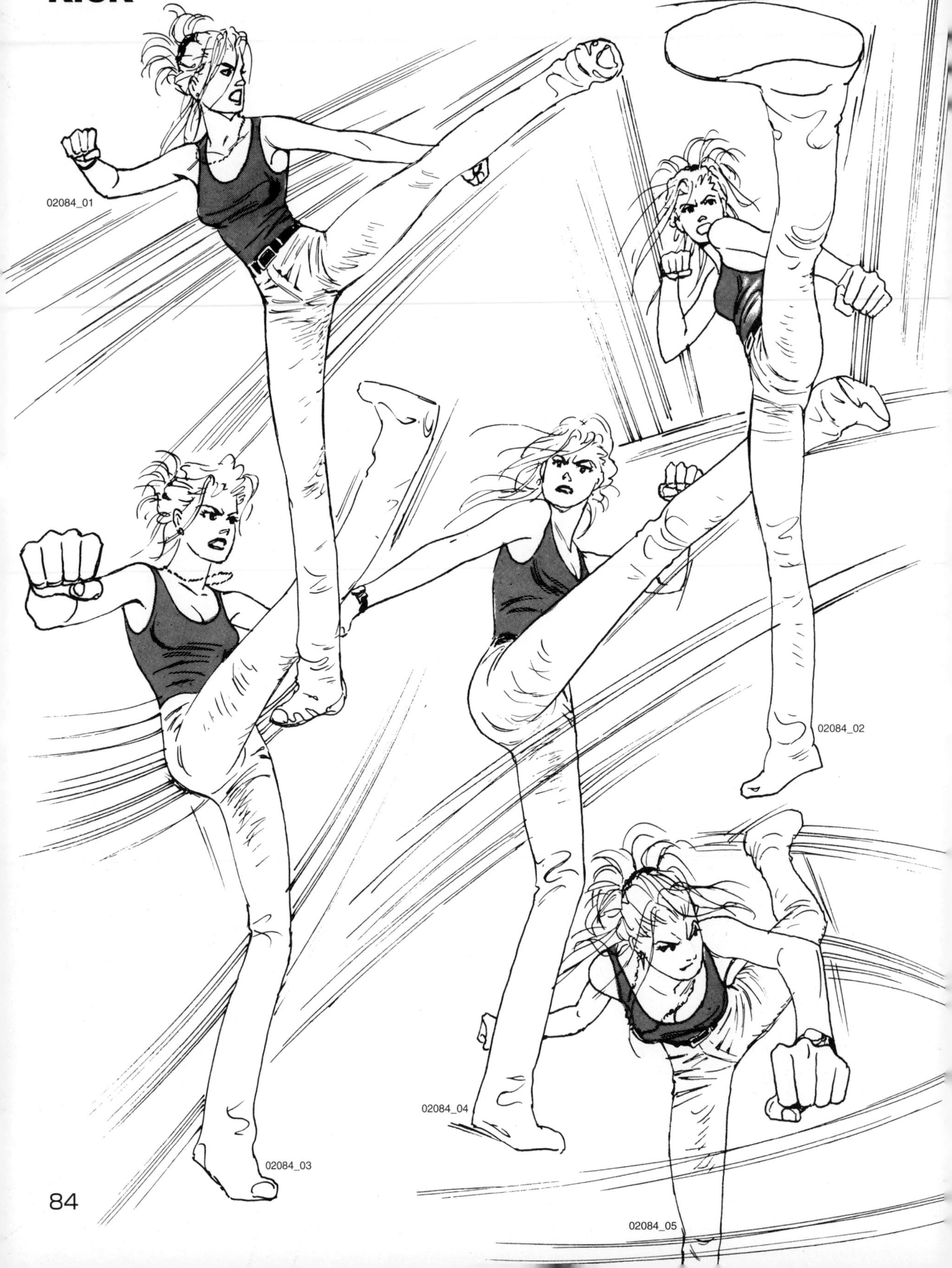

02084_01
02084_02
02084_03
02084_04
02084_05

BLADE

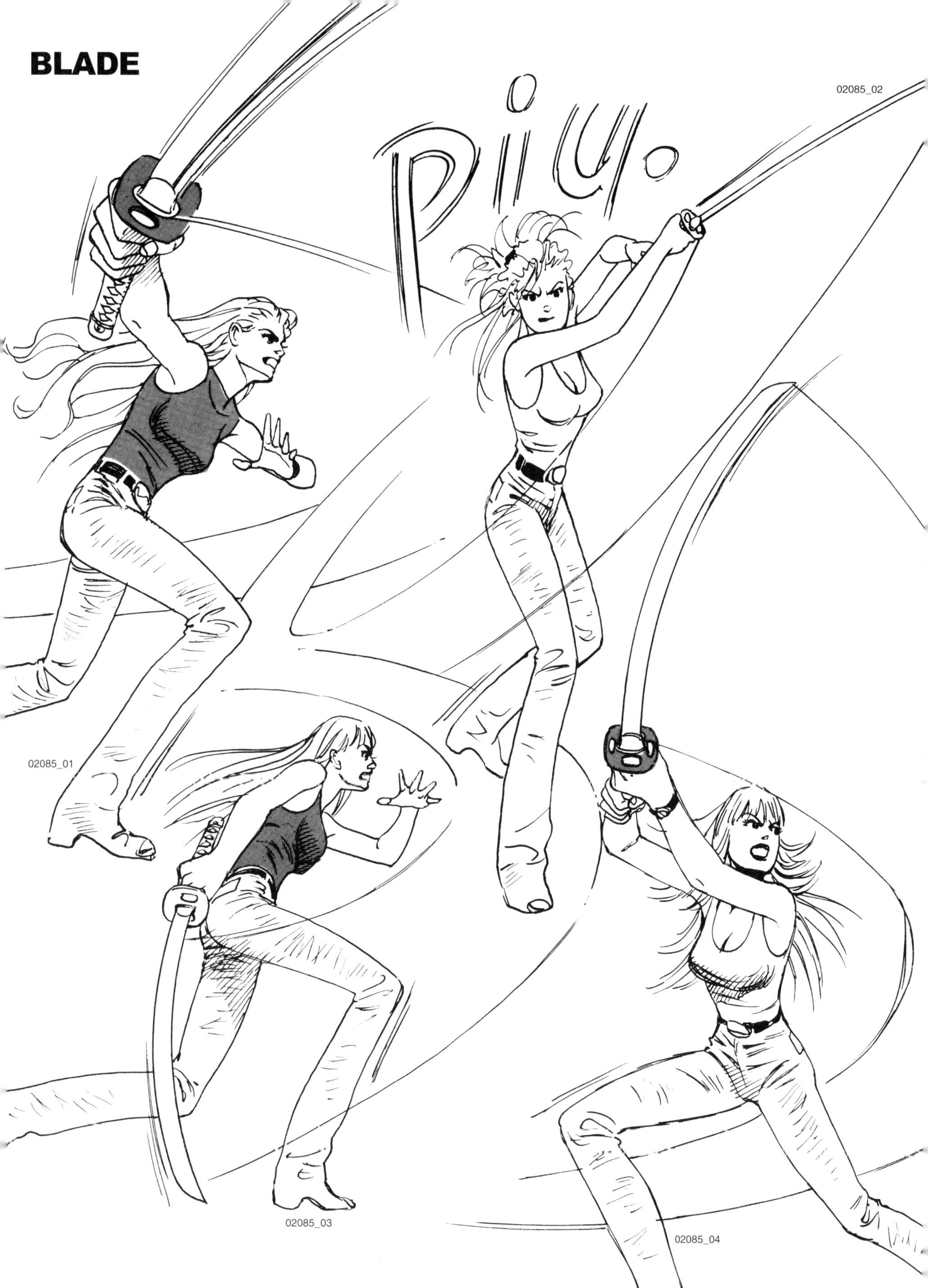
piu

02085_01
02085_02
02085_03
02085_04

BLADE

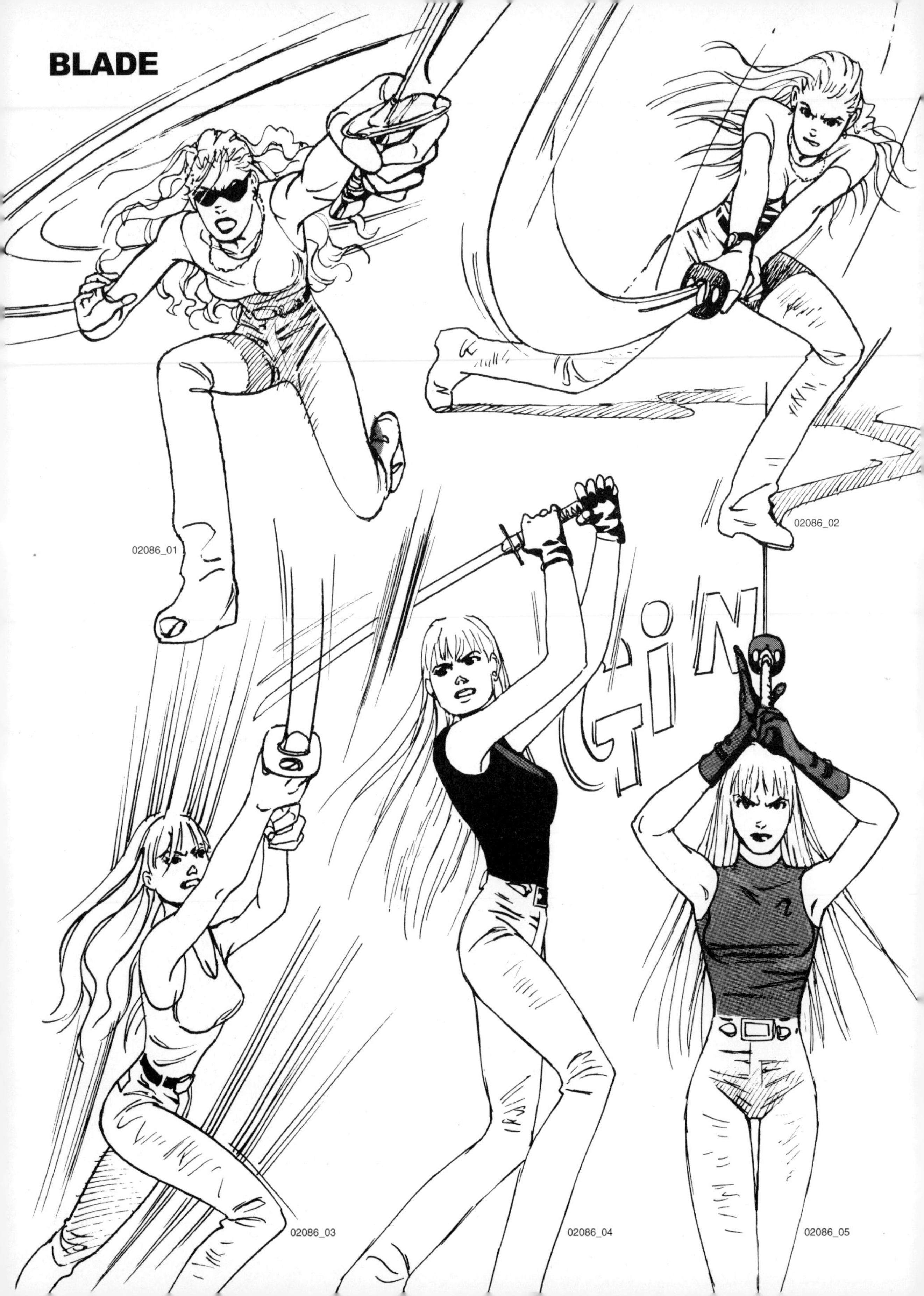

02086_01

02086_02

02086_03

02086_04

02086_05

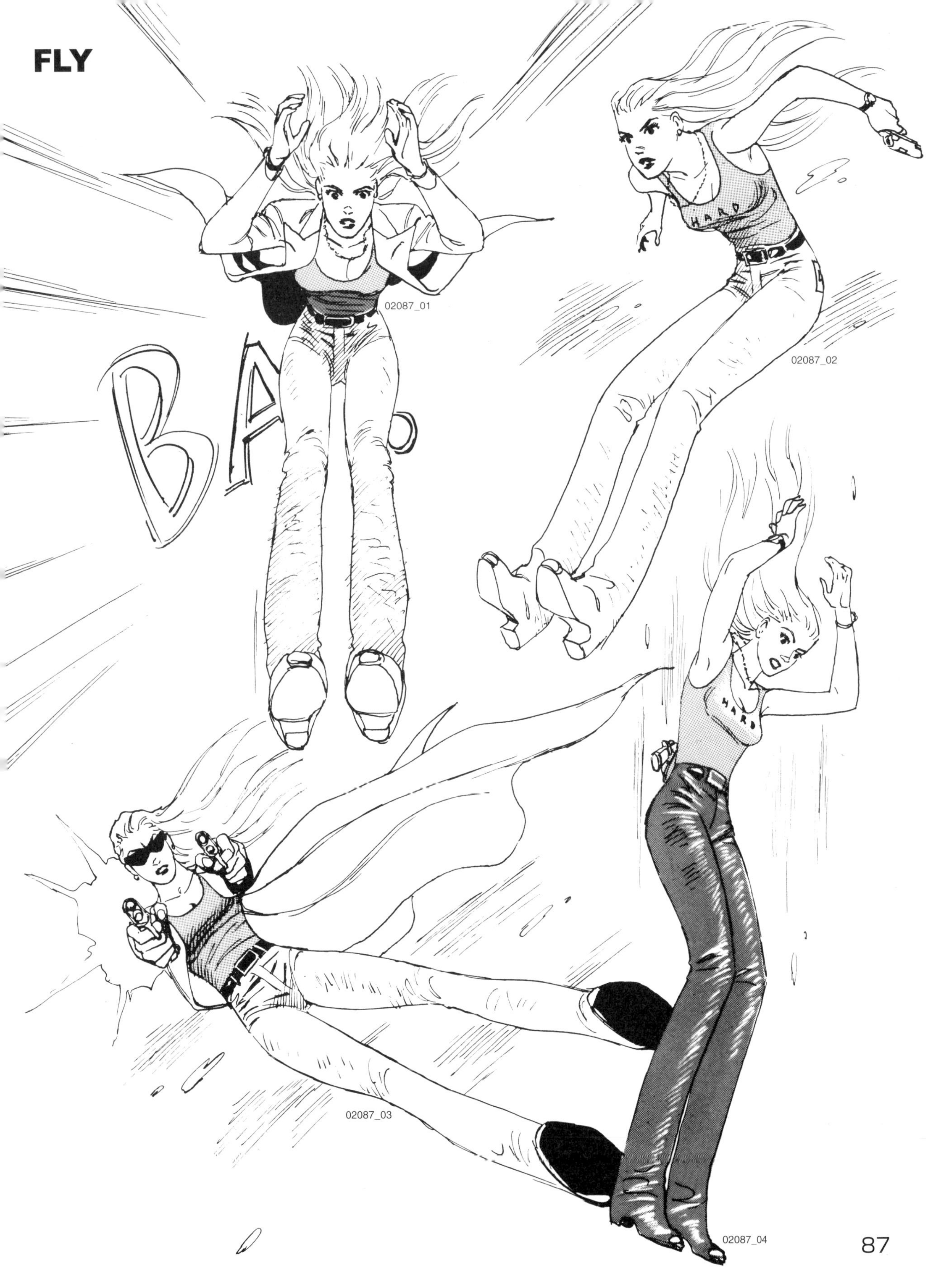

02087_01

02087_02

02087_03

02087_04

FLY

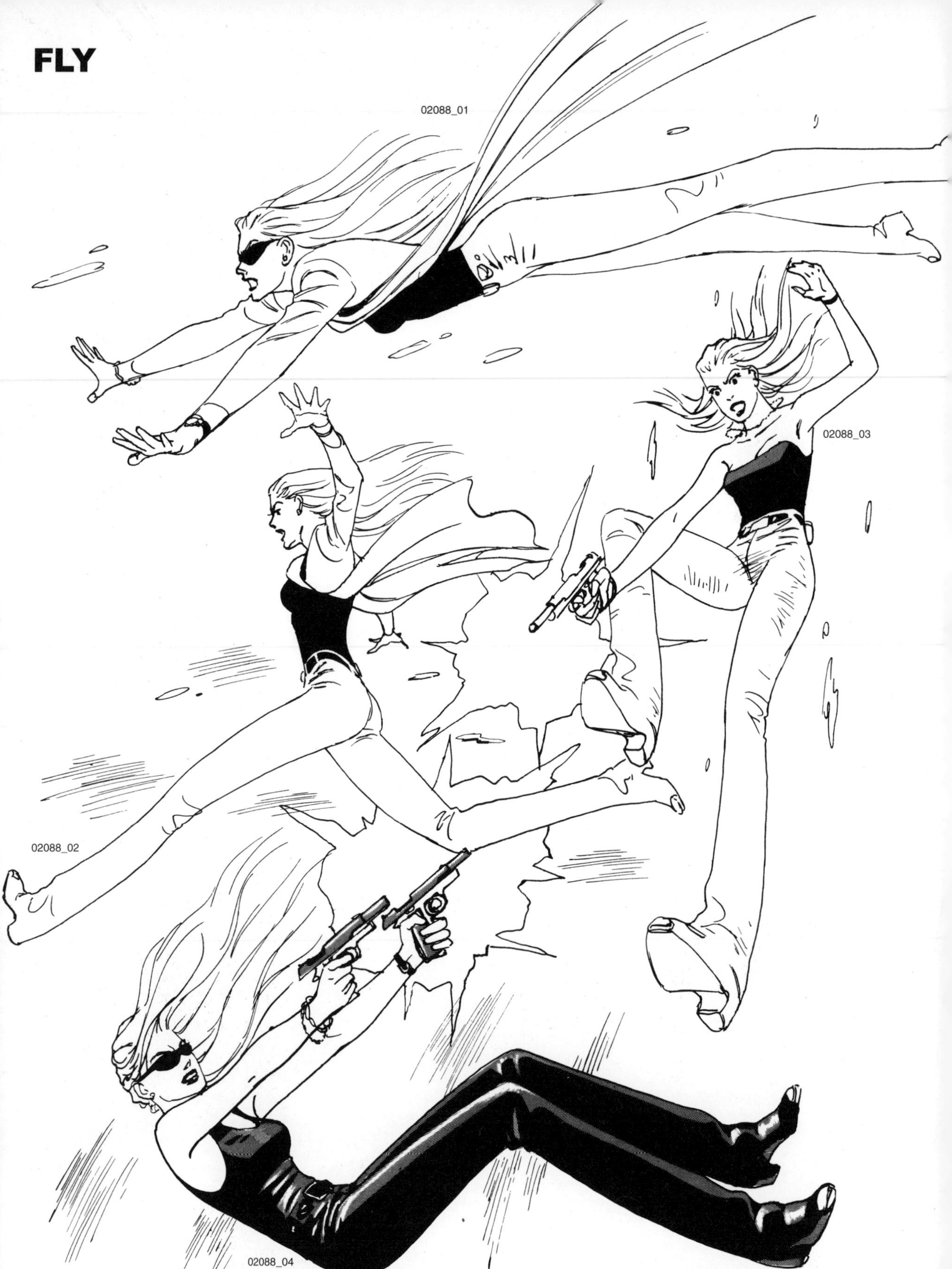
02088_01
02088_03
02088_02
02088_04

SHOT

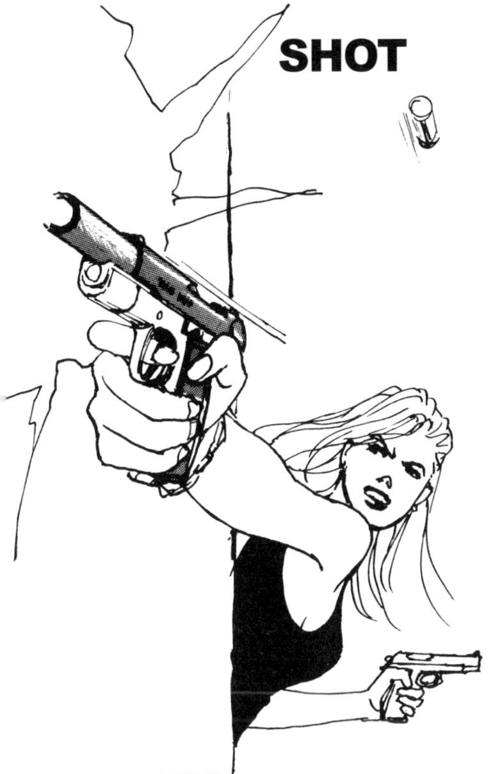

02089_01

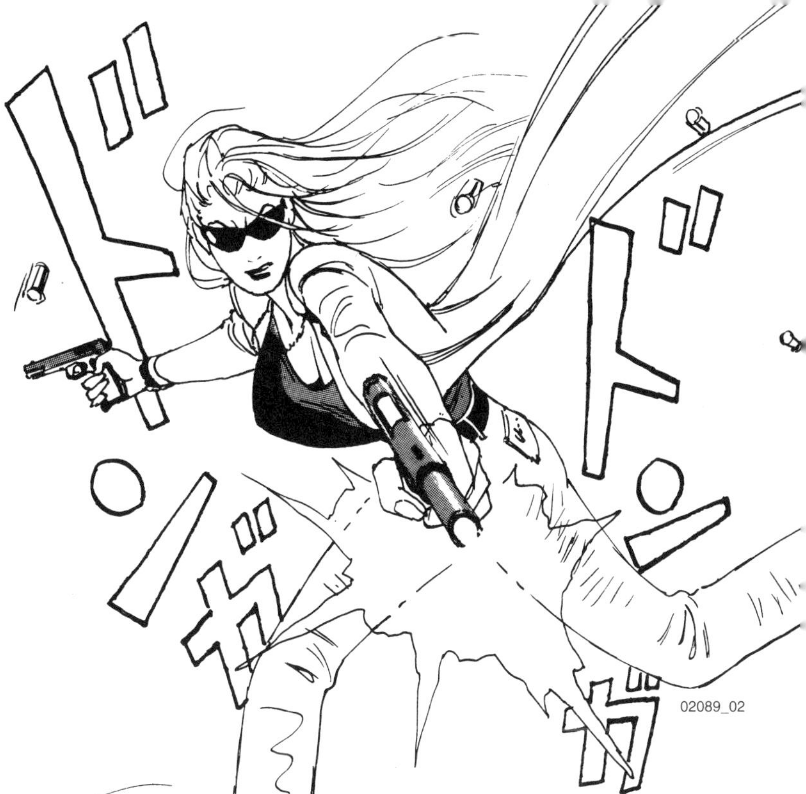

02089_02

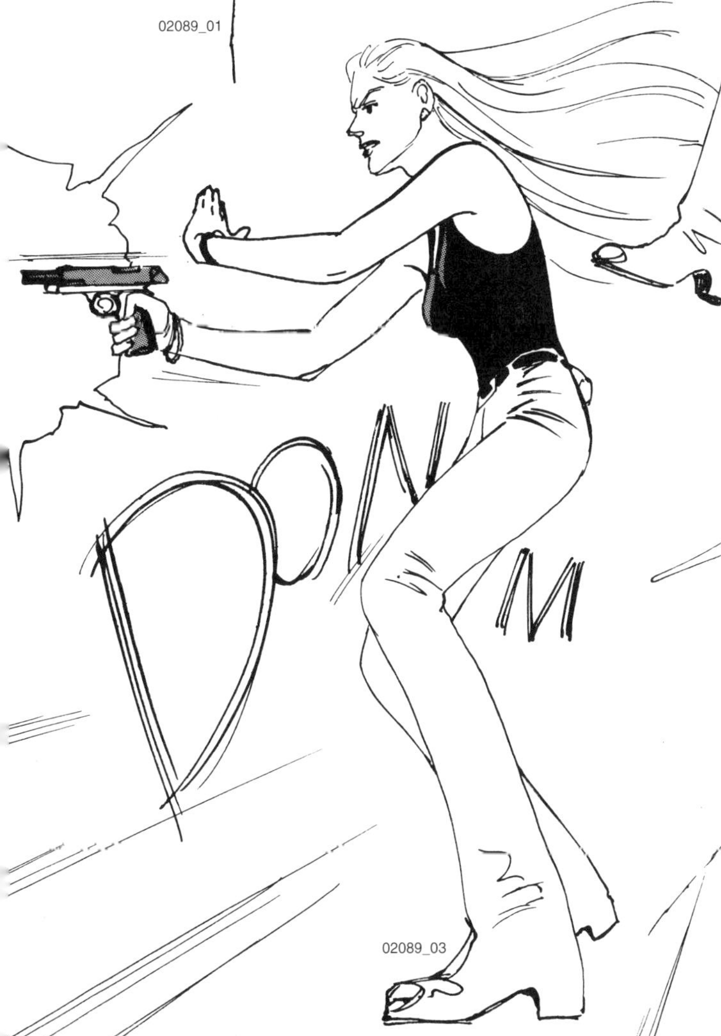

02089_03

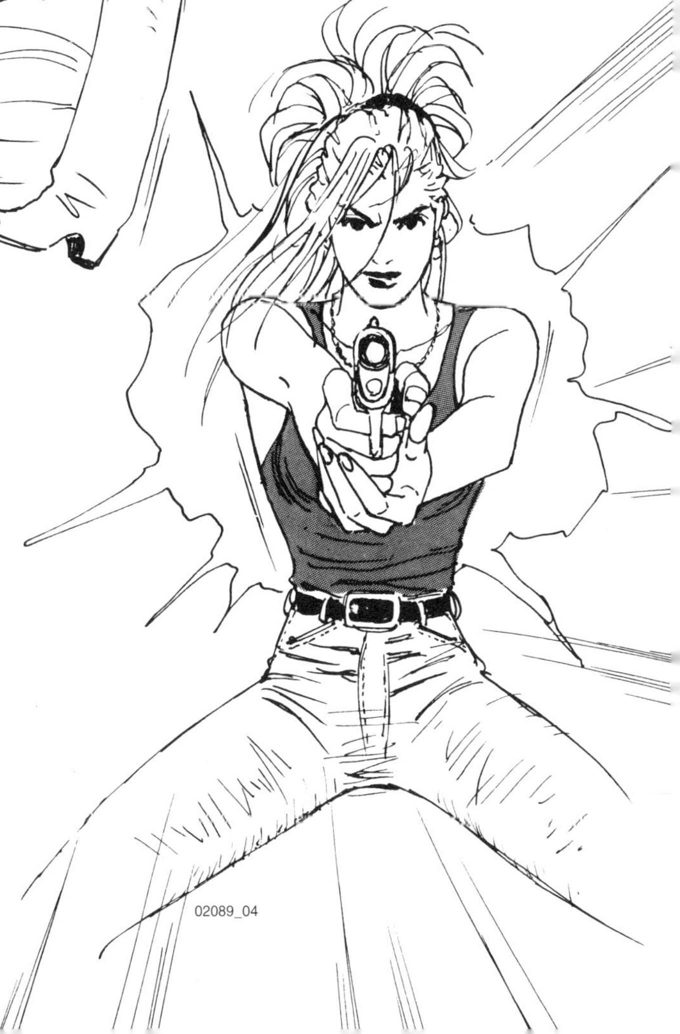

02089_04

SHOT

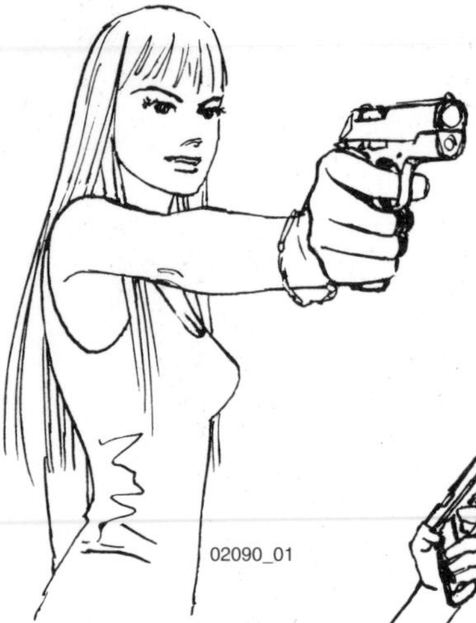
02090_01

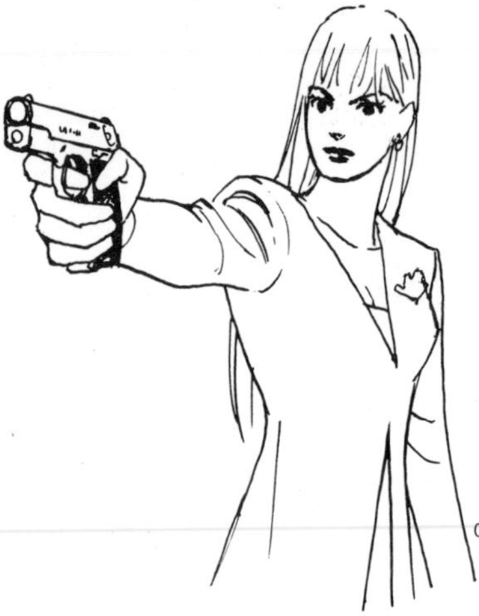
02090_02

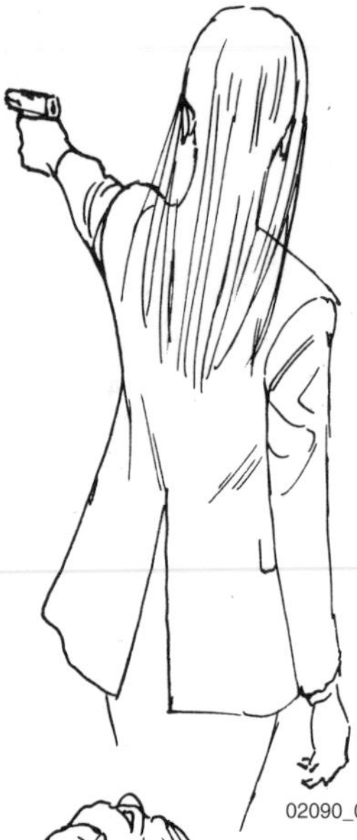
02090_03

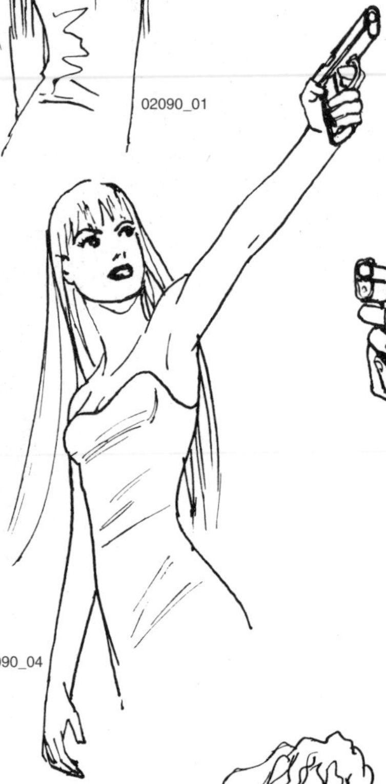
02090_04

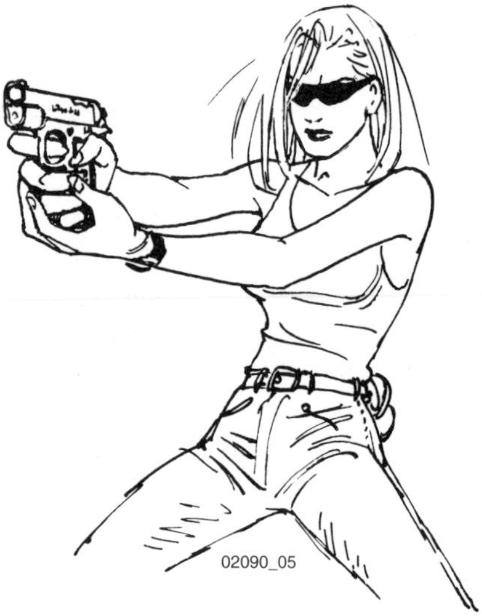
02090_05

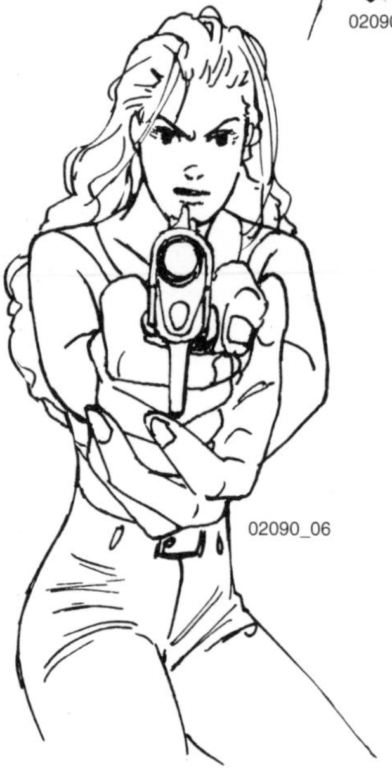
02090_06

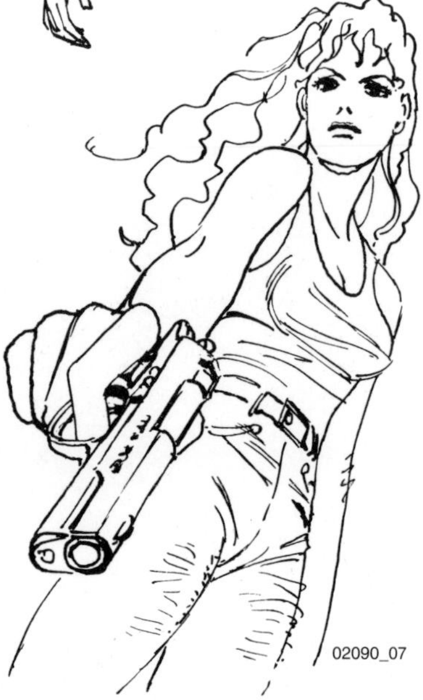
02090_07

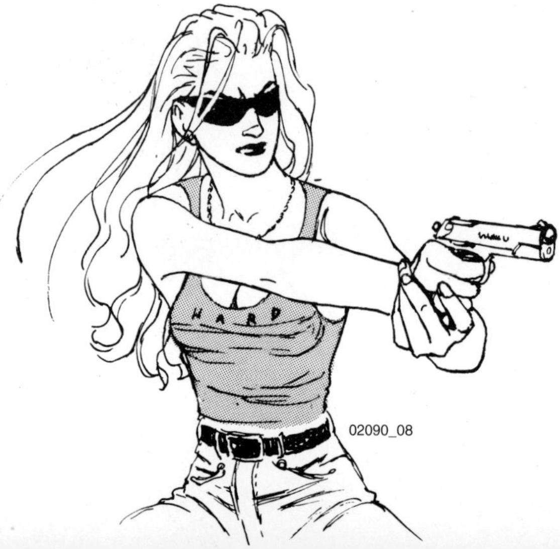
HARD
02090_08

SHOT

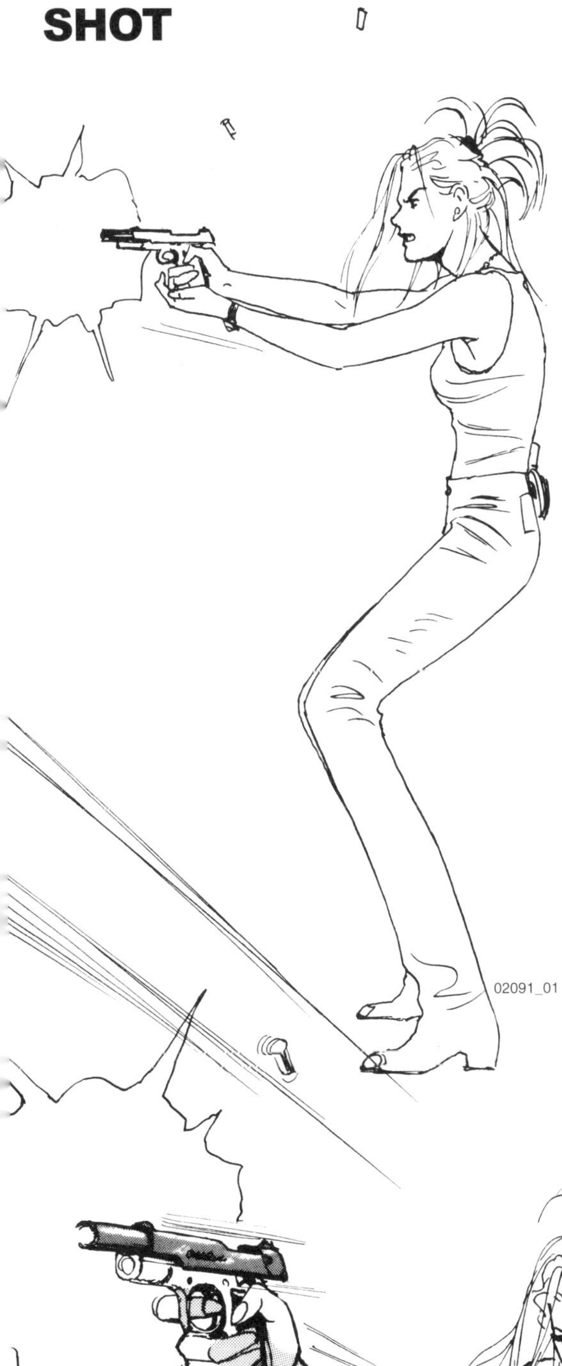

02091_01

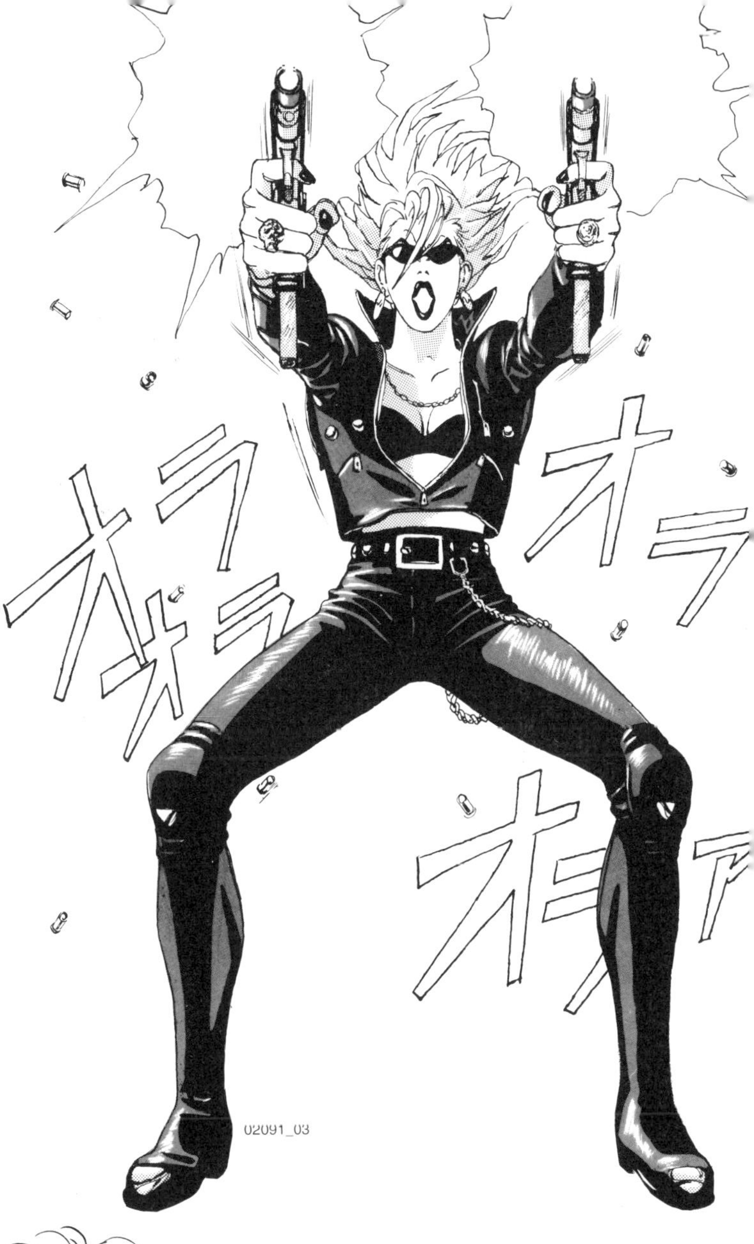
オラ
オラ
オラ
オラ
オラア

02091_03

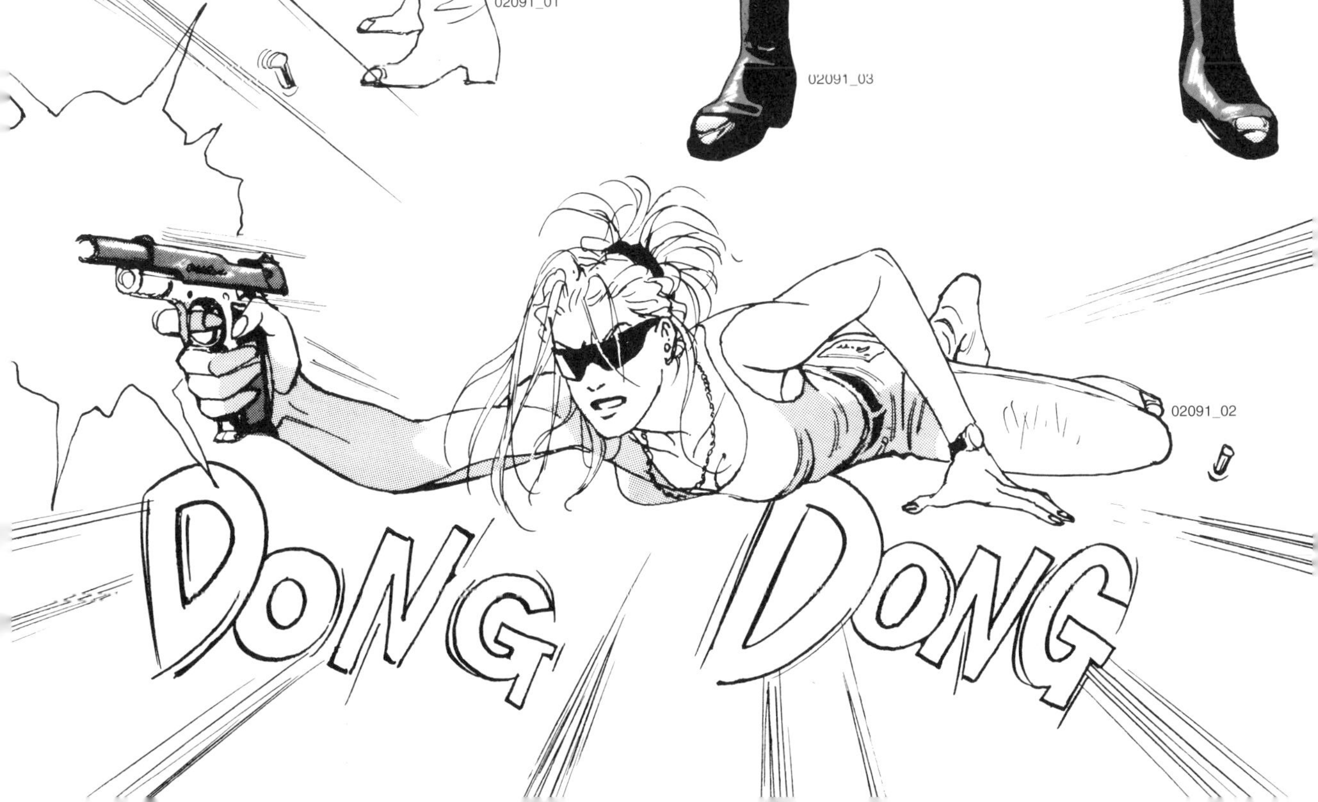
DONG
DONG

02091_02

SEXY

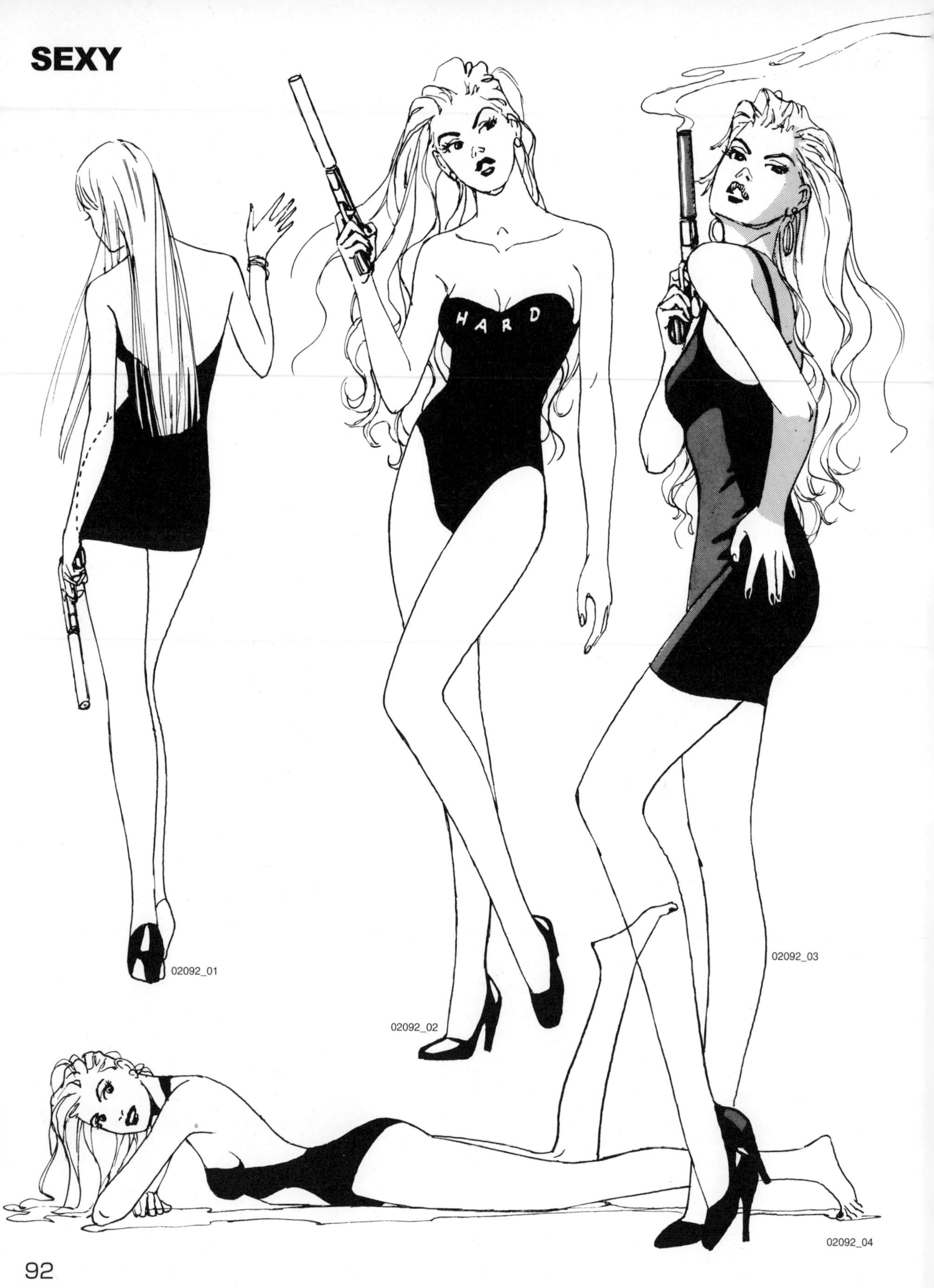
HARD

02092_01

02092_02

02092_03

02092_04

SEXY

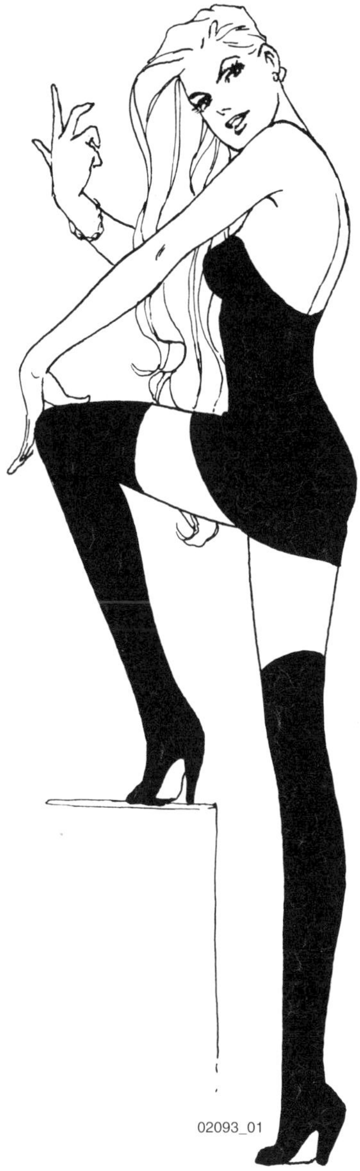

02093_01

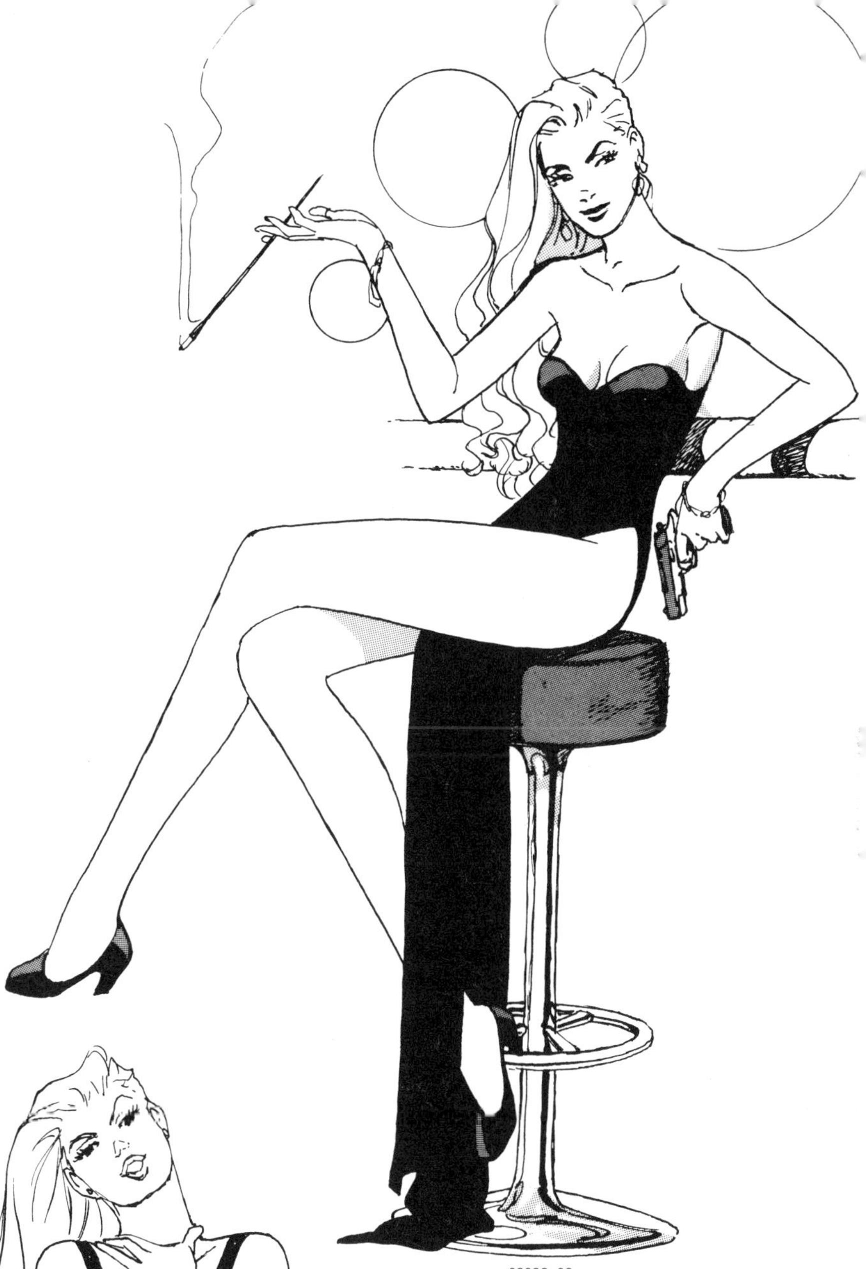

02093_02

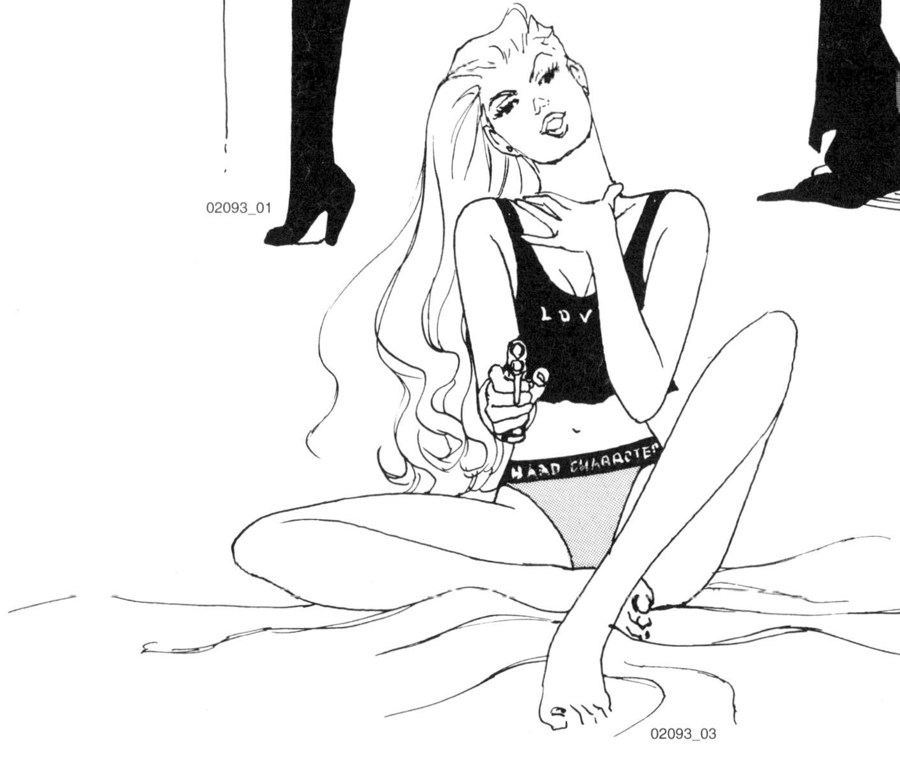
LOV
HARD CHARACTE

02093_03

SEXY

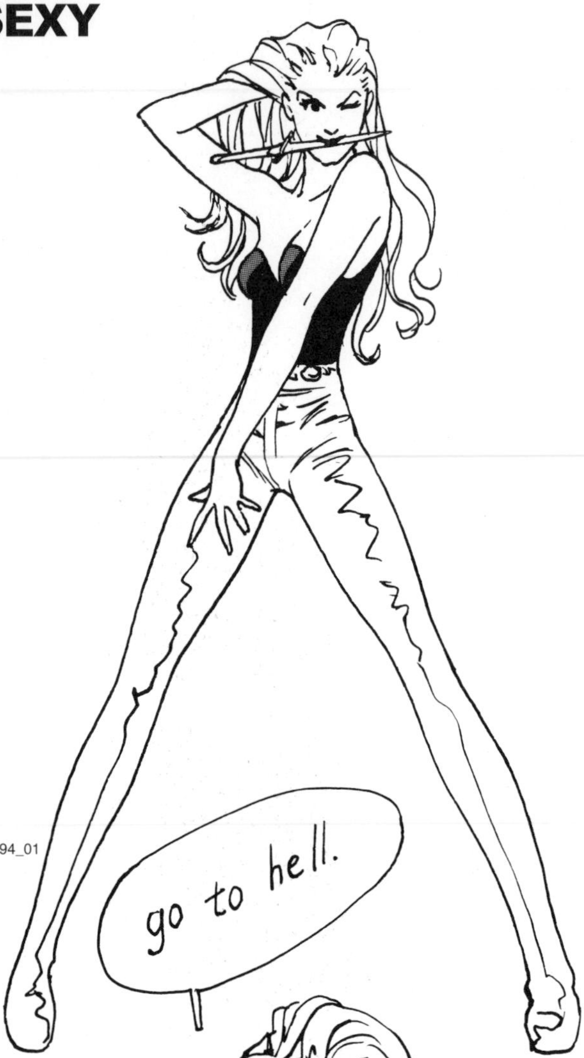

02094_01

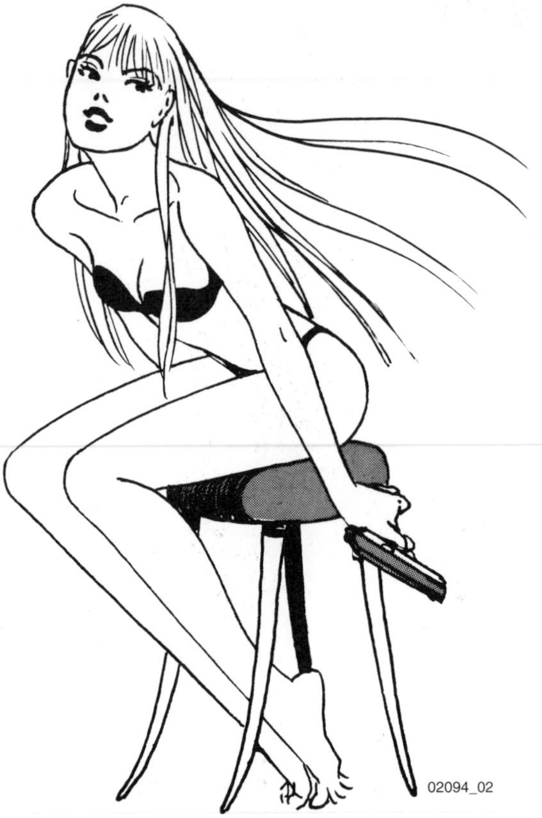

02094_02

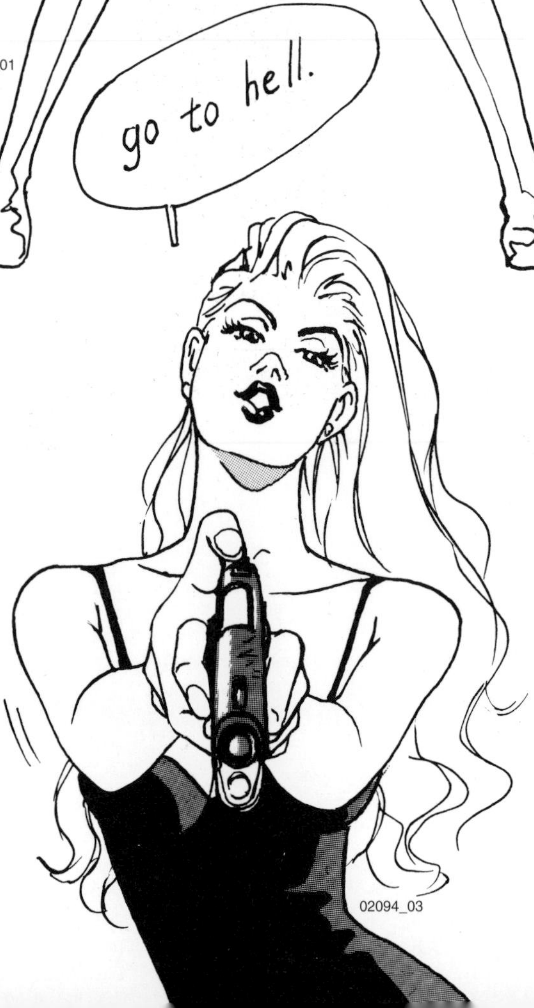
go to hell.

02094_03

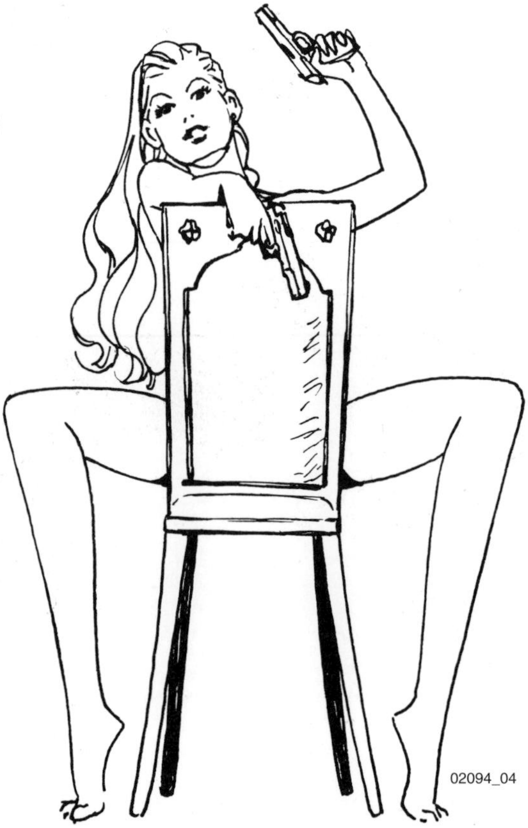

02094_04

SEXY

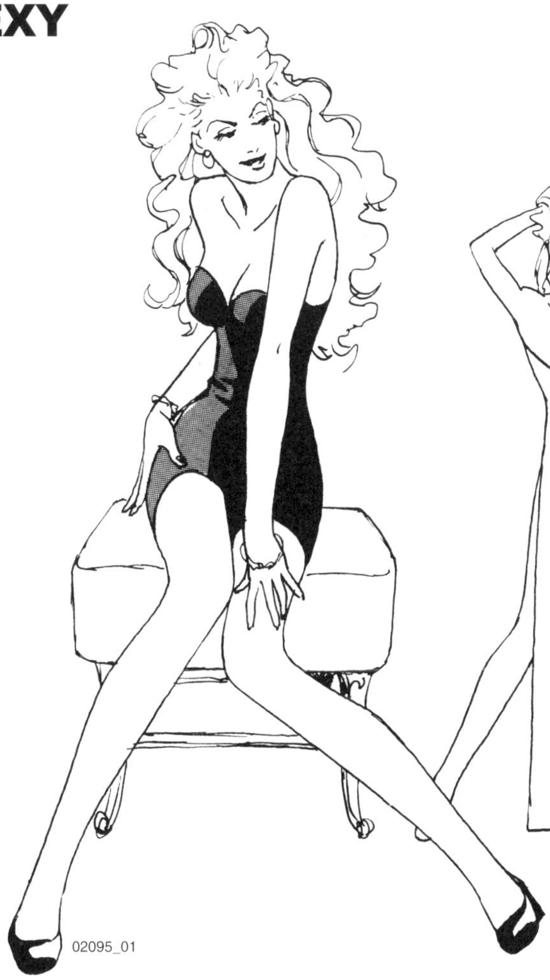

02095_01

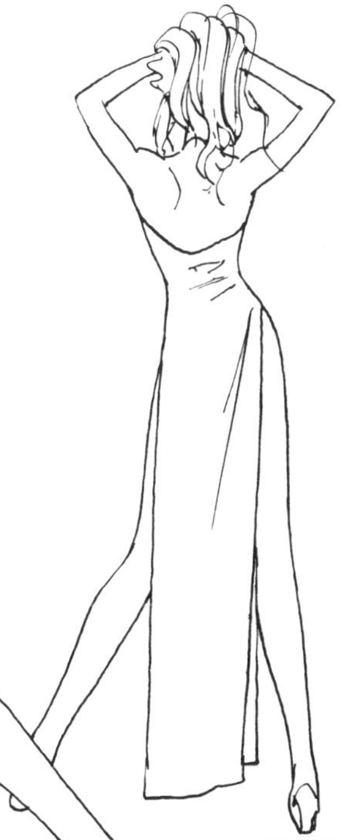

02095_02

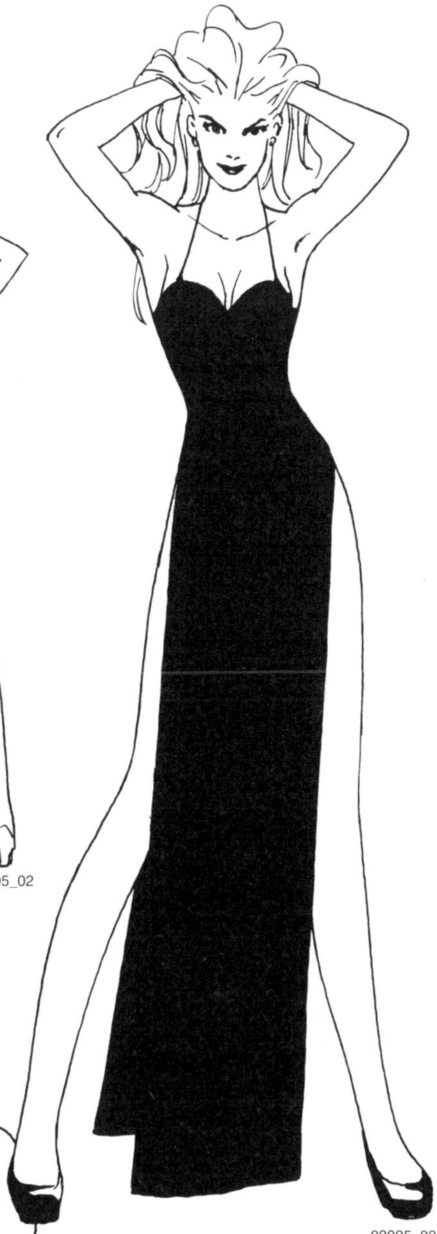

02095_03

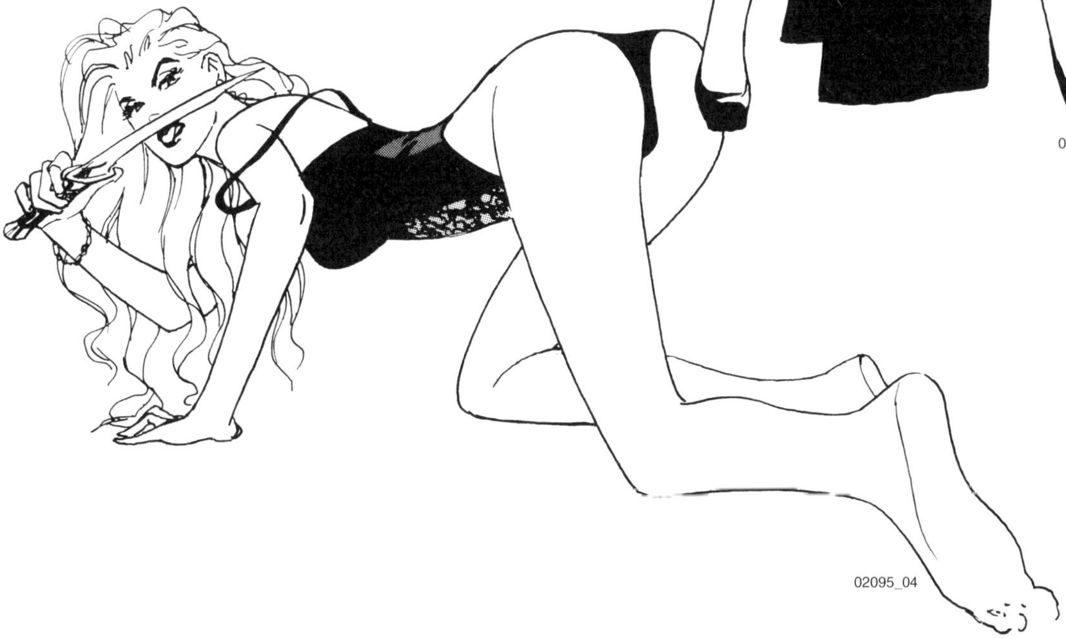

02095_04

SEXY

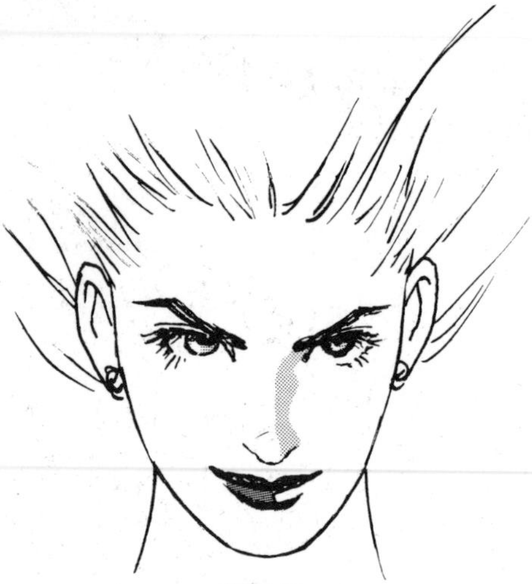

02096_01

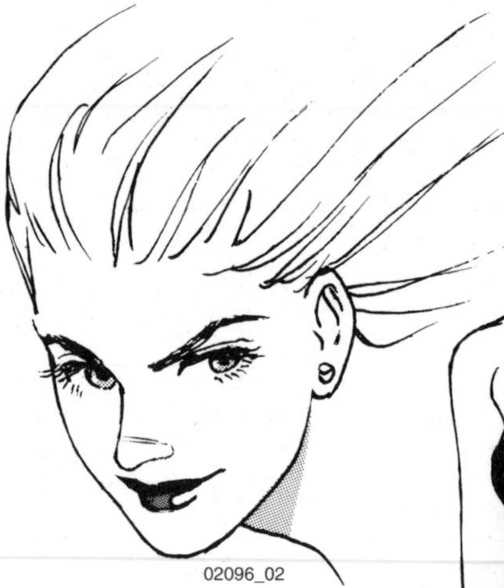

02096_02

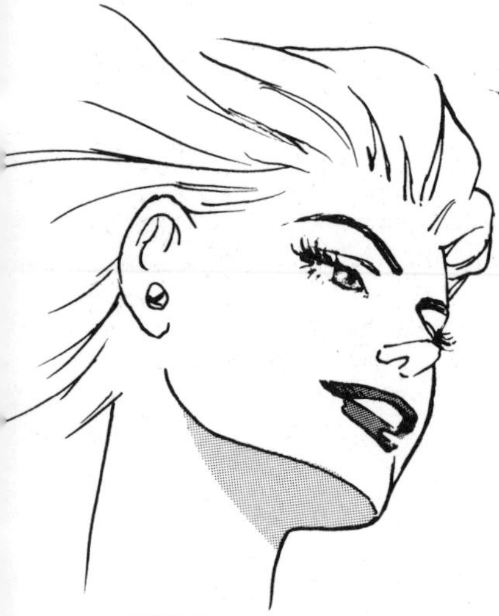

02096_03

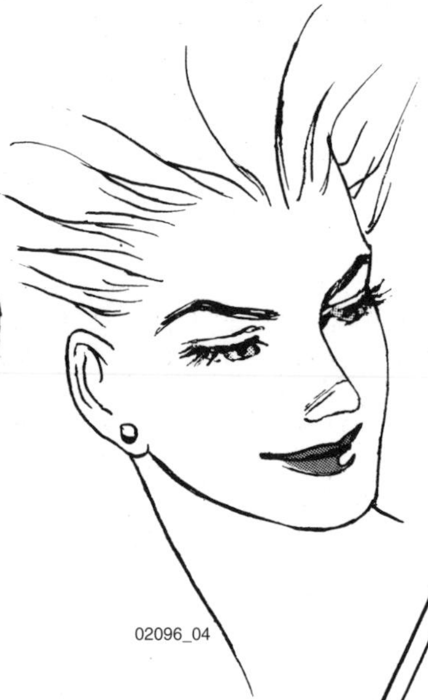

02096_04

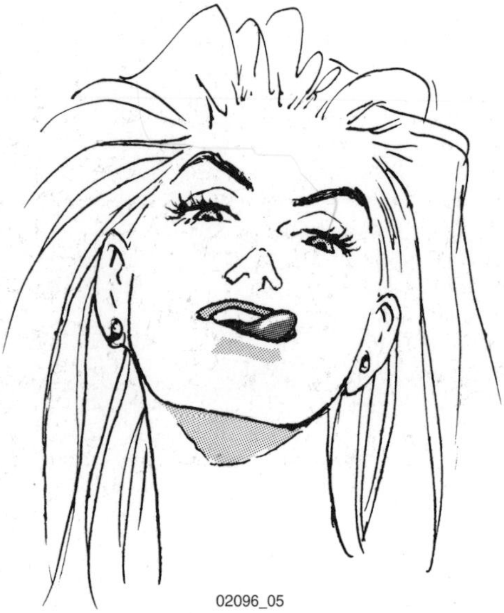

02096_05

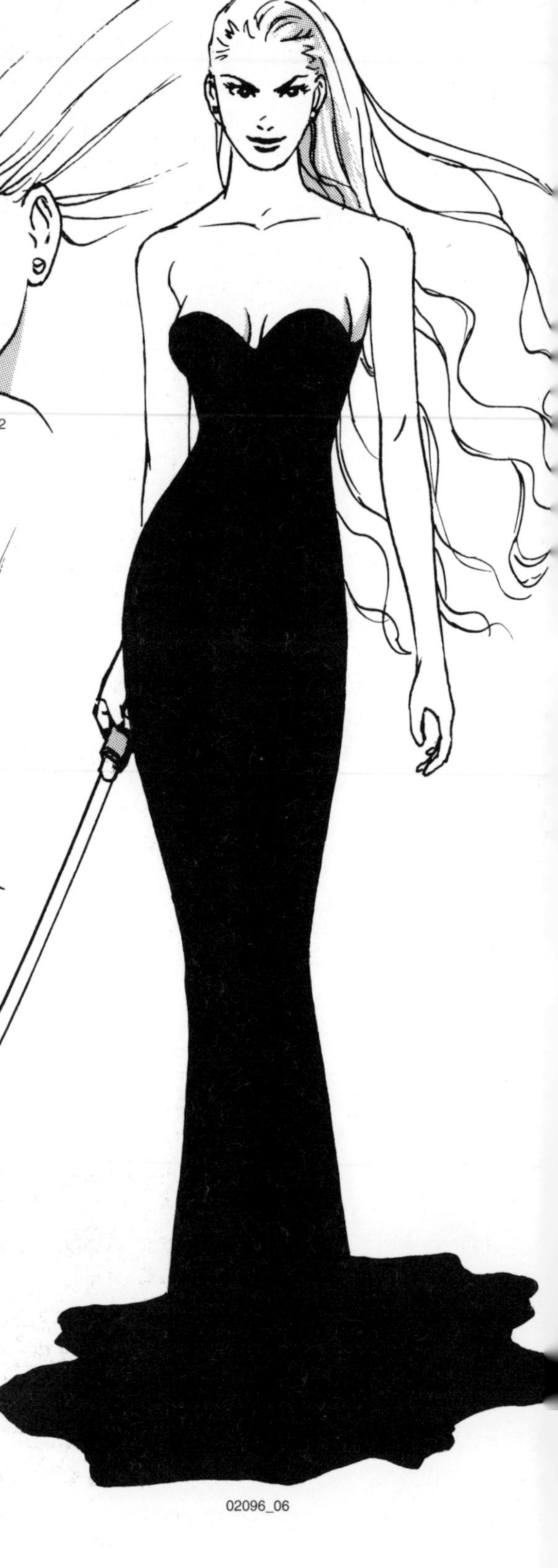

02096_06

ATTACK

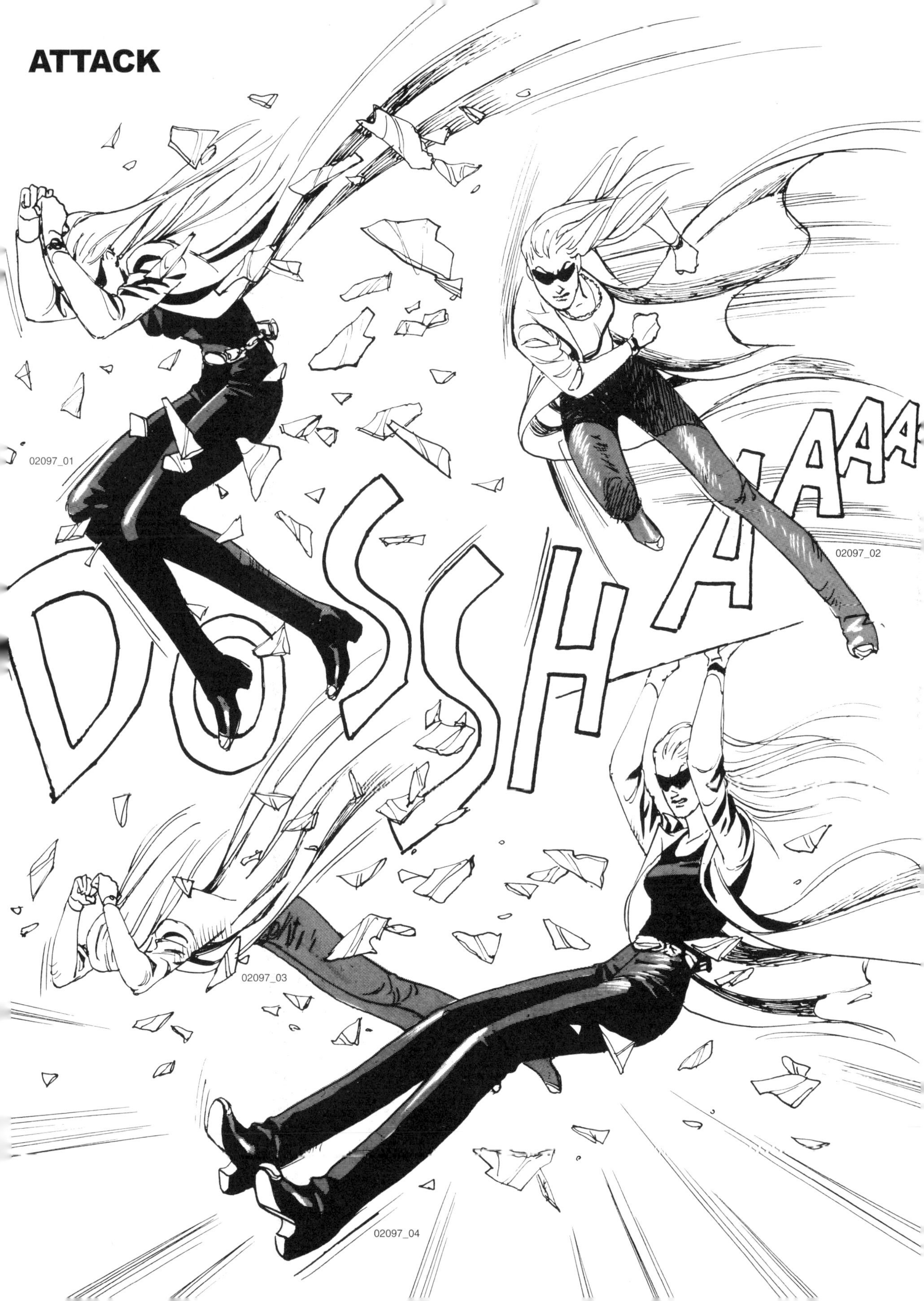
DOSSHAAAAA

02097_01

02097_02

02097_03

02097_04

RIFLE

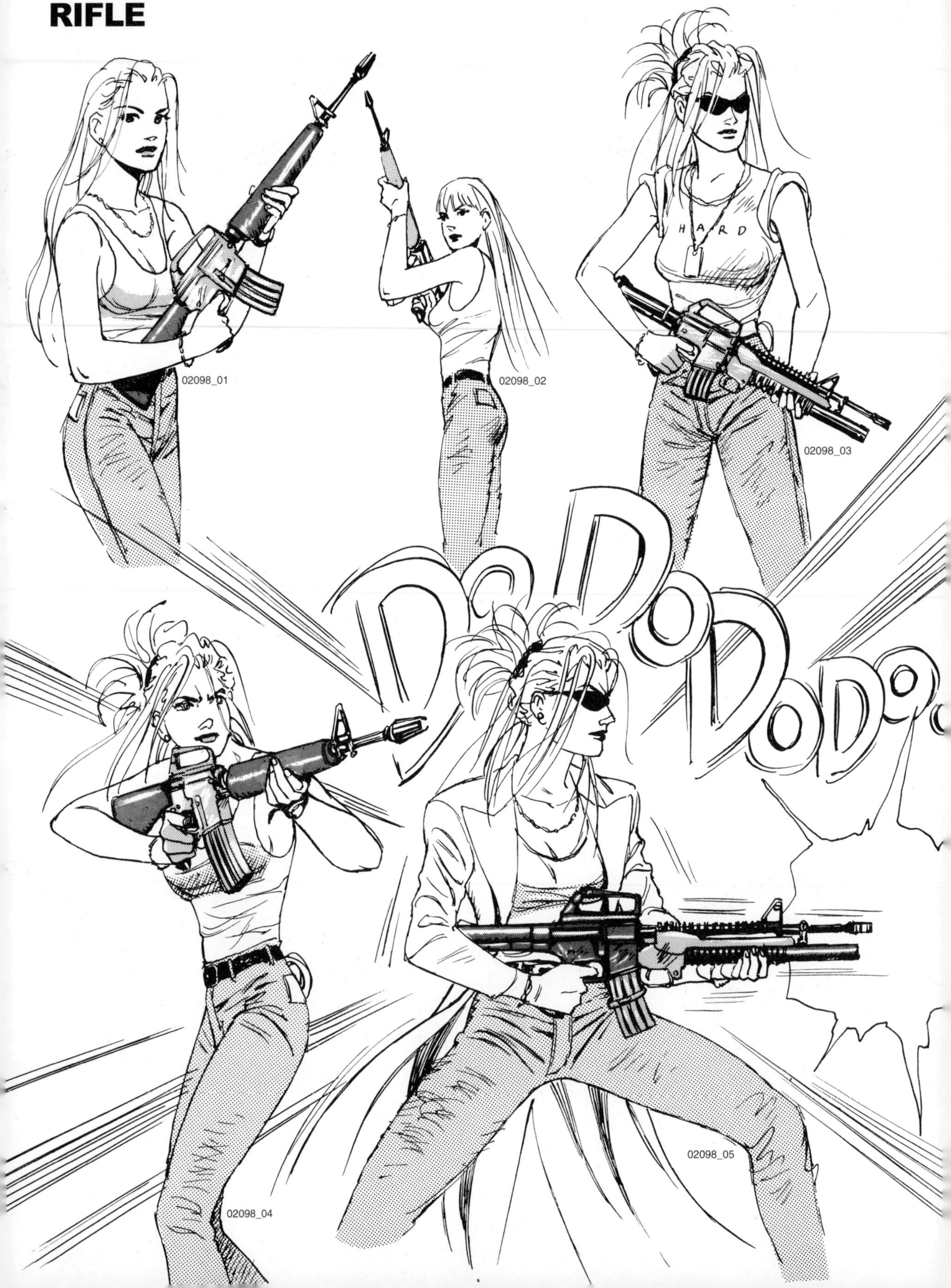
HARD
DoDoDoDo

02098_01 02098_02 02098_03 02098_04 02098_05

RIFLE

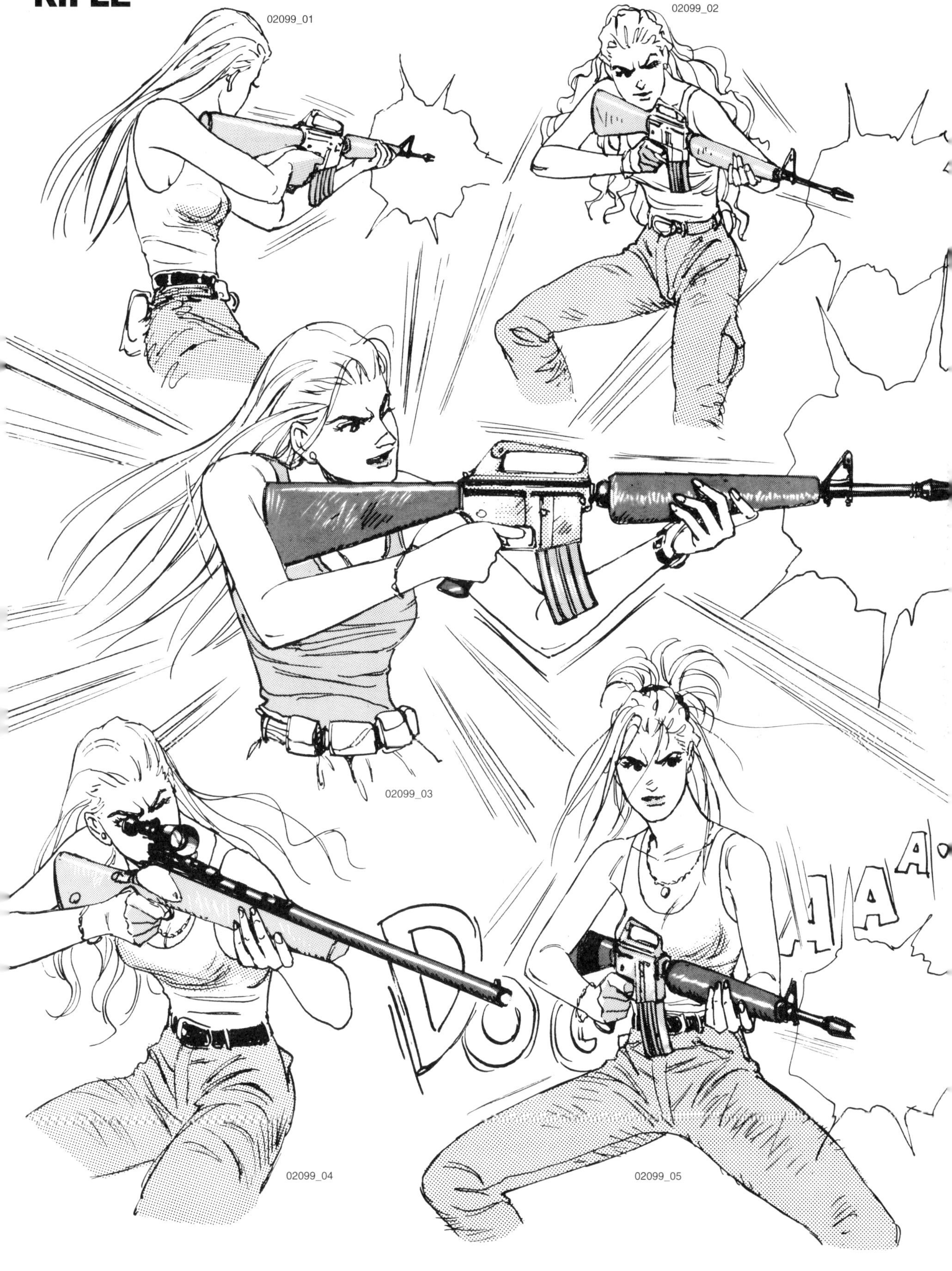

02099_01

02099_02

02099_03

02099_04

02099_05

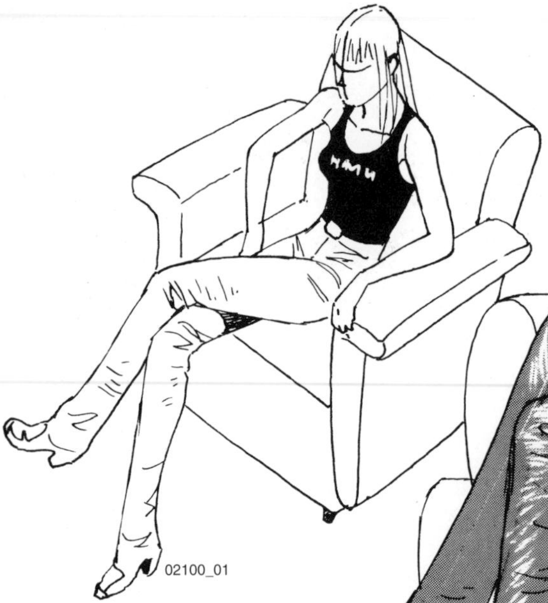

02100_01

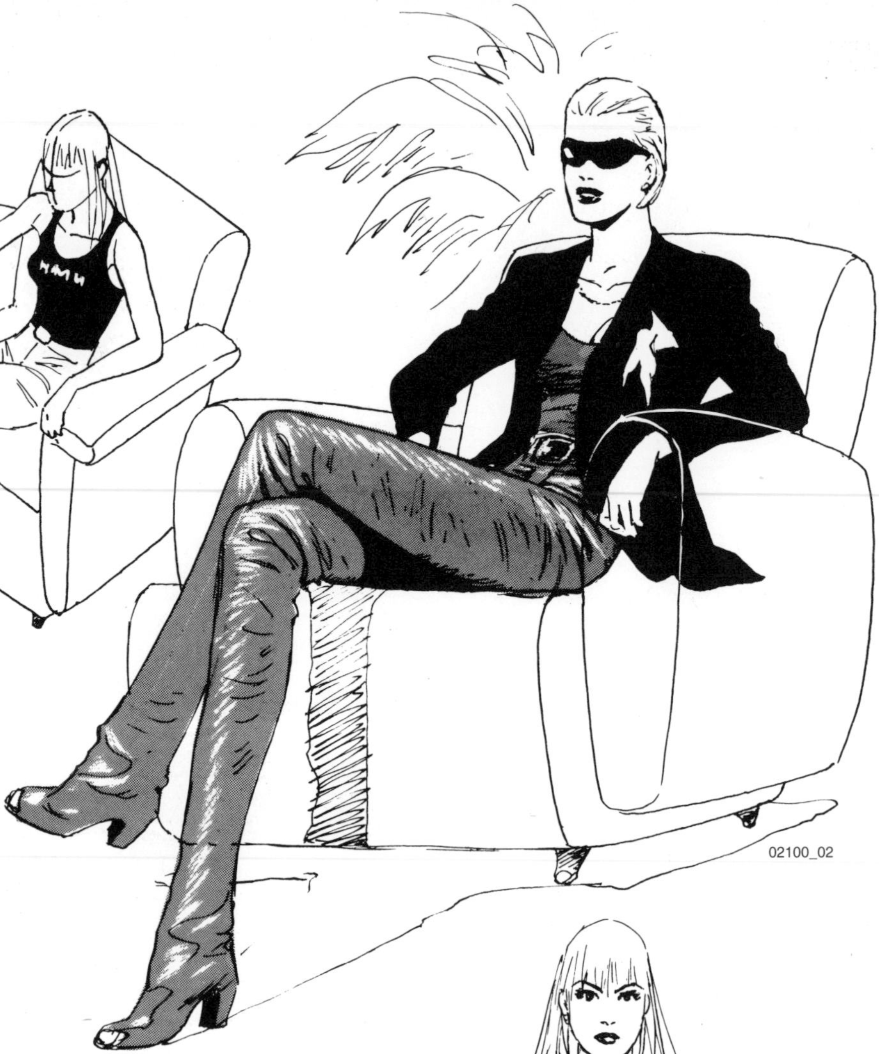

02100_02

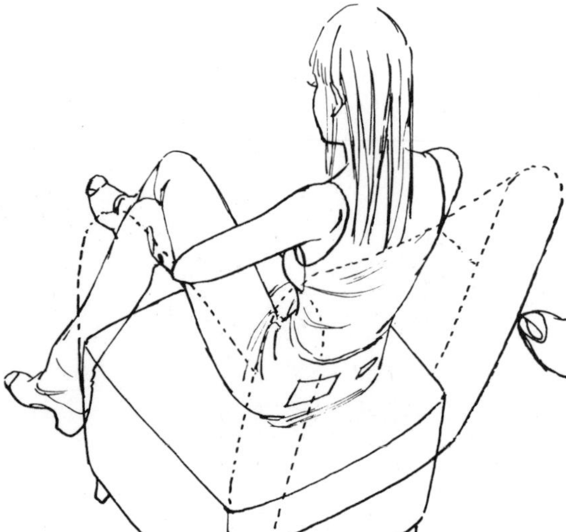

02100_03

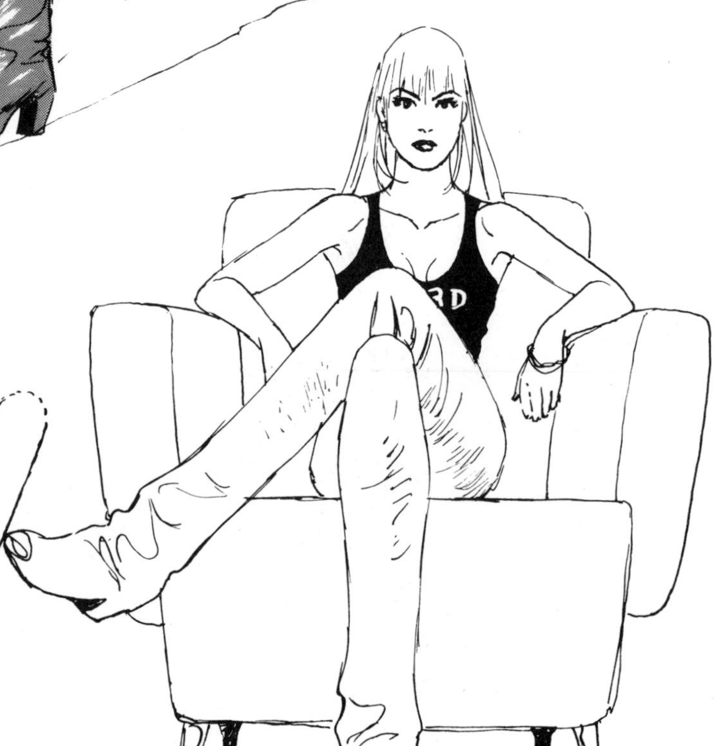

02100_04

SIT

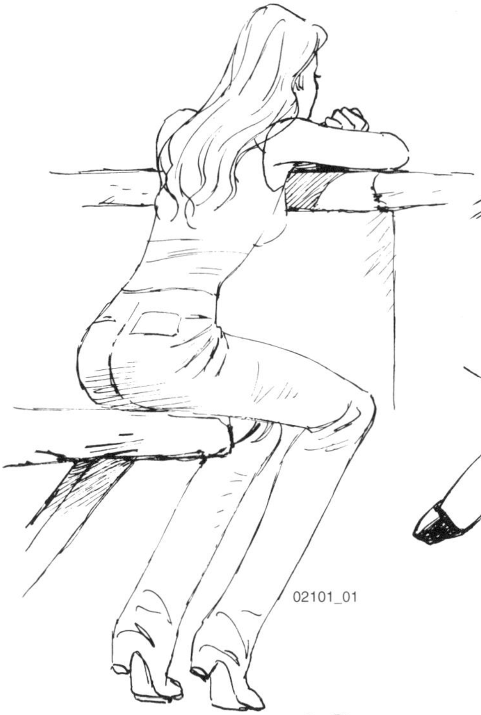

02101_01

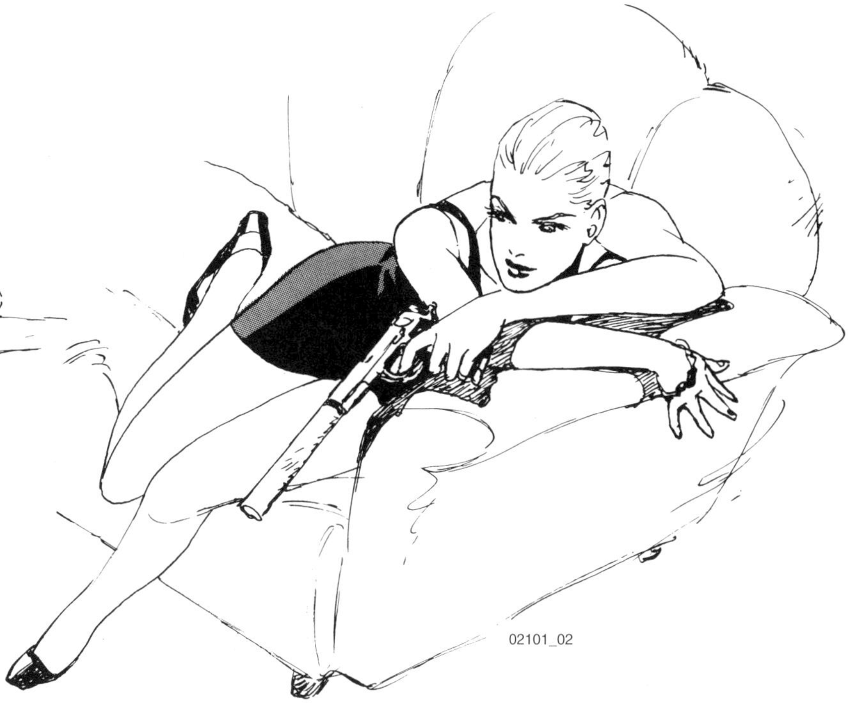

02101_02

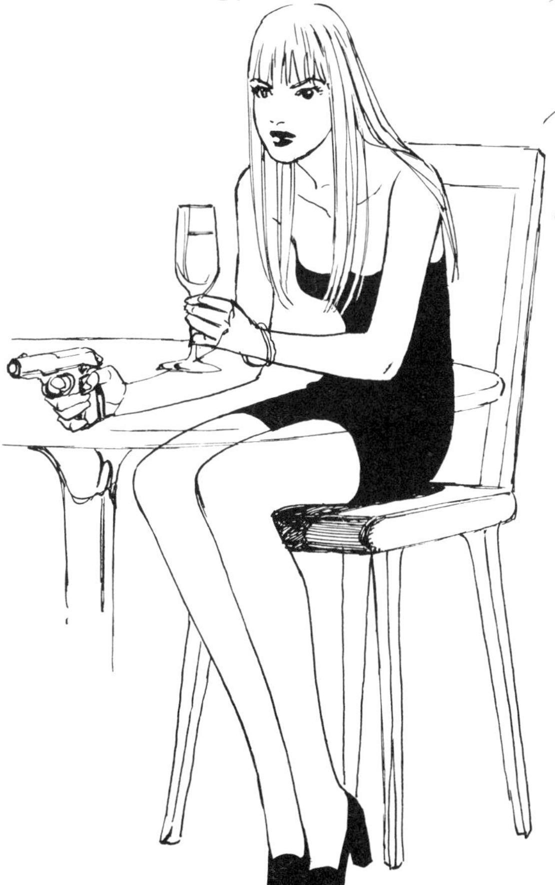

02101_03

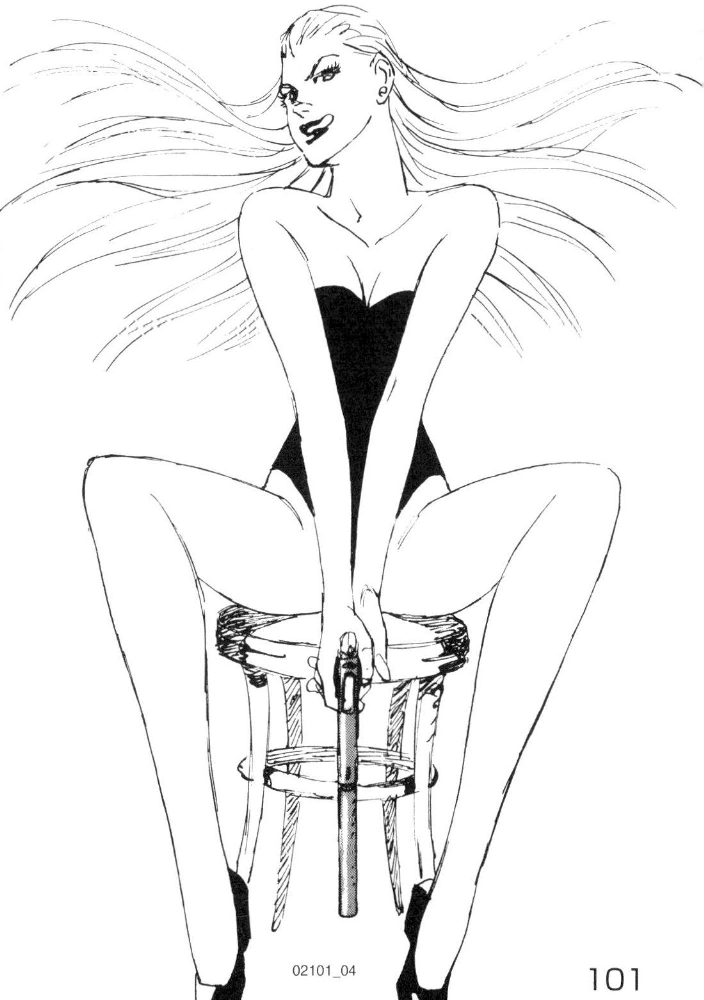

02101_04

SIT

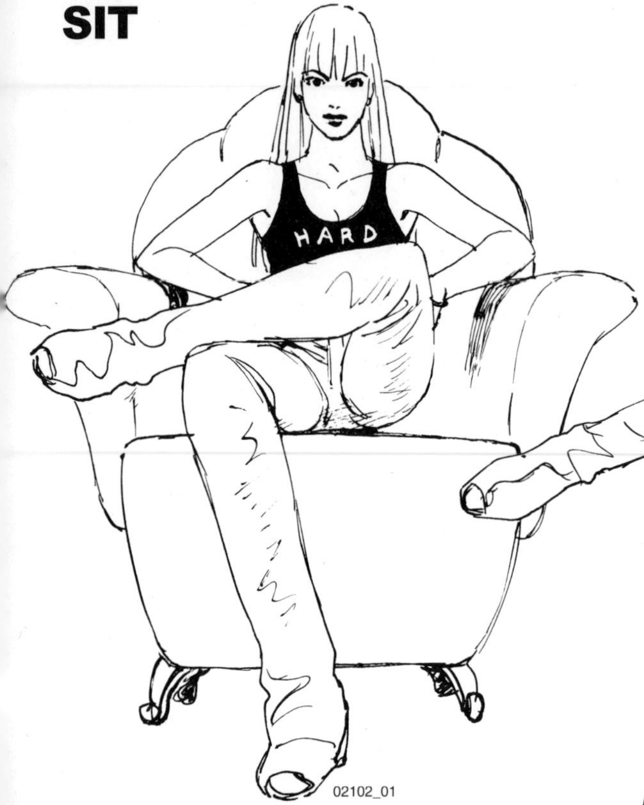
HARD

02102_01

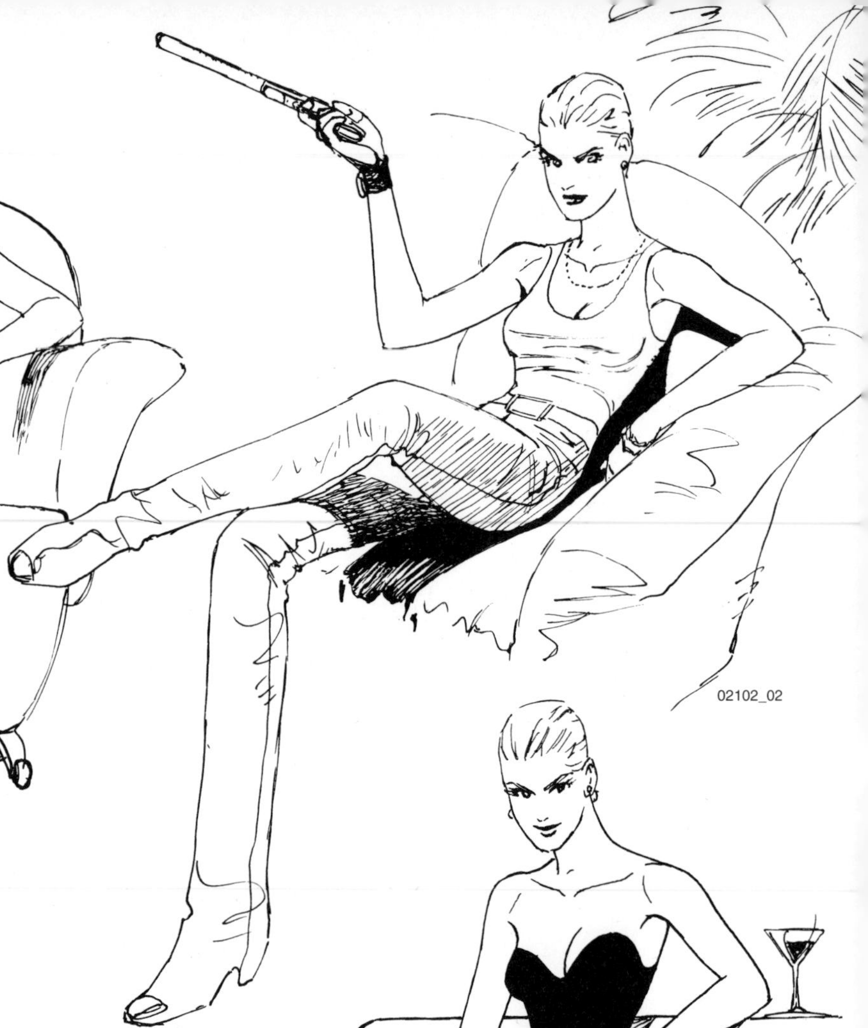

02102_02

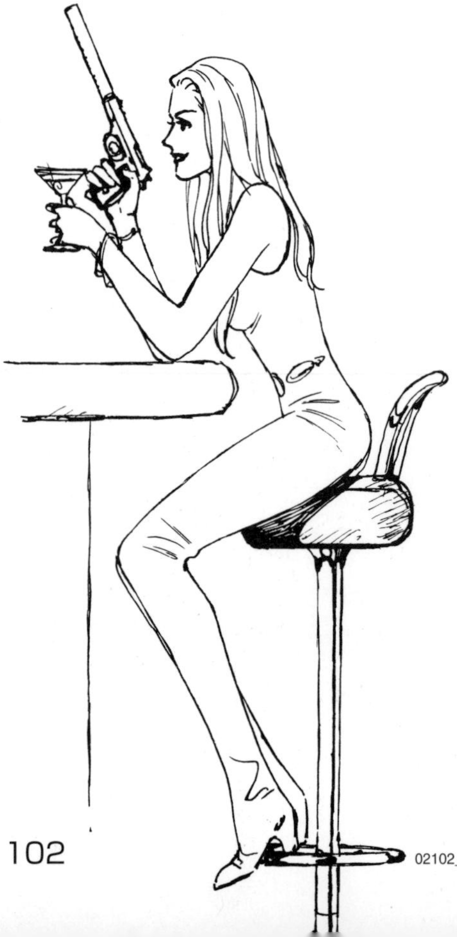

02102_03

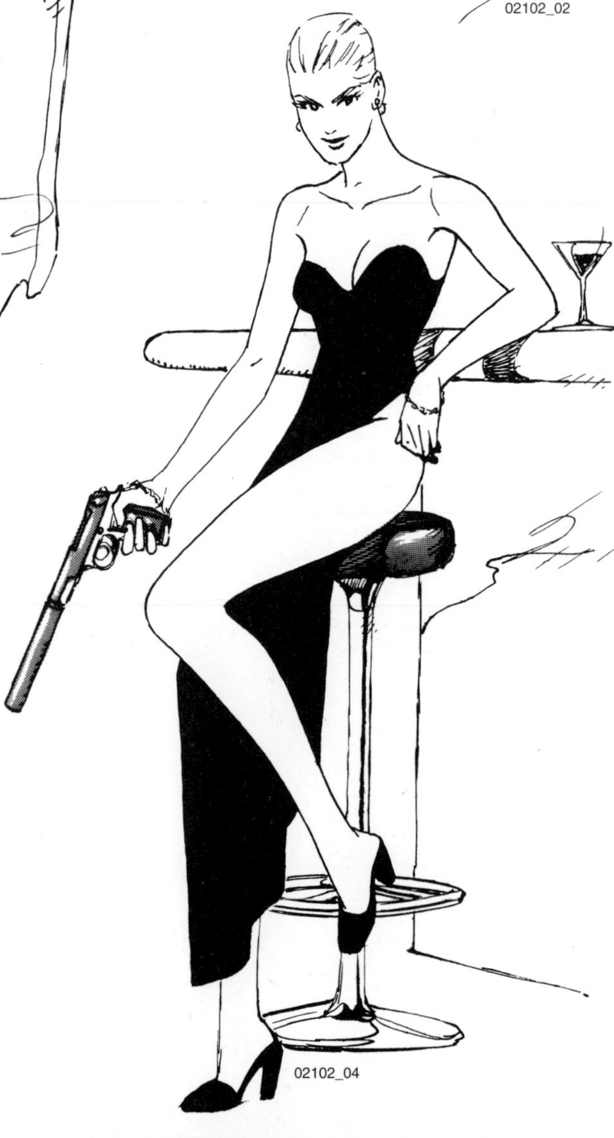

02102_04

SIT

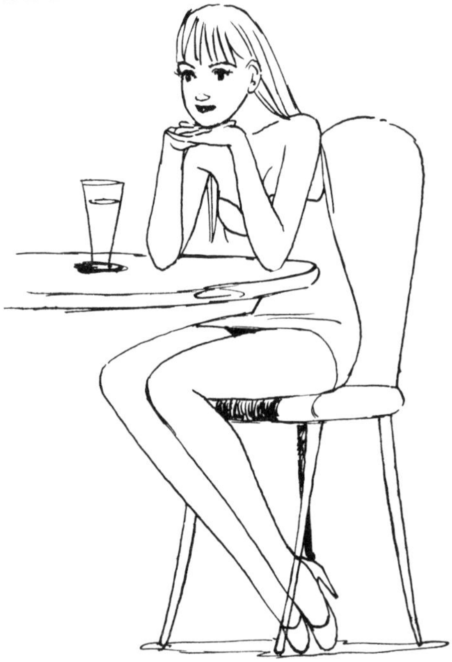

02103_01

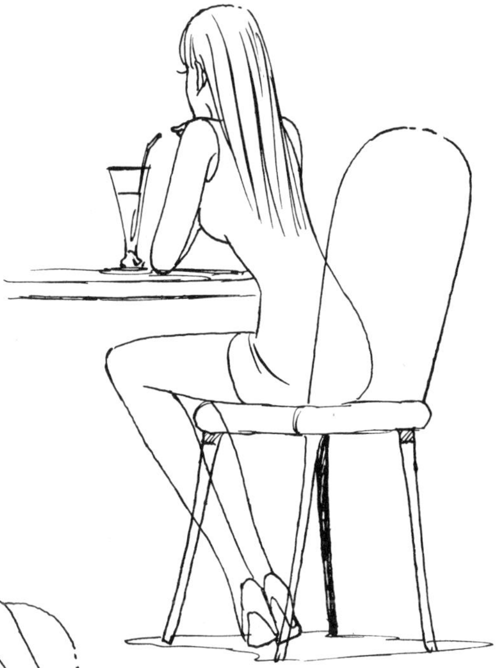

02103_02

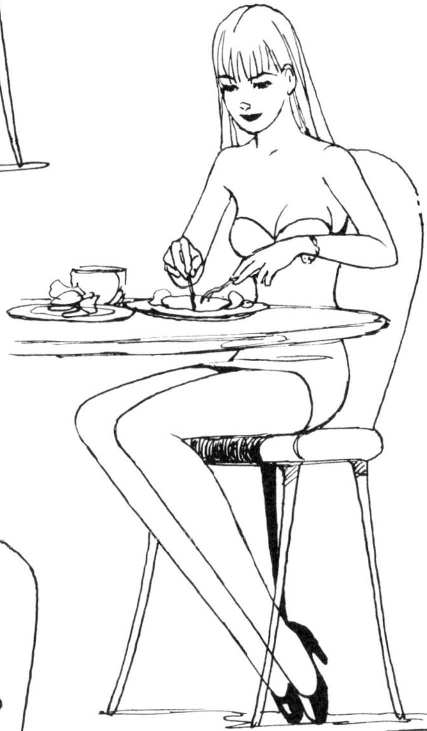

02103_03

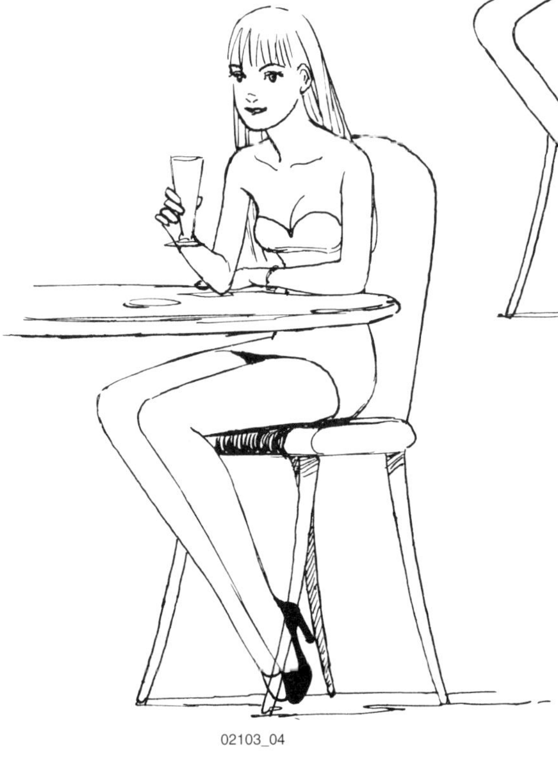

02103_04

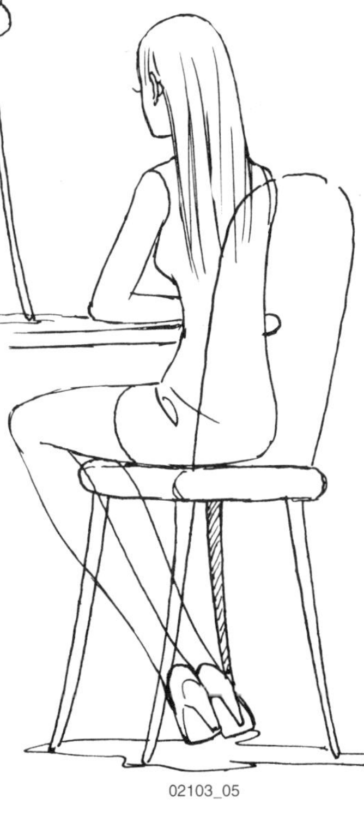

02103_05

SHOWER

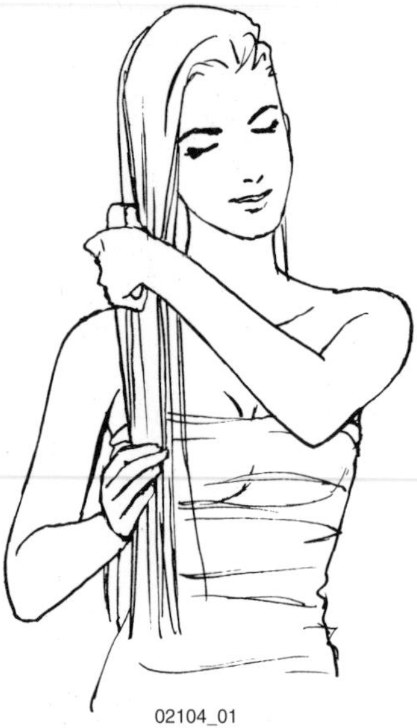
02104_01

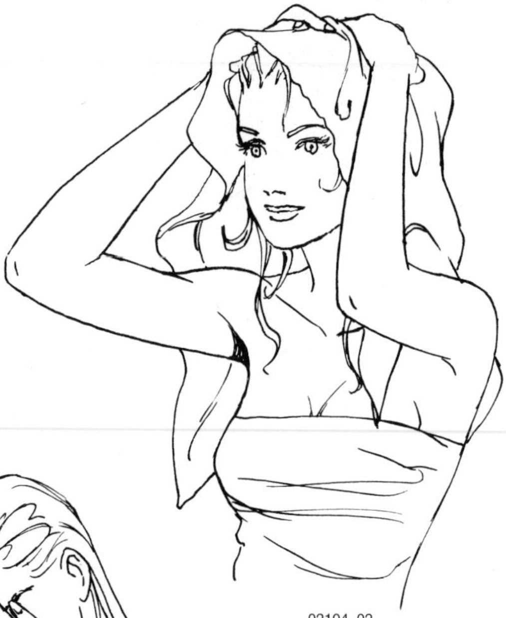
02104_02

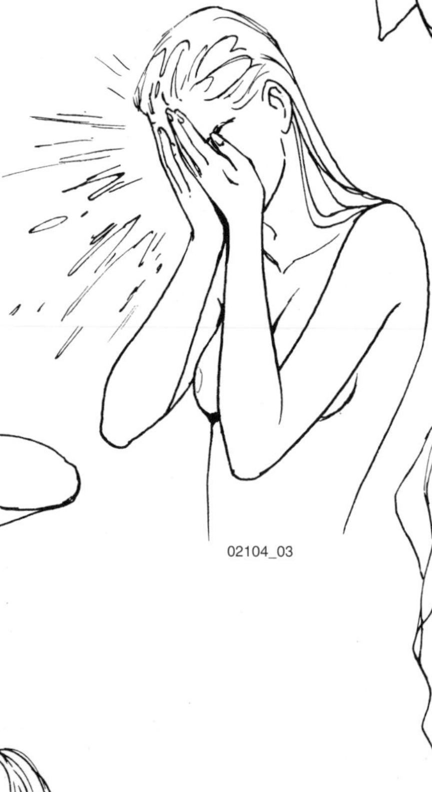
02104_03

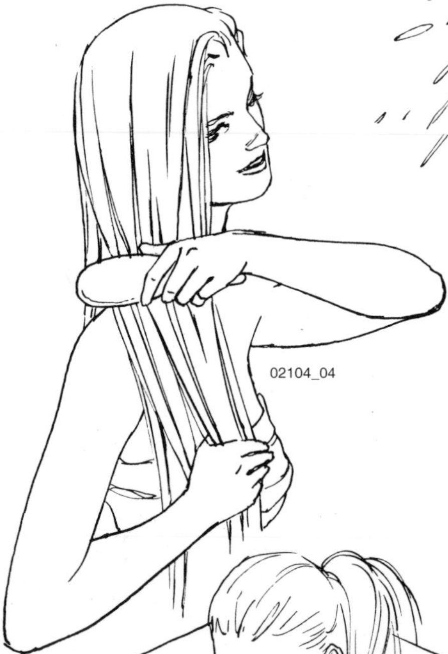
02104_04

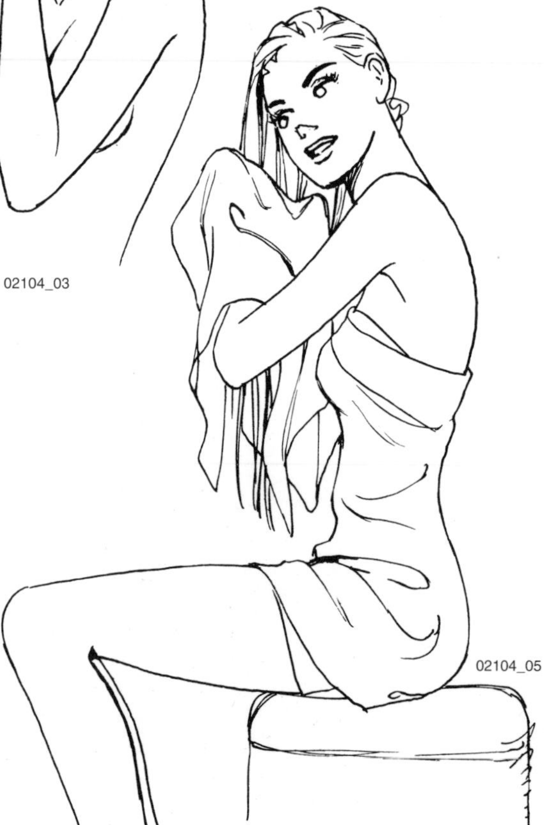
02104_05

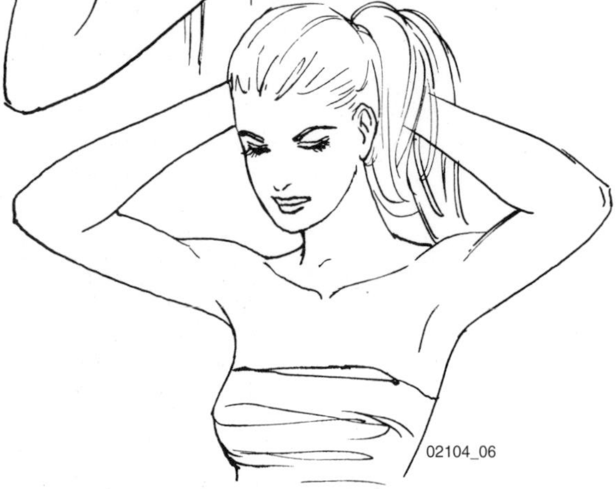
02104_06

SHOWER

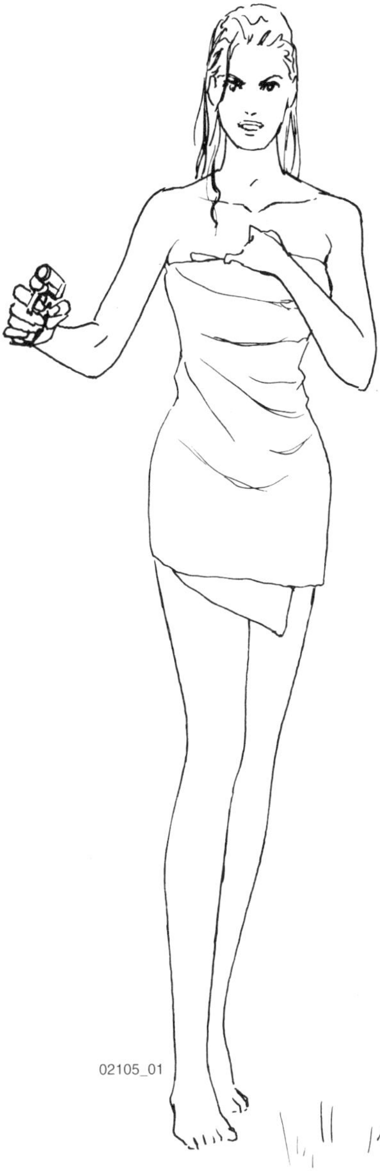

02105_01

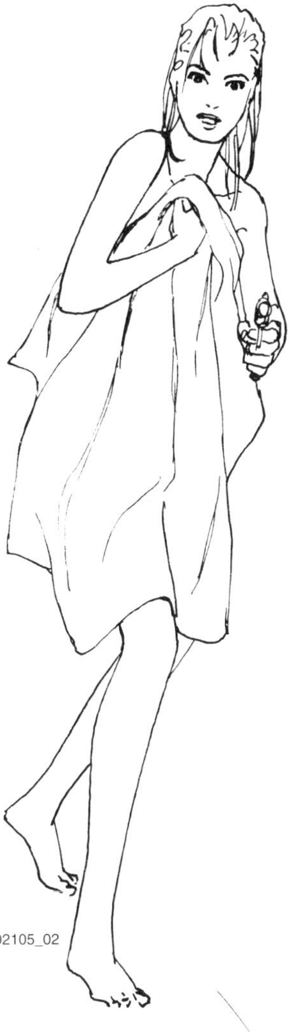

02105_02

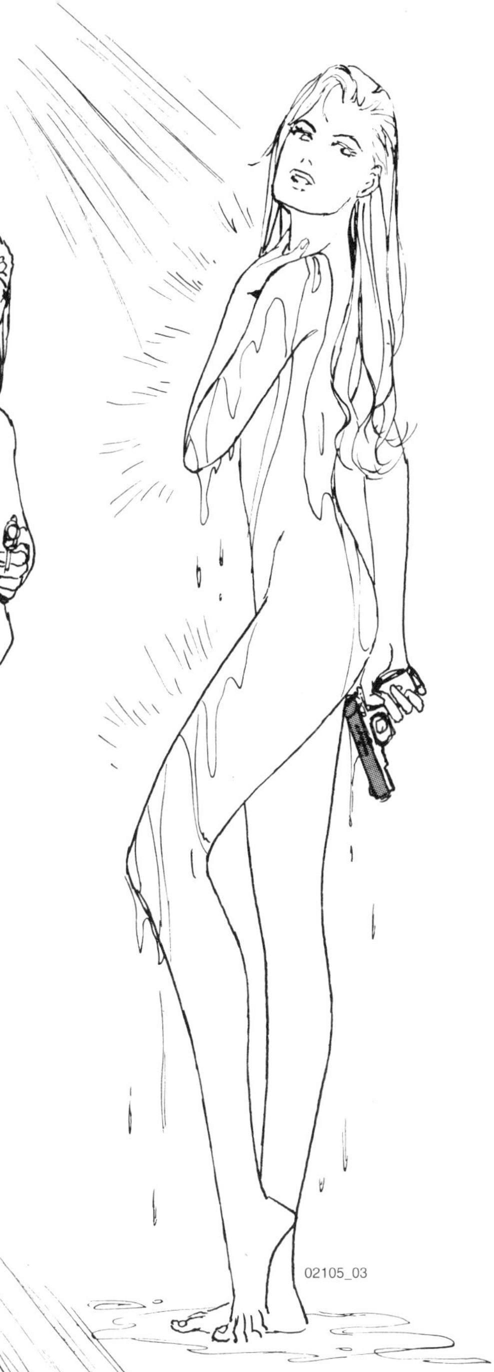

02105_03

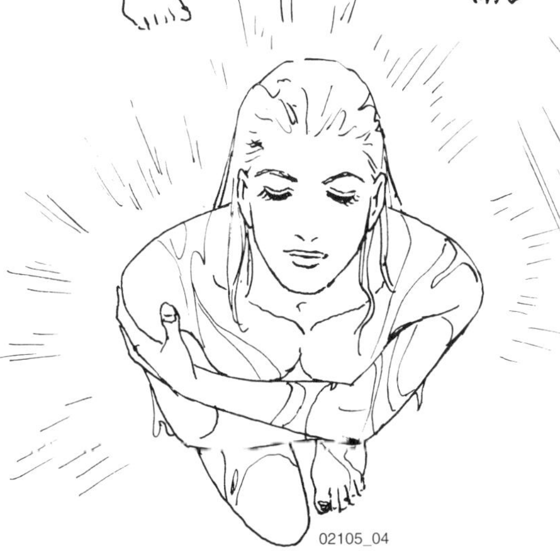

02105_04

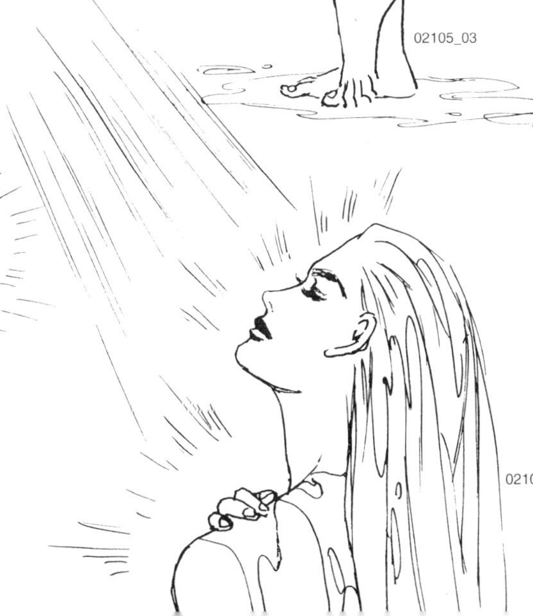

02105_05

BED

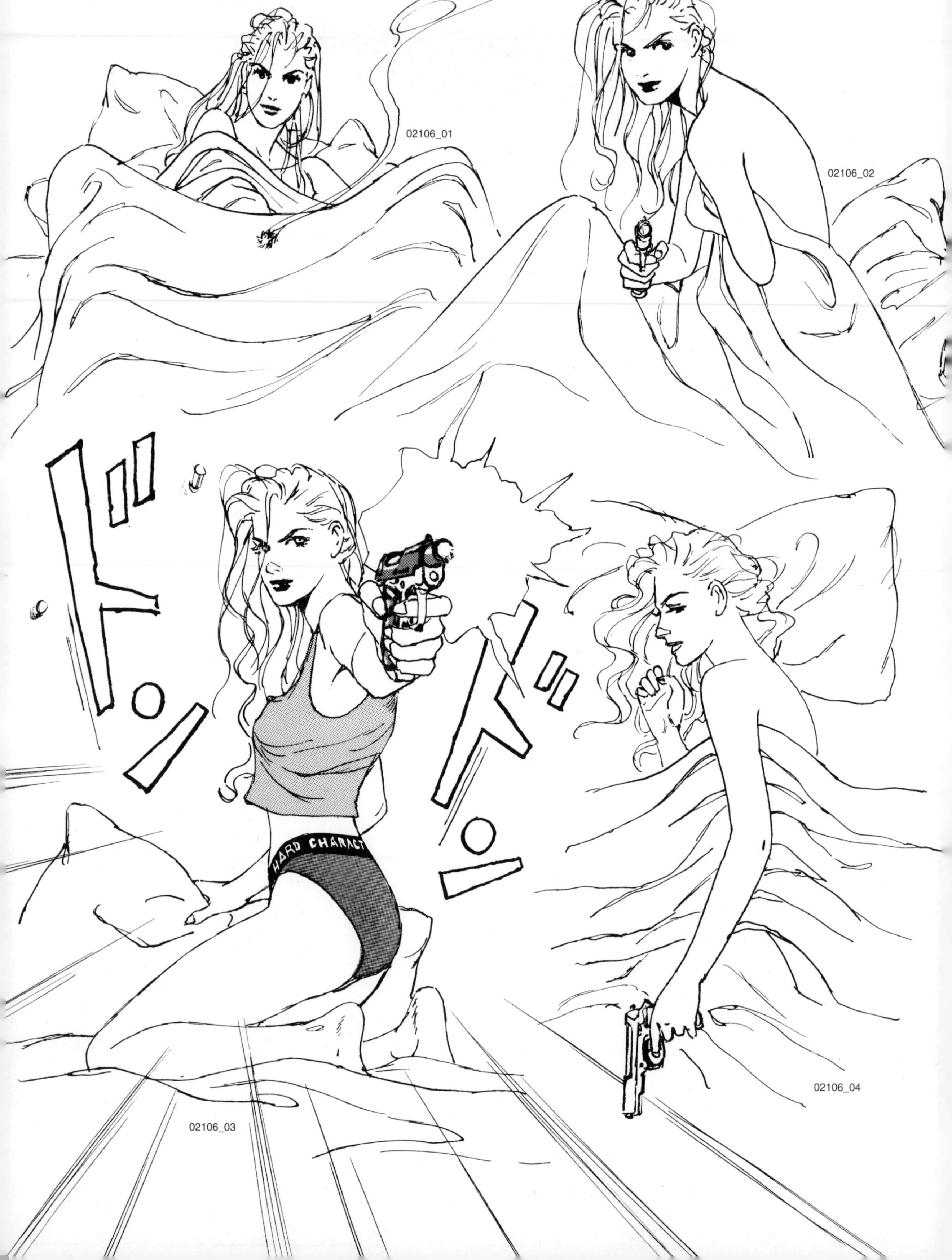
02106_01
02106_02
02106_03
02106_04

DIVING

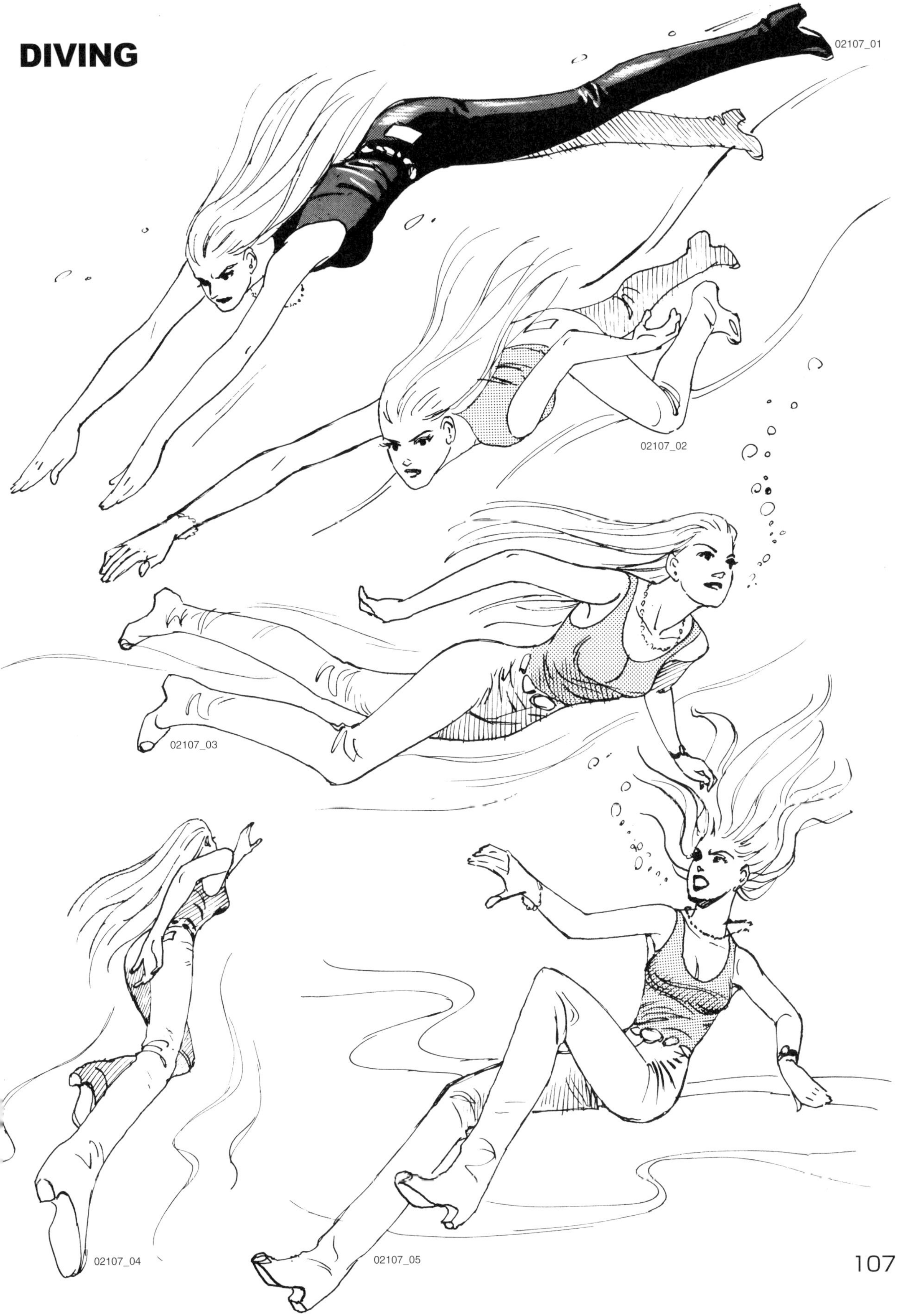

02107_01

02107_02

02107_03

02107_04

02107_05

KISS

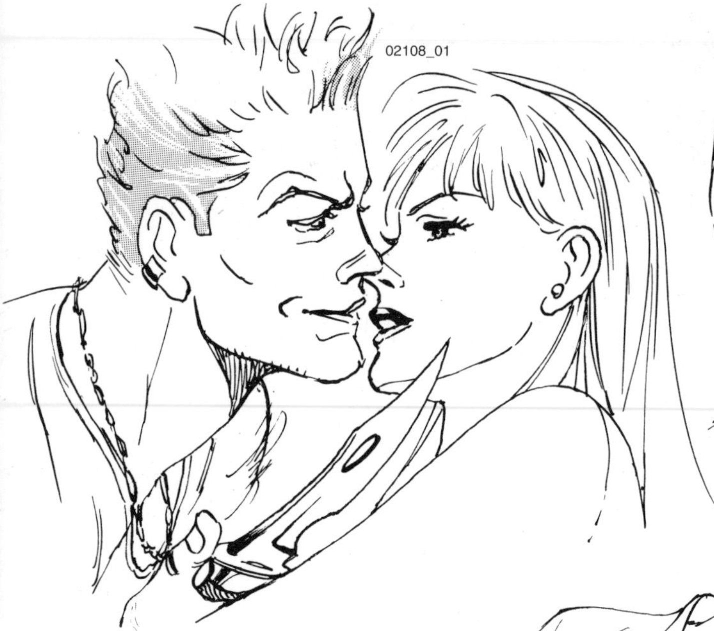

02108_01

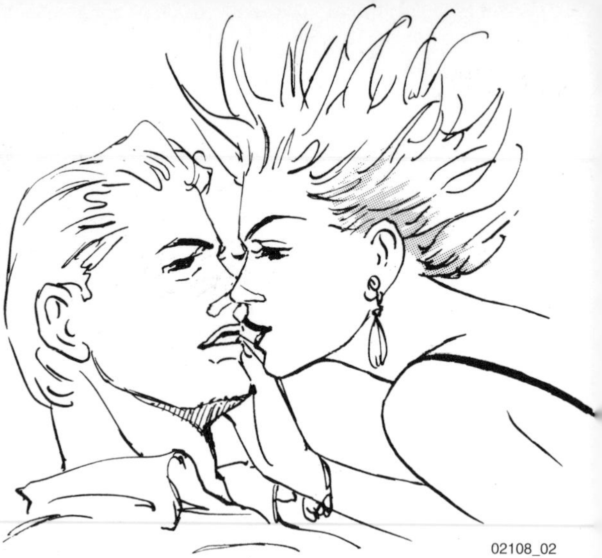

02108_02

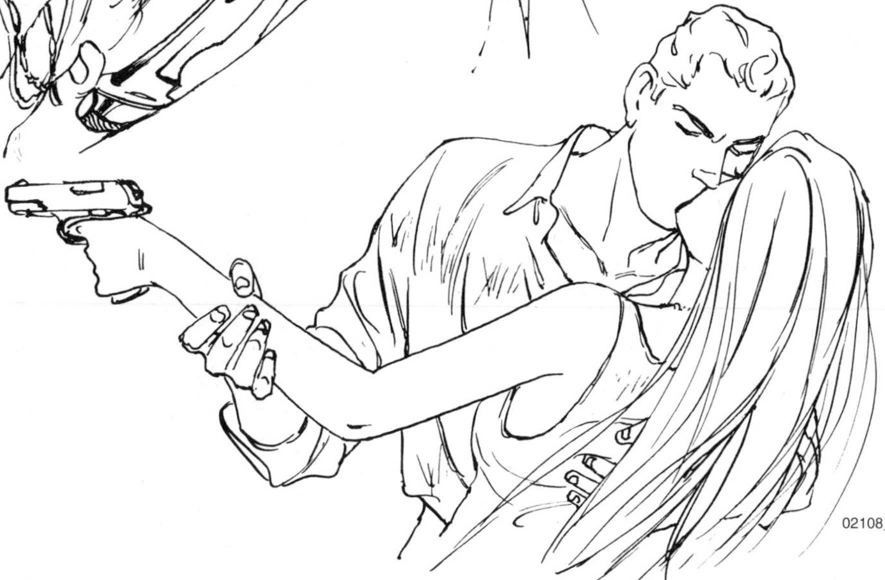

02108_03

02108_04

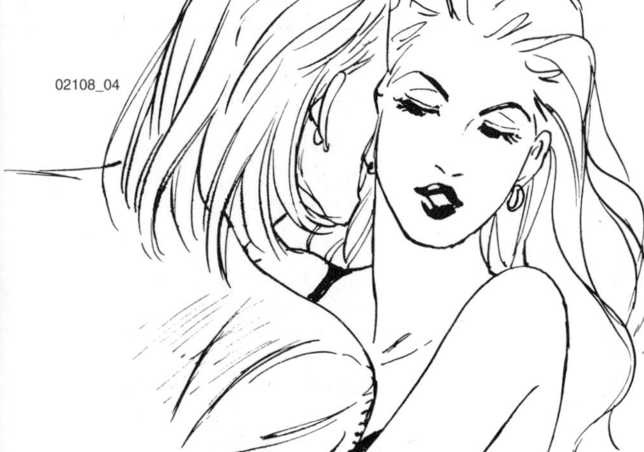

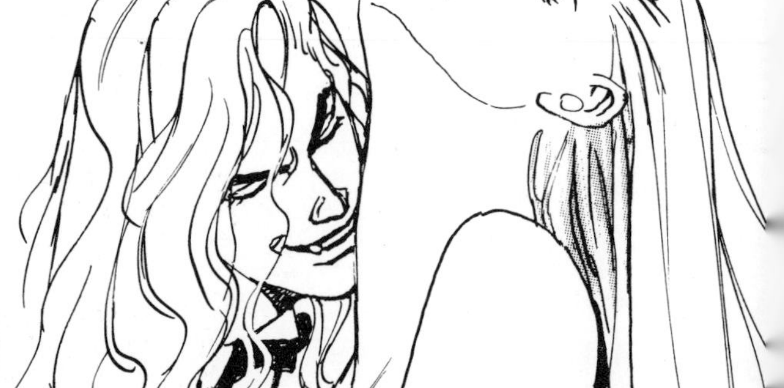

02108_05

COOL

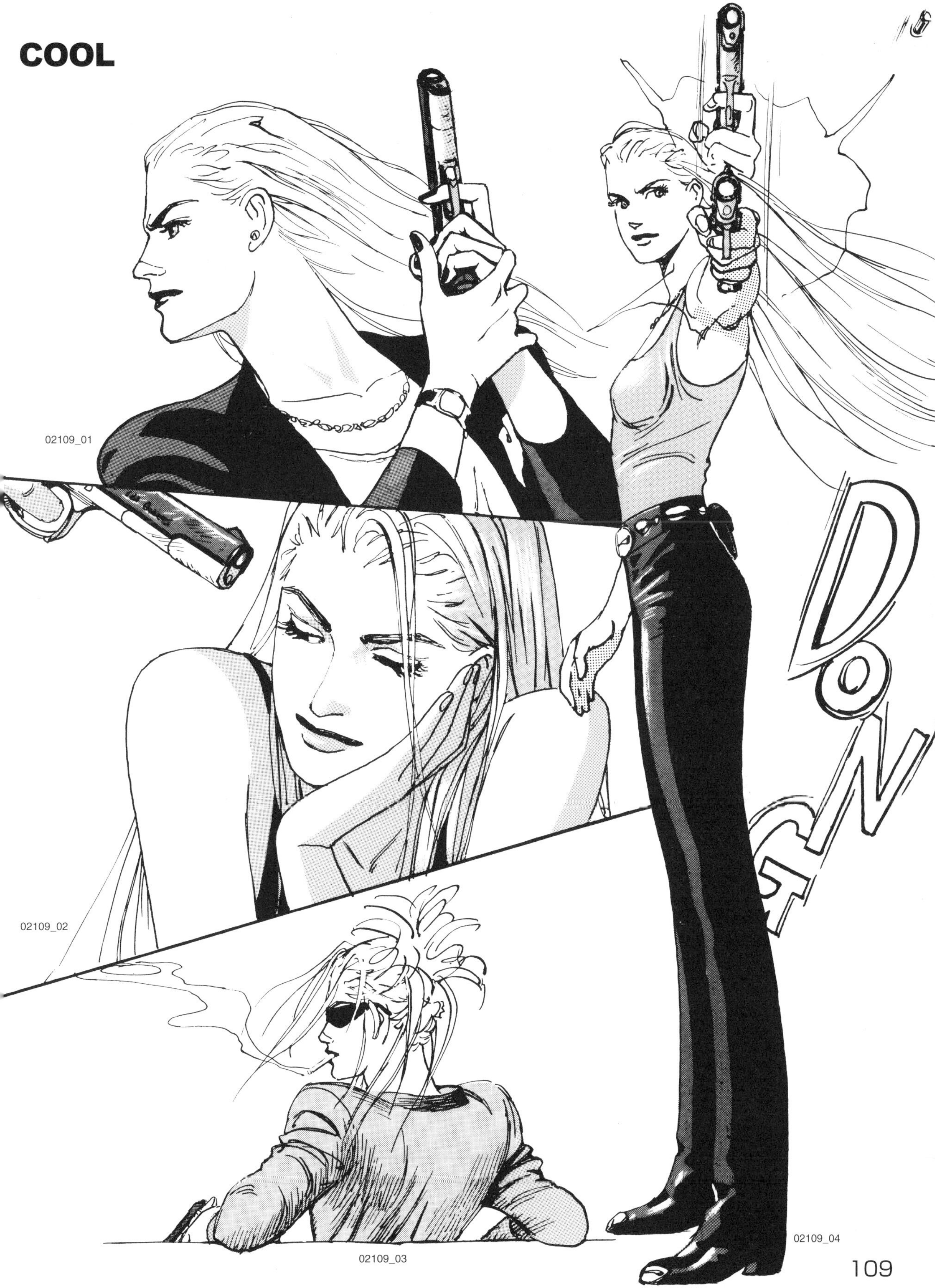
DON

02109_01

02109_02

02109_03

02109_04

DRIVE

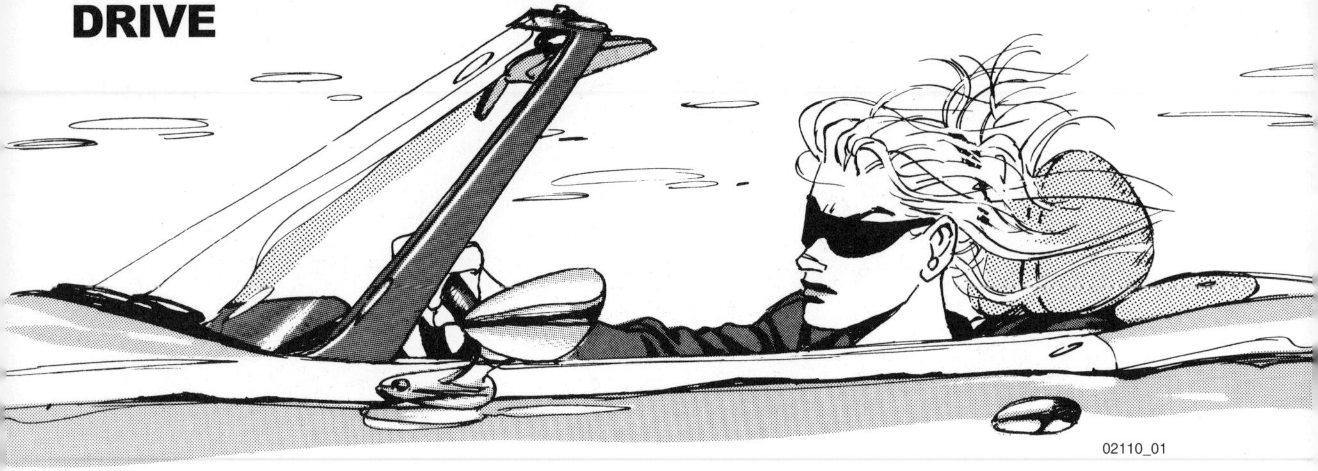

02110_01

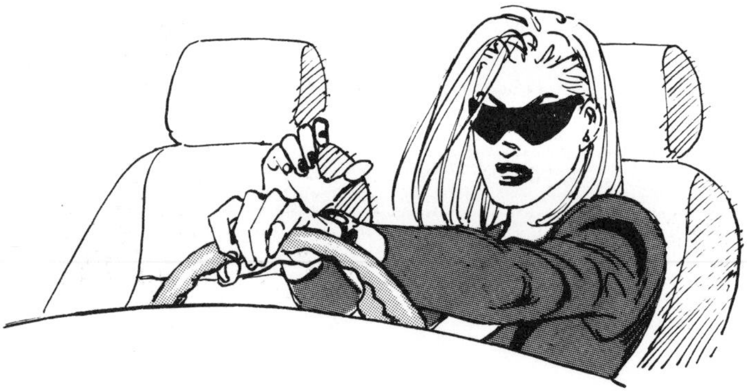

02110_02

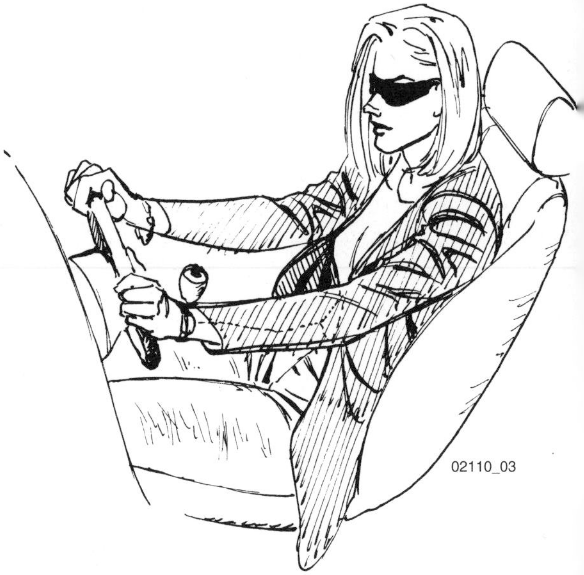

02110_03

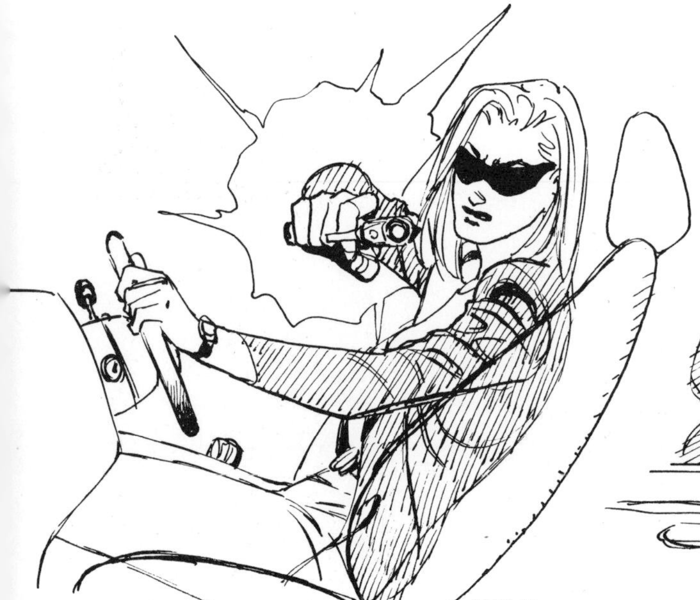

02110_04

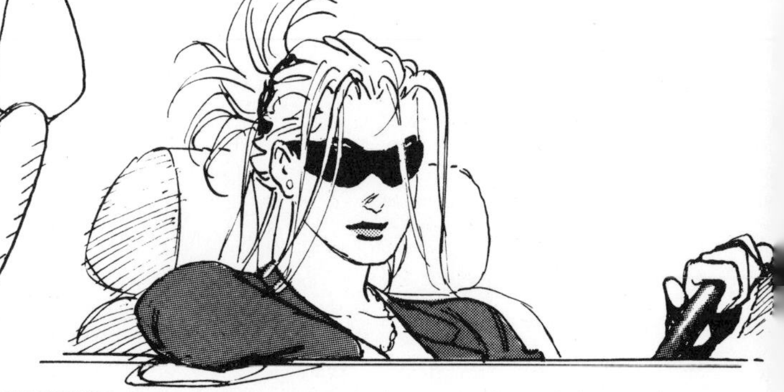

02110_05

DRIVE

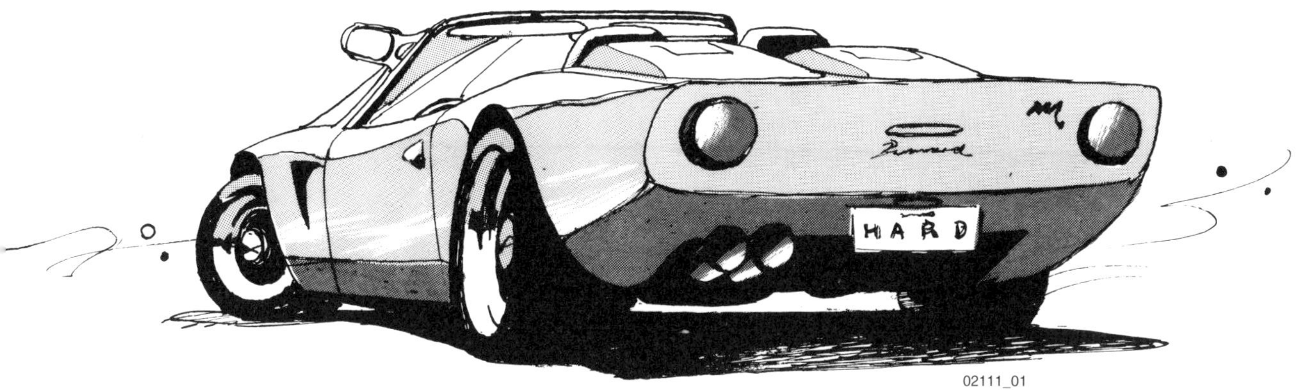
HARD

02111_01

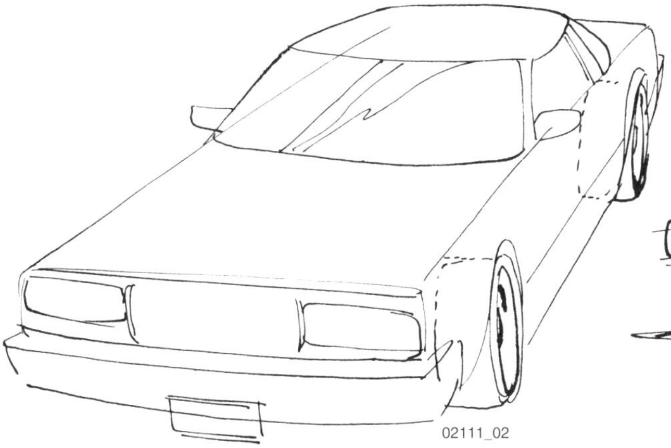

02111_02

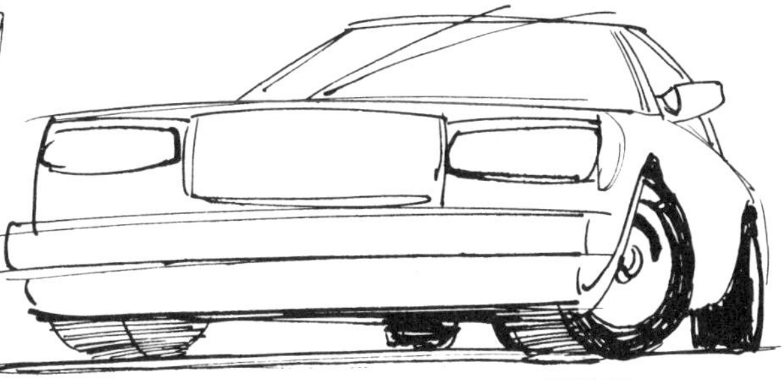

02111_03

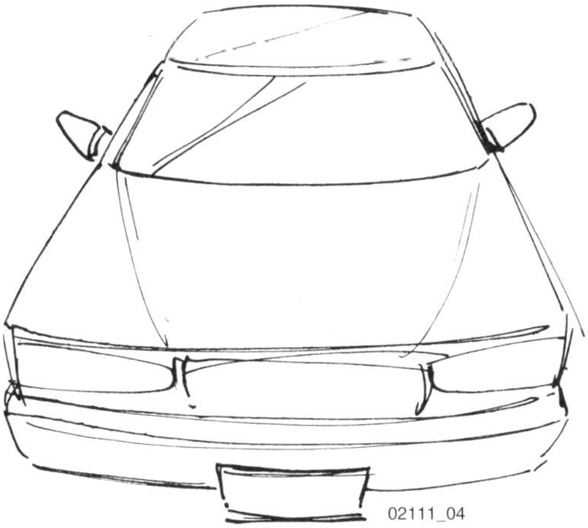

02111_04

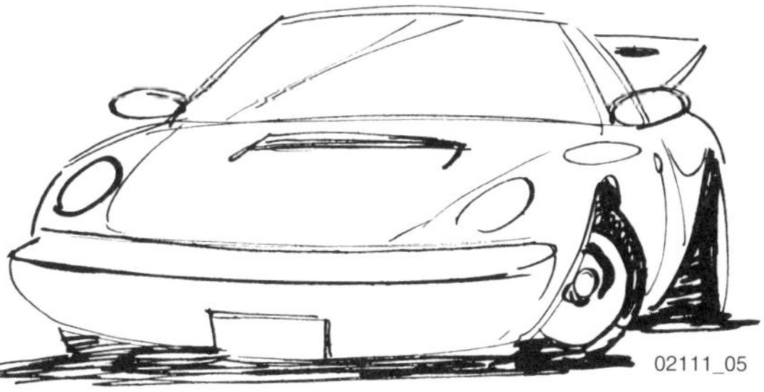

02111_05

※車のフォーマットです。トレースして好きな車の
BODYを上から描けば使いやすいと思います。

※This is a format for cars. I think this is easy to use if you trace this format then add the body of the car you like.

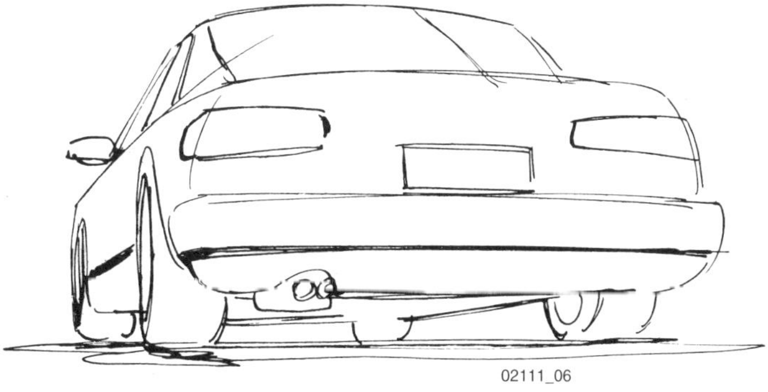

02111_06

PHONE

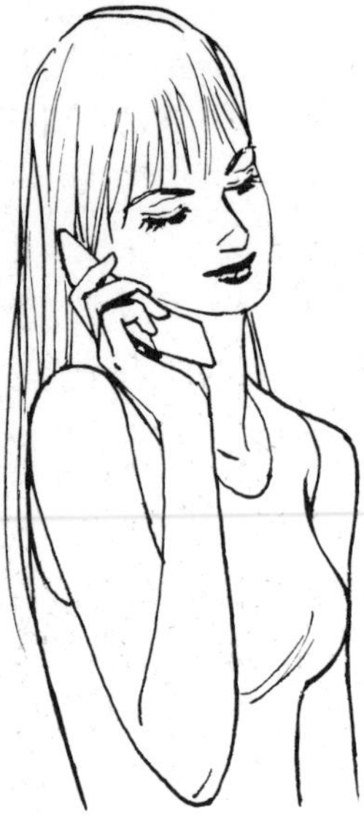

02112_01

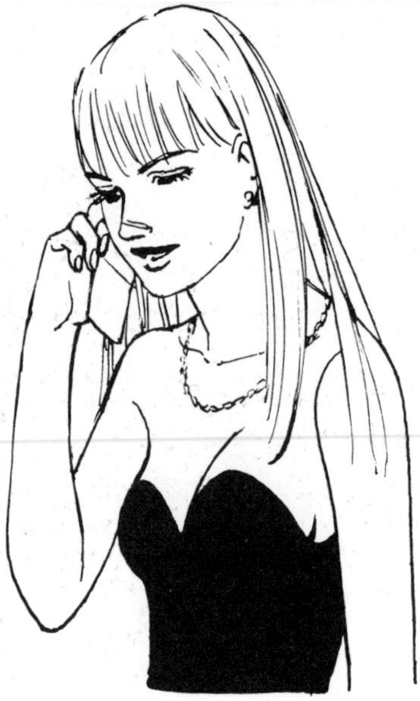

02112_02

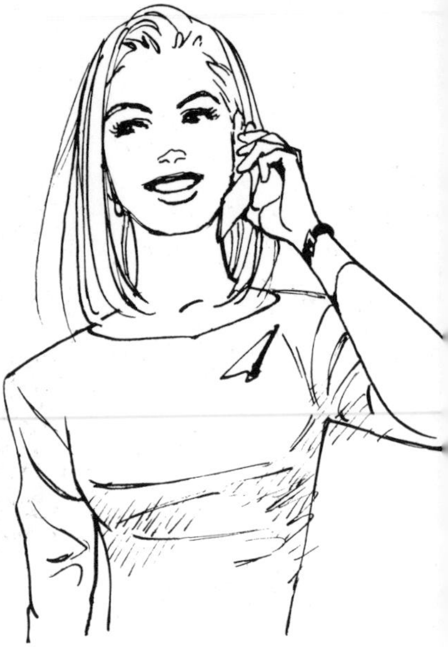

02112_03

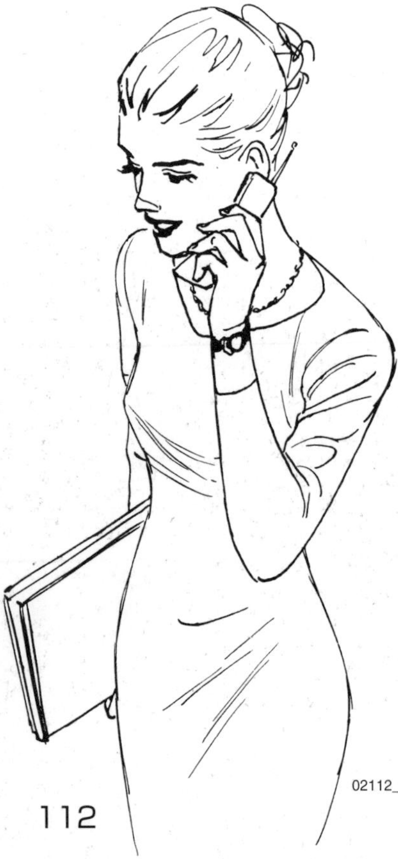

02112_04

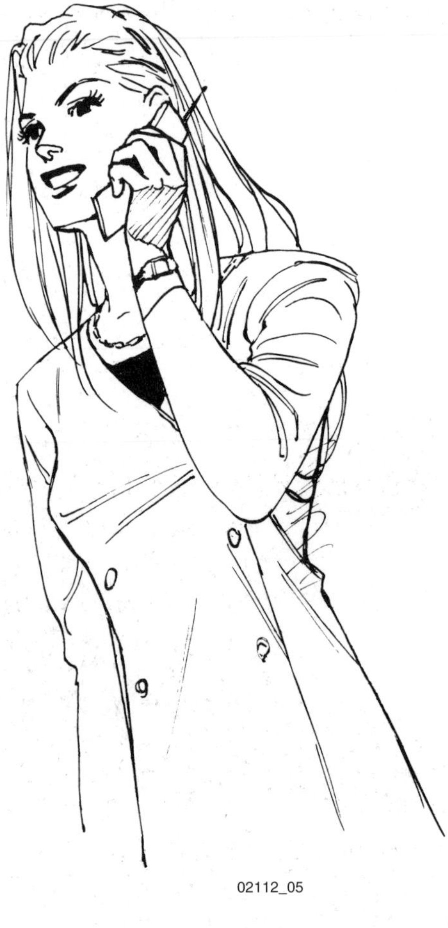

02112_05

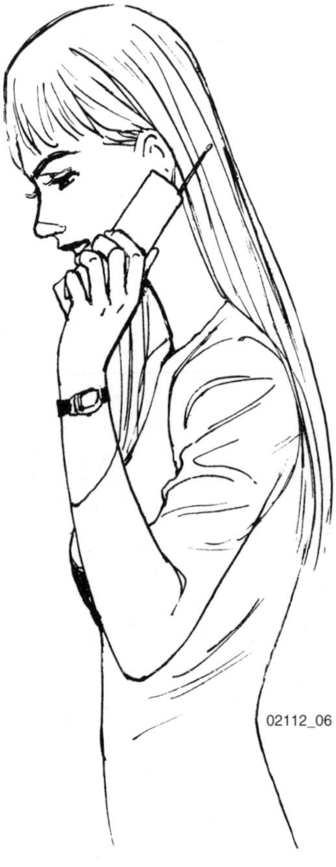

02112_06

BICYCLE

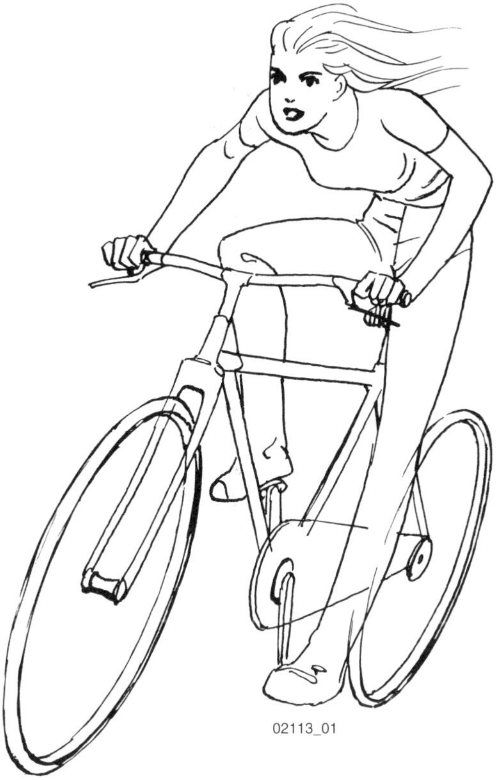

02113_01

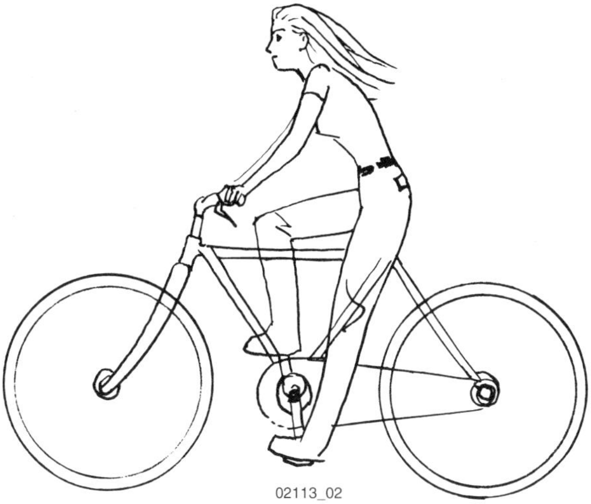

02113_02

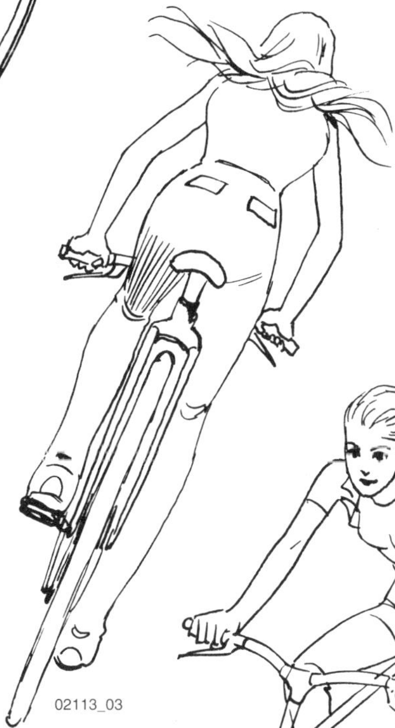

02113_03

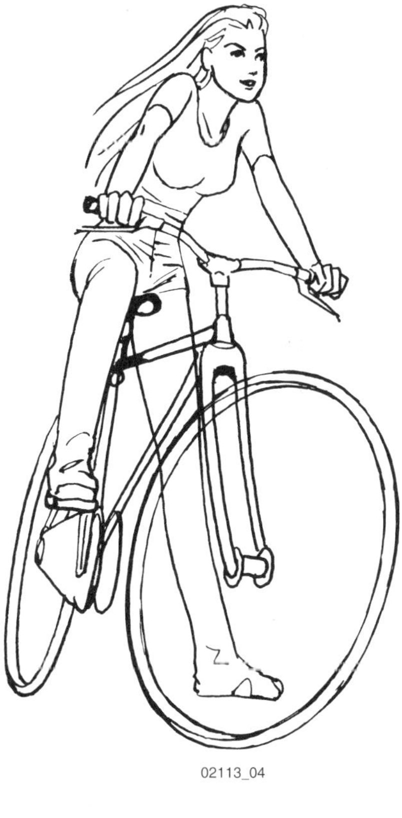

02113_04

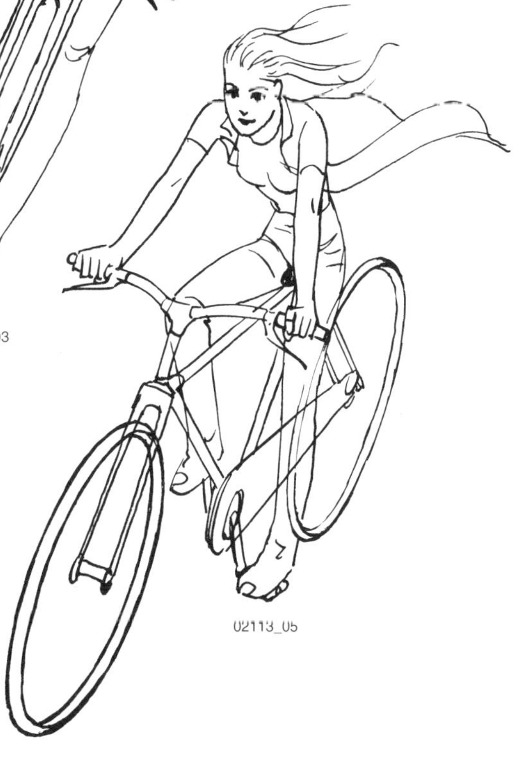

02113_05

STEP

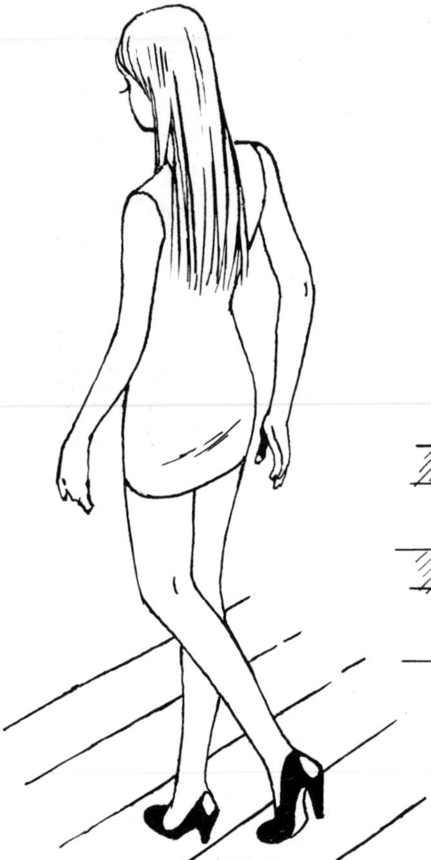

02114_01

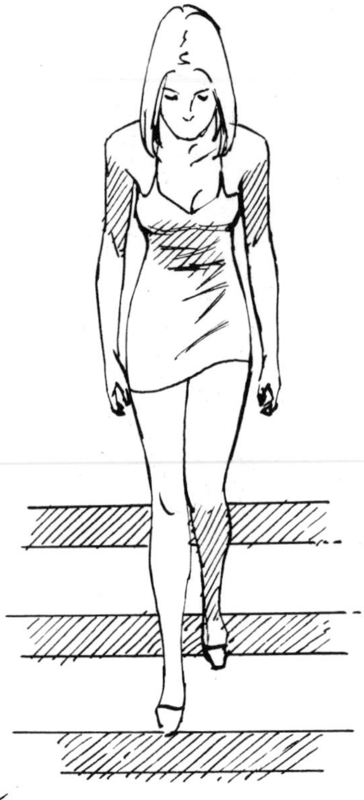

02114_02

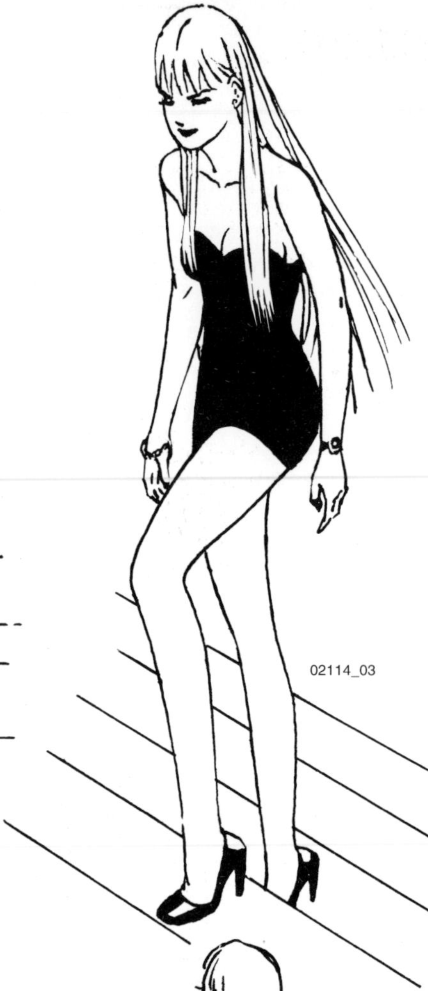

02114_03

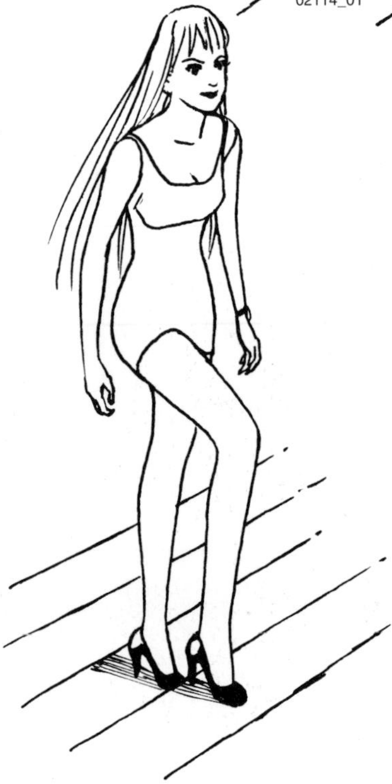

02114_04

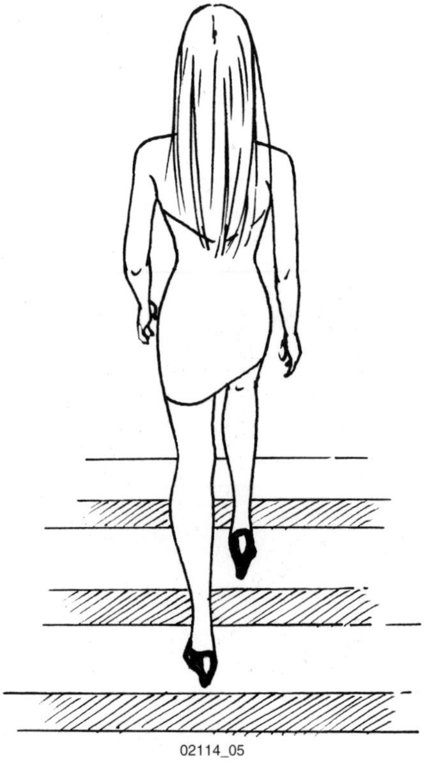

02114_05

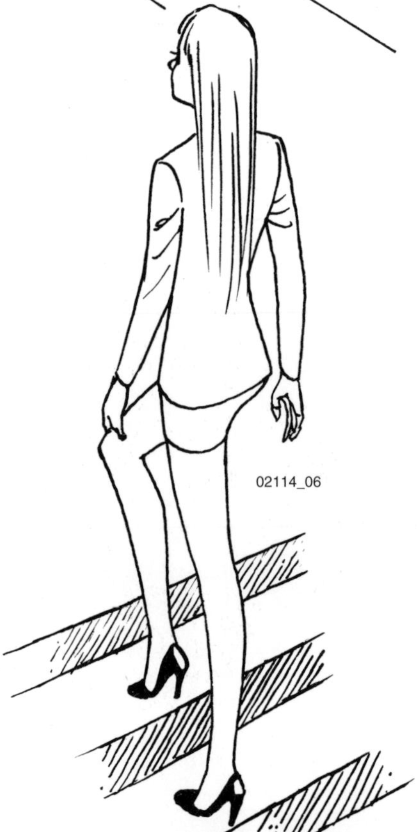

02114_06

DRINK

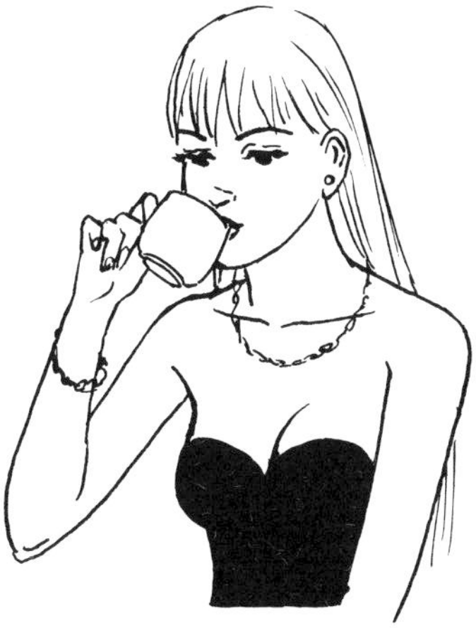
02115_01

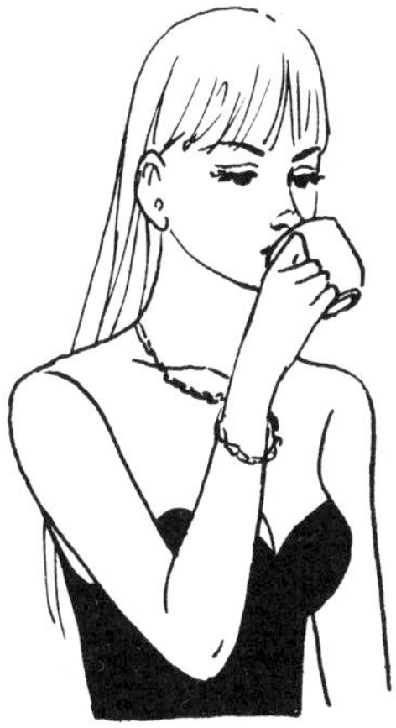
02115_02

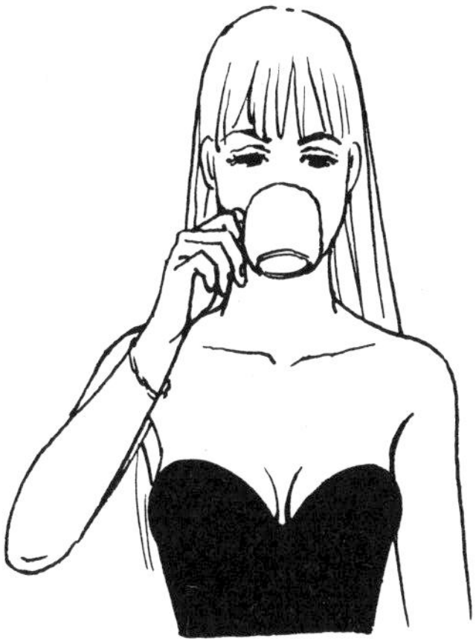
02115_03

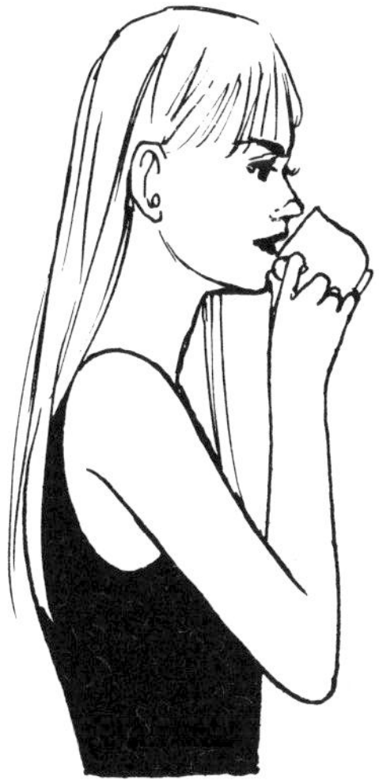
02115_04

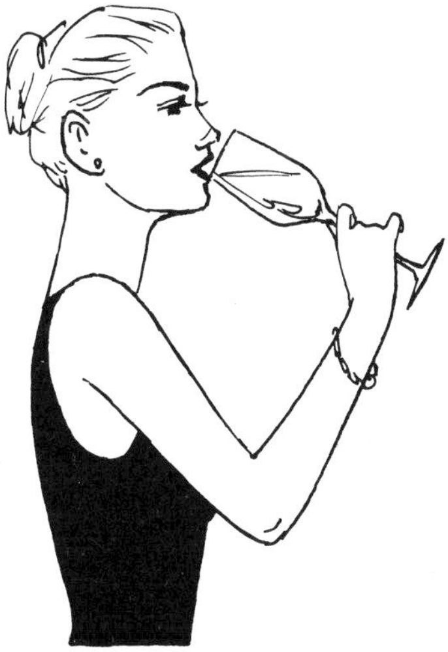
02115_05

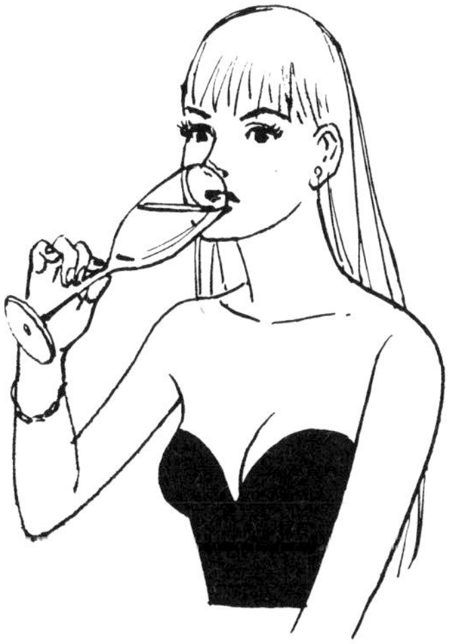
02115_06

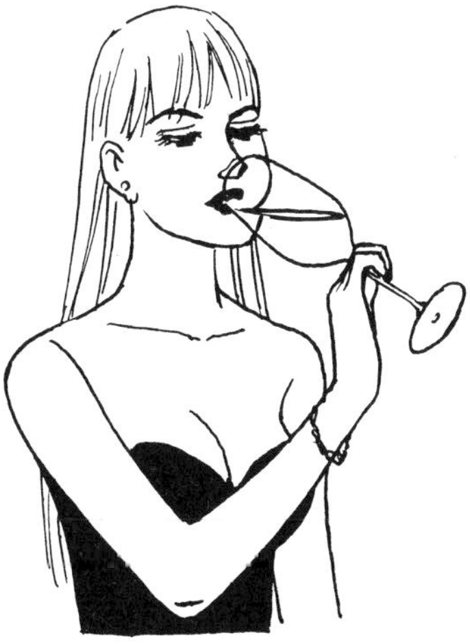
02115_07

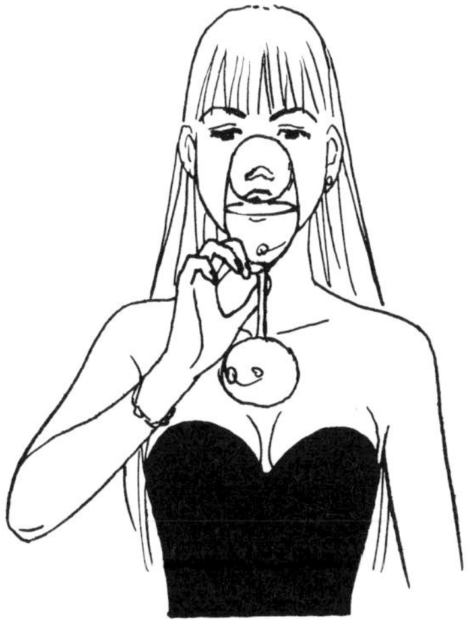
02115_08

■POSE■

CHESTER COAT

チェスターコート

アクションヒーローがよく身につけているファッションだ。黒くて長い丈のコートがかっこいいい。POSEのコーナーにはコートがたくさん登場しているので参考にして欲しい。

Coats are often used on action heroes. Long black coats are very cool. There are a lot of coats appearing in this POSE section so please refer to them.

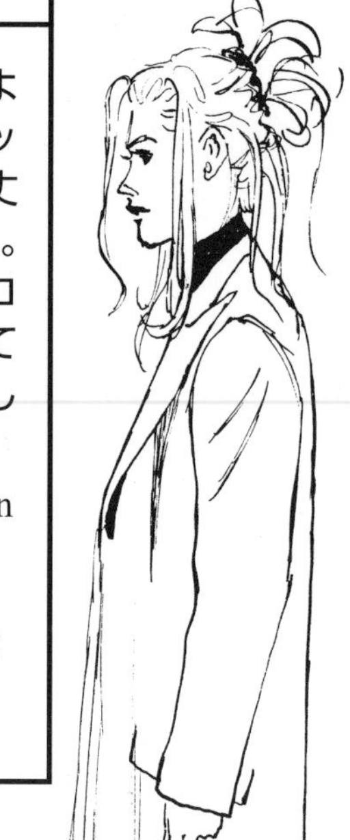

ゆったりとしていて肩で着る感じだ。ドレープの利いたマントのようなイメージだ。ボタンををとめないで着た方が風になびいてかっこいい。

Loosely worn over the shoulders. It is draped to look like a mantle unbuttoned so it flutters in the wind cool.

02116_01

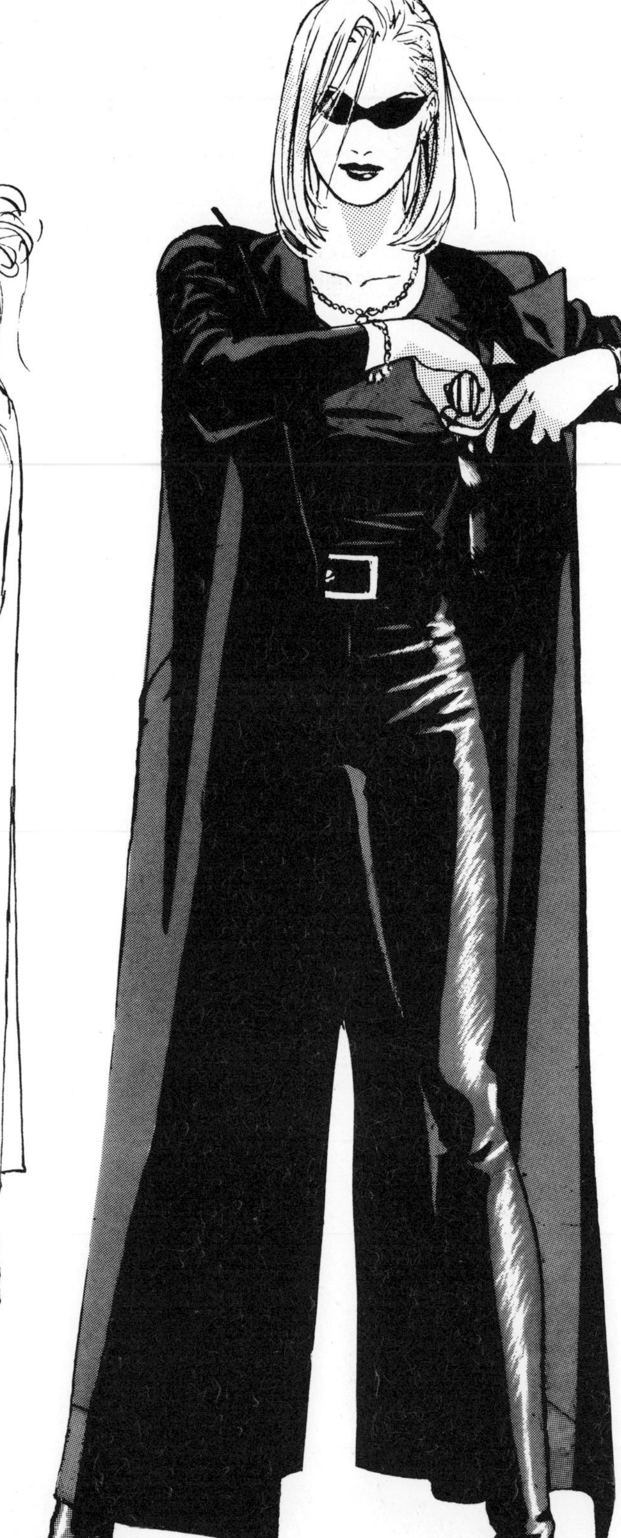

02116_02

■POSE■

JACKET

ジャケット

いわゆる背広だが、ハードなキャラクターには欠かせない。大人の女にとって大切なファッションだ。構造を理解して描けるようになりたい。ファッション誌などを見て研究しよう。

Suits are an important fashion for grown-up women and they often accompany tough women. Understand the structure of suits and you will want to learn to draw them. Look at fashion magazines etc and study.

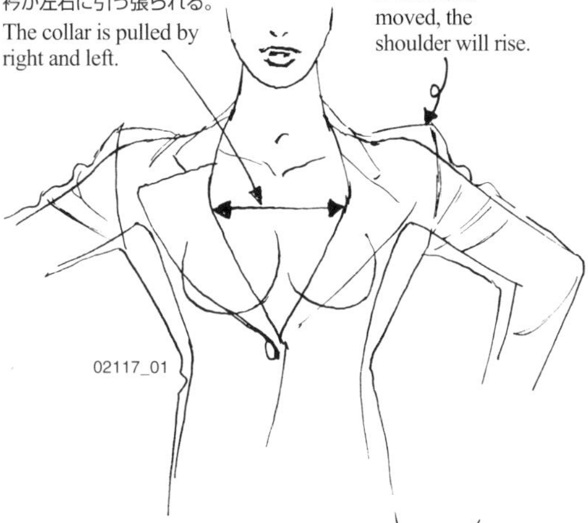

衿が左右に引っ張られる。
The collar is pulled by right and left.
腕を上げると
肩が盛り上がる。
If an arm is moved, the shoulder will rise.

02117_01

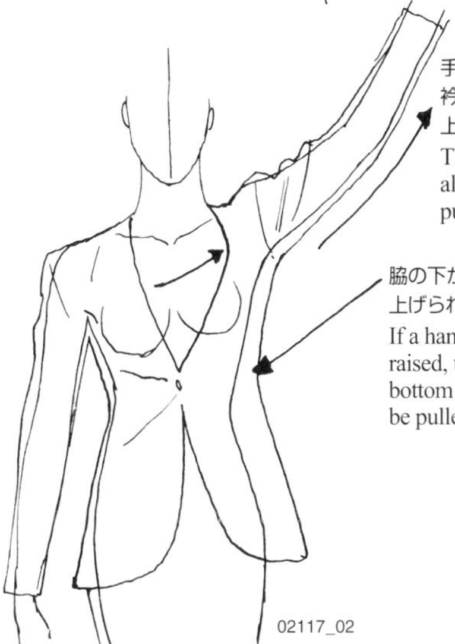

手を上げると
衿が引っ張り
上げられる。
The collar has also been pulled.
脇の下が引っ張り
上げられる。
If a hand is raised, the bottom side will be pulled up.

02117_02

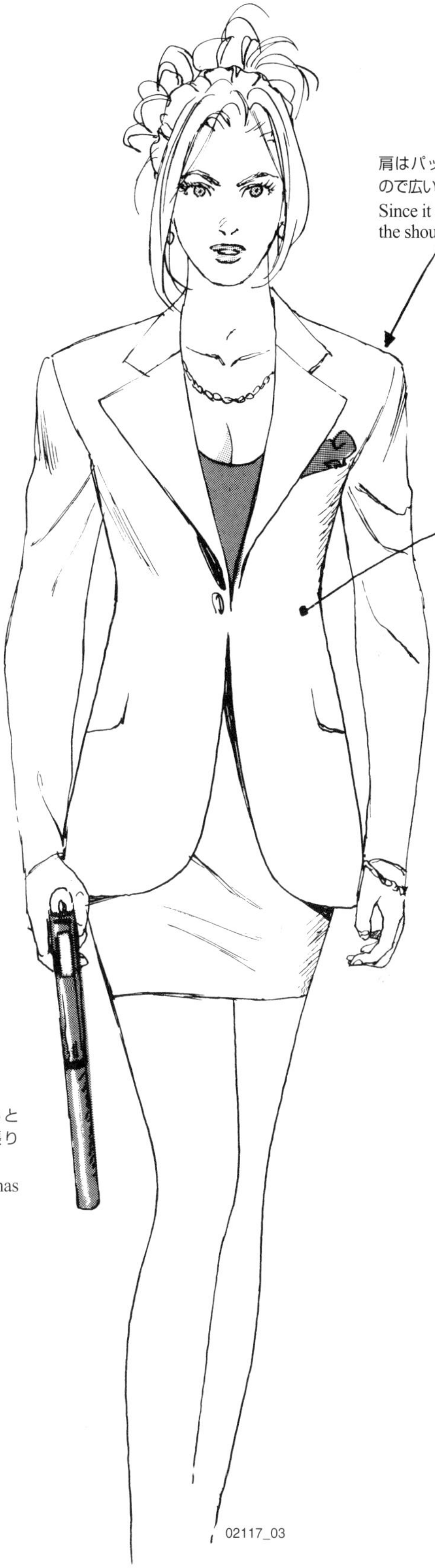

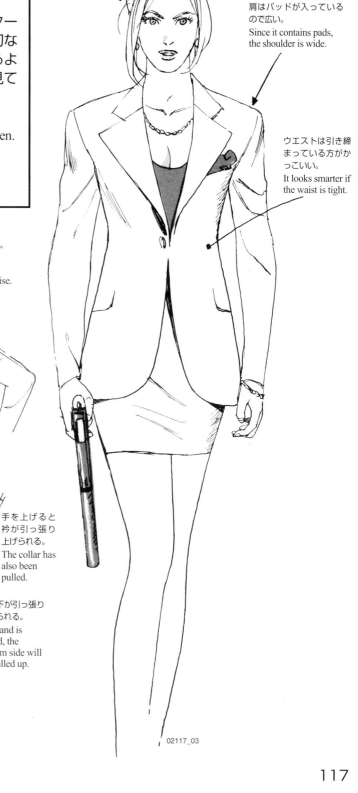

肩はパッドが入っている
ので広い。
Since it contains pads, the shoulder is wide.
ウエストは引き締
まっている方がか
っこいい。
It looks smarter if the waist is tight.

02117_03

■POSE■

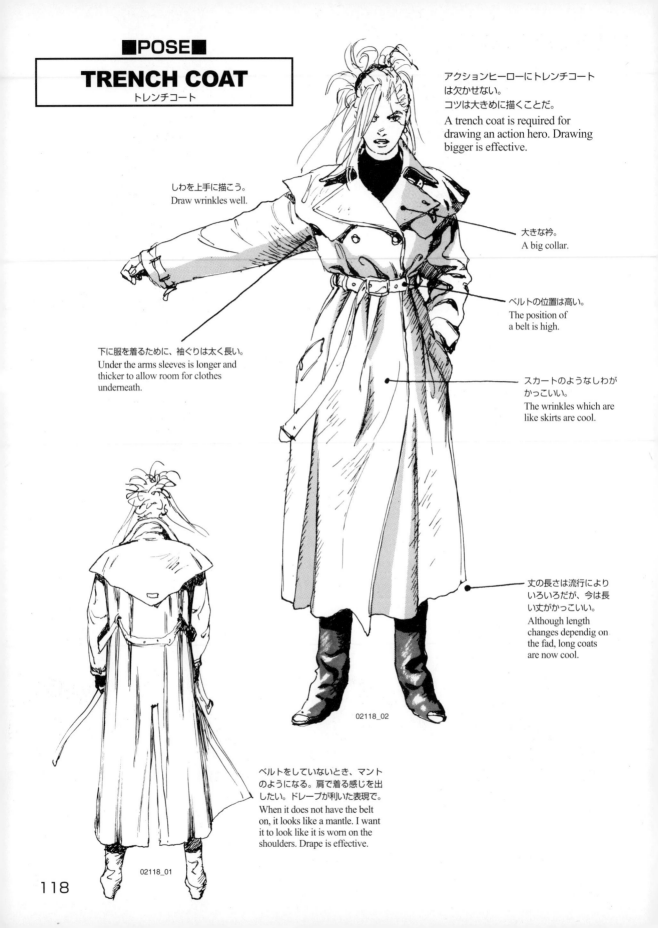

TRENCH COAT

トレンチコート

アクションヒーローにトレンチコートは欠かせない。
コツは大きめに描くことだ。

A trench coat is required for drawing an action hero. Drawing bigger is effective.

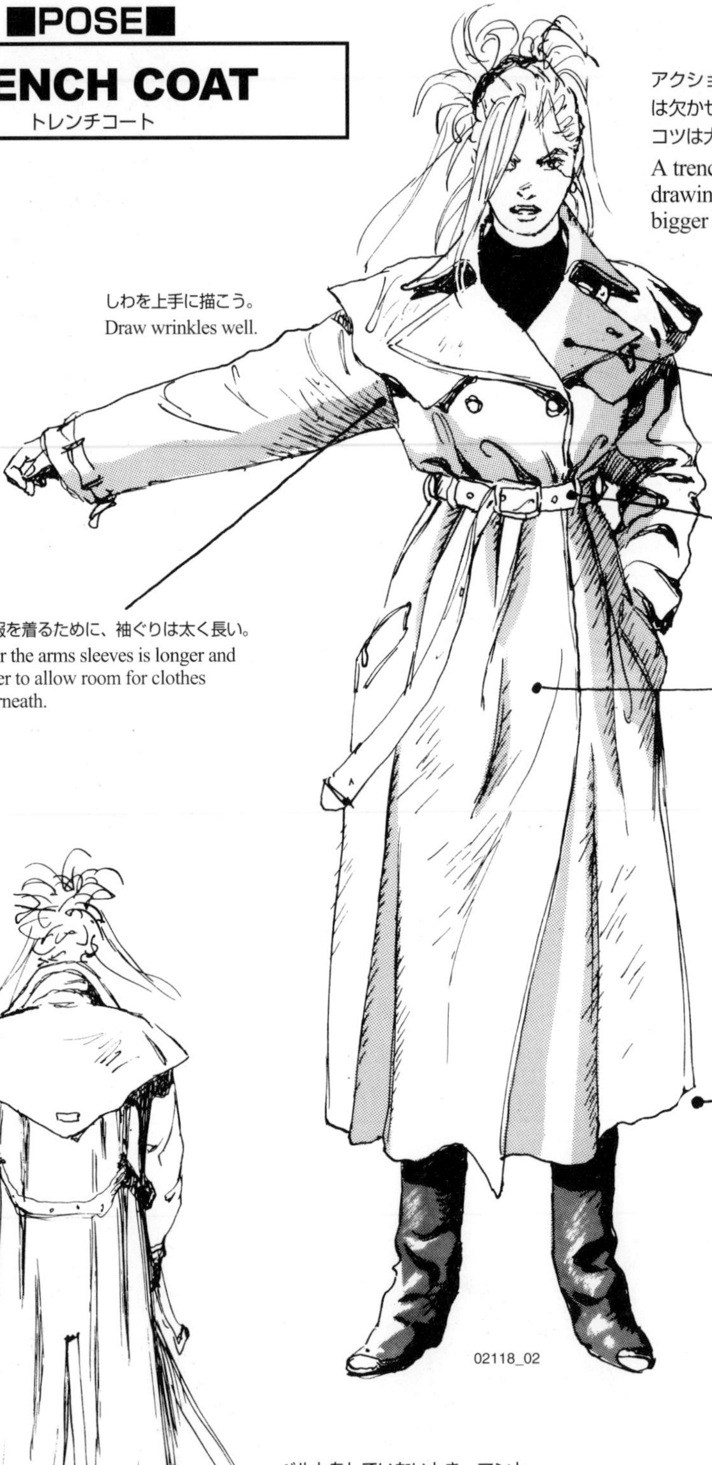

02118_02

しわを上手に描こう。
Draw wrinkles well.

大きな衿。
A big collar.

ベルトの位置は高い。
The position of a belt is high.

下に服を着るために、袖ぐりは太く長い。
Under the arms sleeves is longer and thicker to allow room for clothes underneath.

スカートのようなしわがかっこいい。
The wrinkles which are like skirts are cool.

丈の長さは流行によりいろいろだが、今は長い丈がかっこいい。
Although length changes dependig on the fad, long coats are now cool.

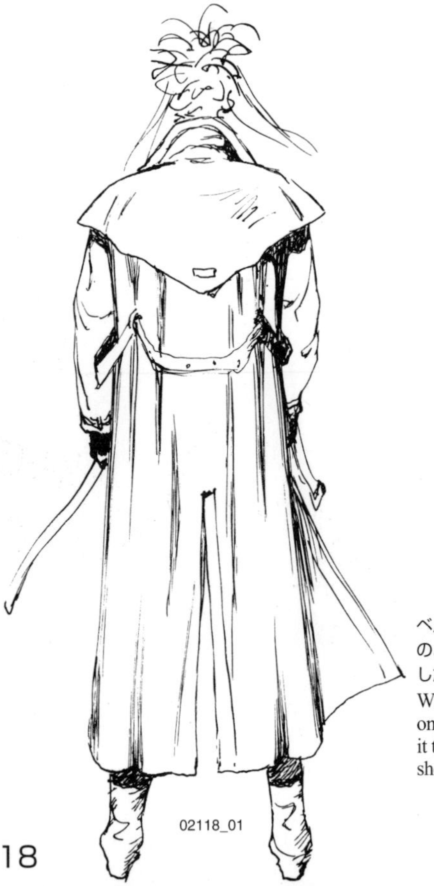

02118_01

ベルトをしていないとき、マントのようになる。肩で着る感じを出したい。ドレープが利いた表現で。
When it does not have the belt on, it looks like a mantle. I want it to look like it is worn on the shoulders. Drape is effective.

TRENCH COAT

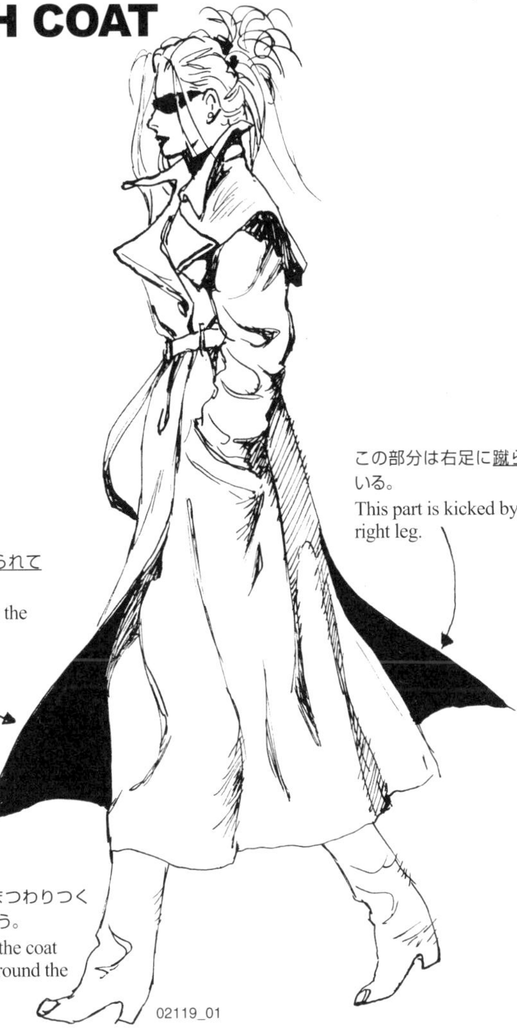
この部分は右足に蹴られている。
This part is kicked by the right leg.
この部分は左足に蹴られている。
This part is kicked by the left leg.
足にコートがまつわりつく様子を表現しよう。
Try to express the coat being caught around the leg.

02119_01

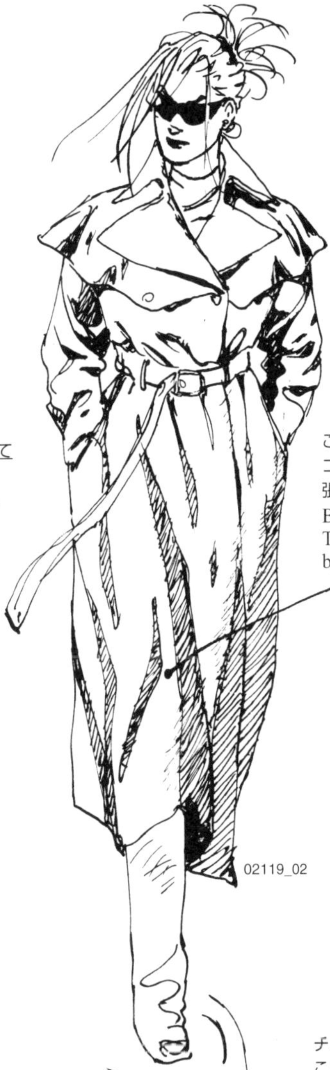
この部分に注意。コートが膝に引っ張られている。
Be careful here! The coat is pulled by the knee.

02119_02

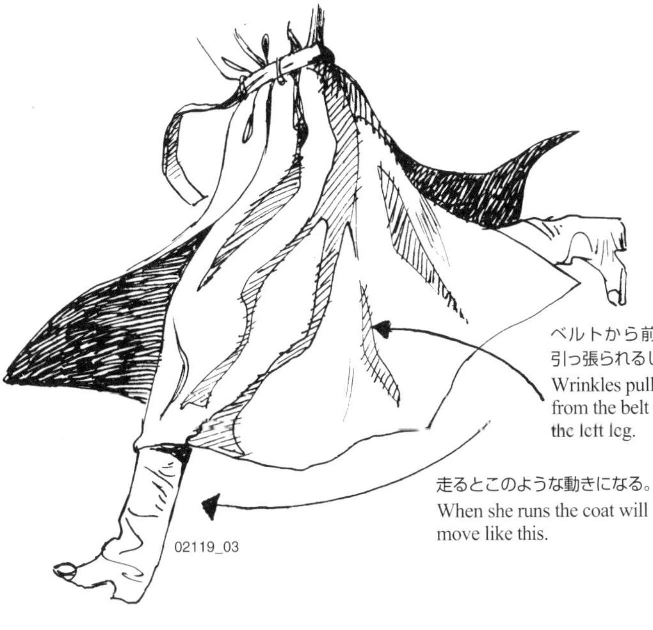
ベルトから前足へ引っ張られるしわ。
Wrinkles pulled from the belt to the left leg.
走るとこのような動きになる。
When she runs the coat will move like this.

02119_03

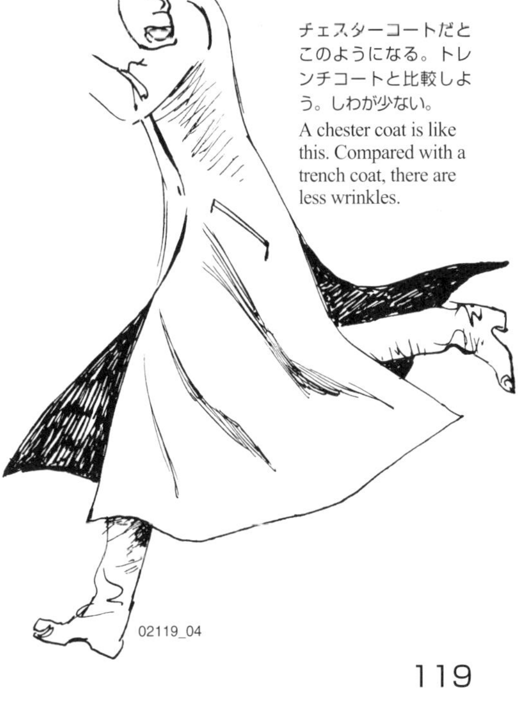
チェスターコートだとこのようになる。トレンチコートと比較しよう。しわが少ない。
A chester coat is like this. Compared with a trench coat, there are less wrinkles.

02119_04

HIHEEL

02120_01

02120_02

02120_03

02120_04

02120_05

02120_06

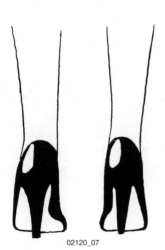

02120_07

02120_08

02120_09

HAND

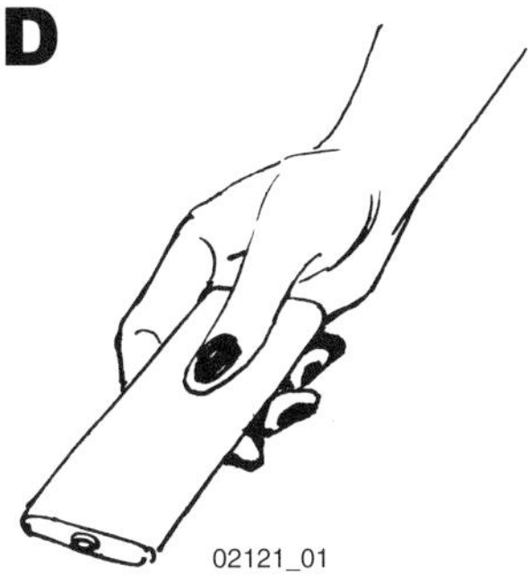
02121_01

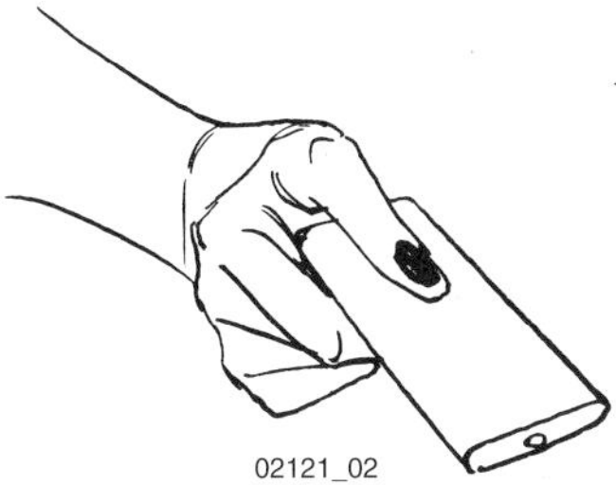
02121_02

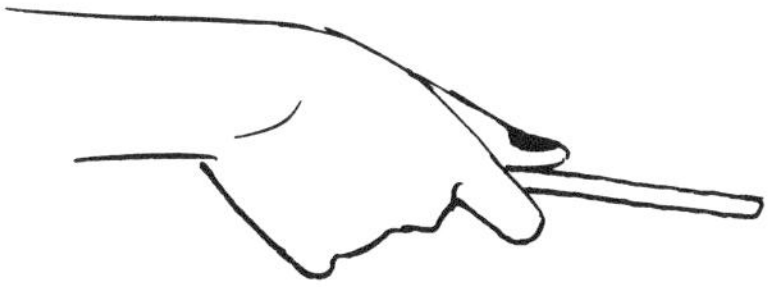
02121_03

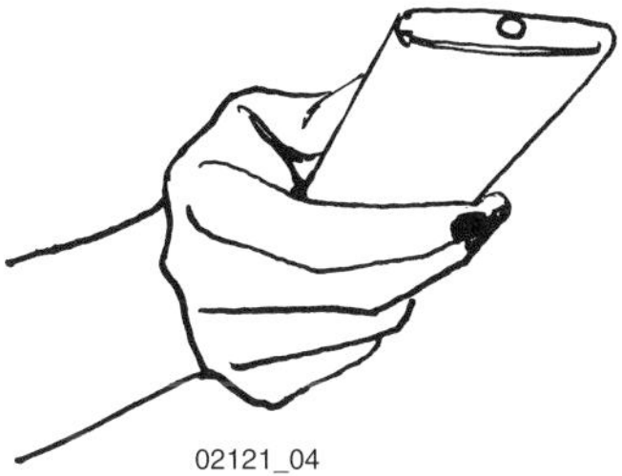
02121_04

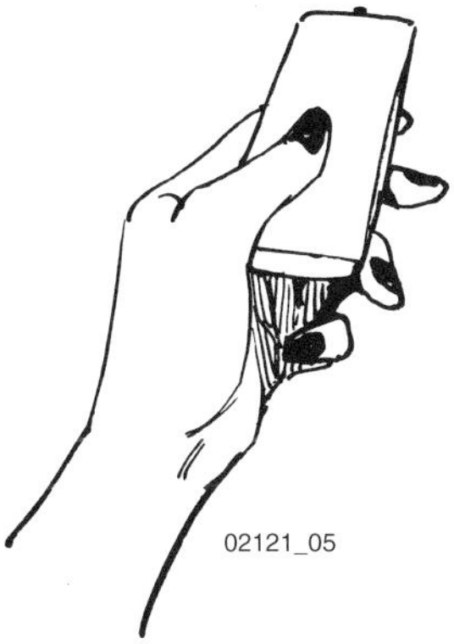
02121_05

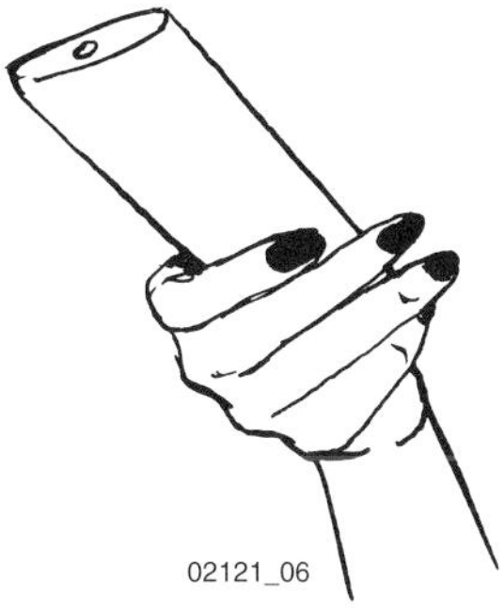
02121_06

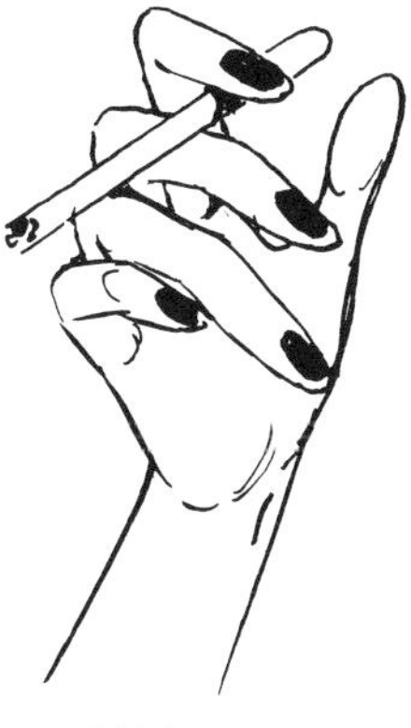
02121_07

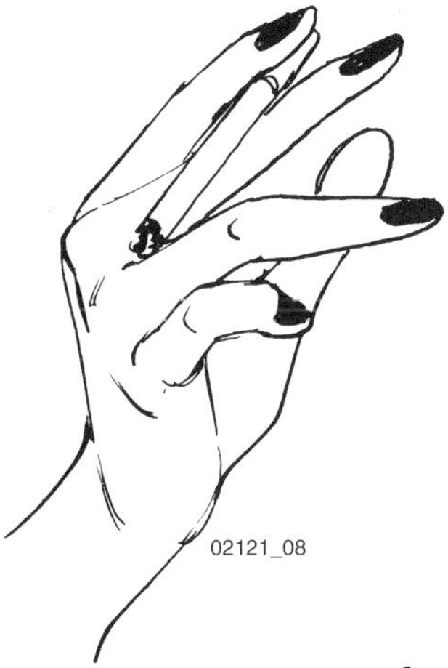
02121_08

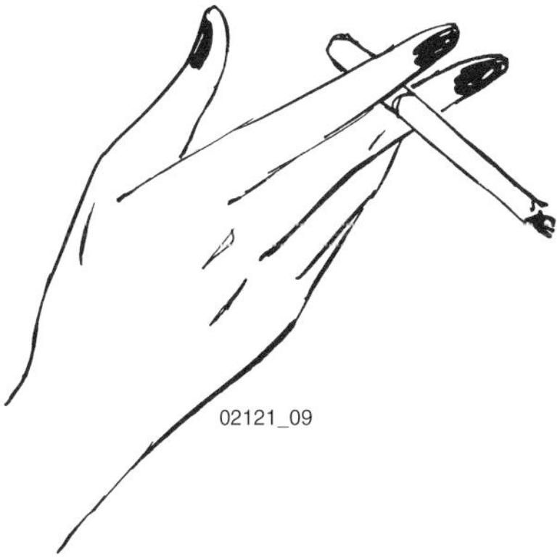
02121_09

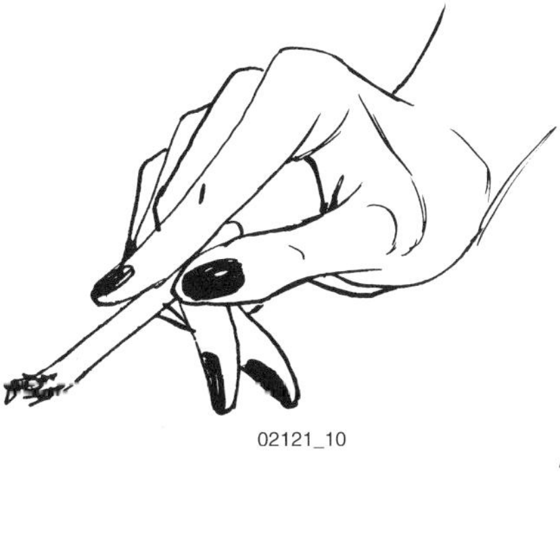
02121_10

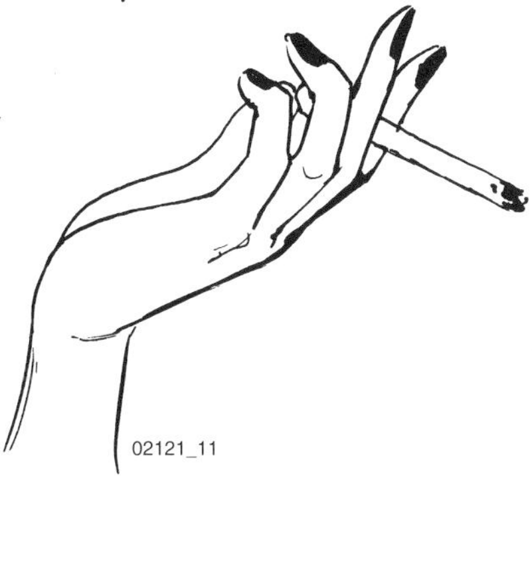
02121_11

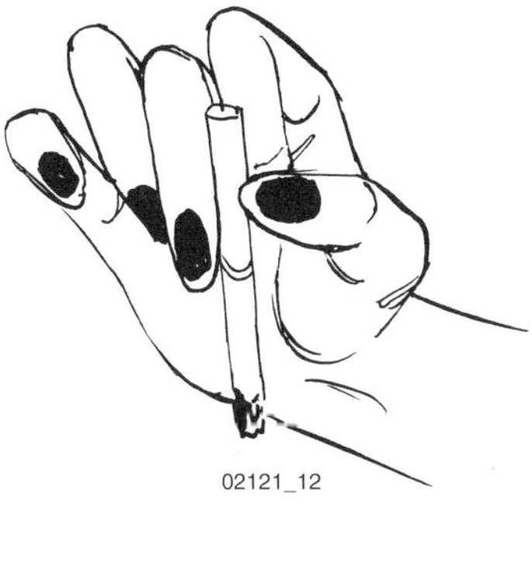
02121_12

HAND

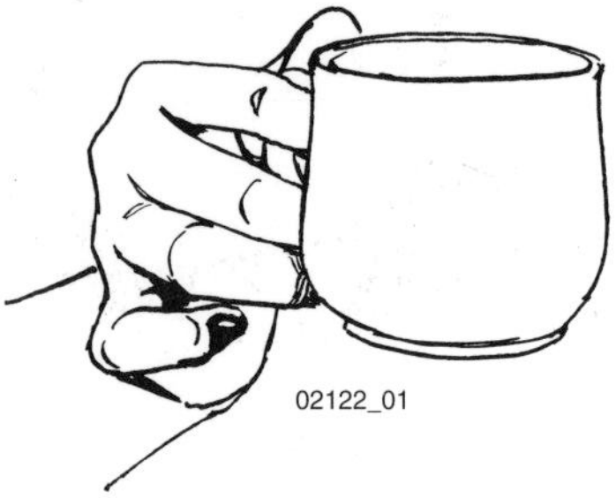
02122_01

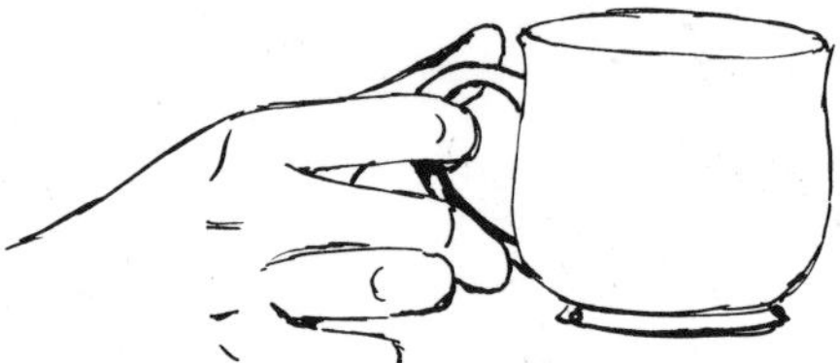
02122_02

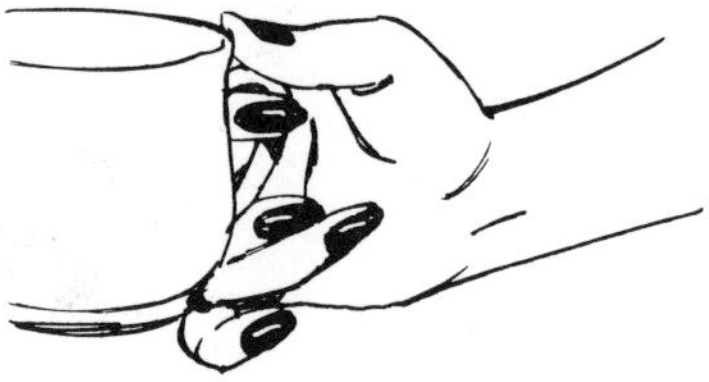
02122_03

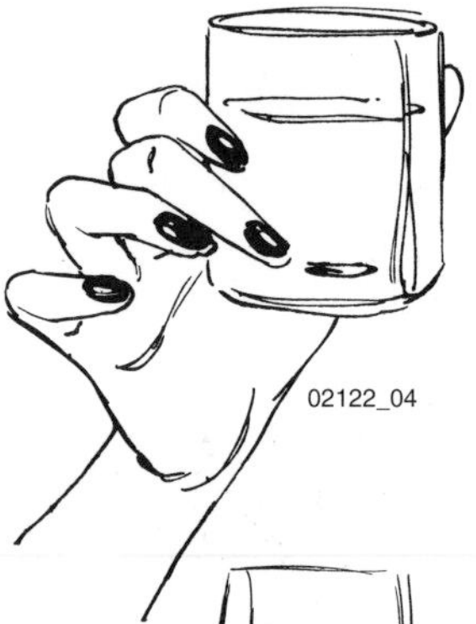
02122_04

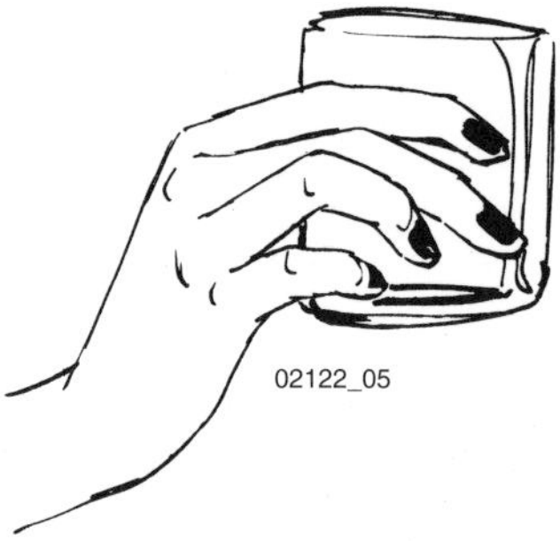
02122_05

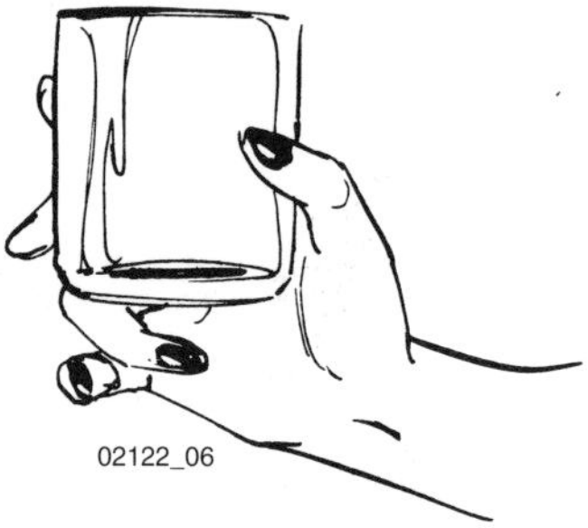
02122_06

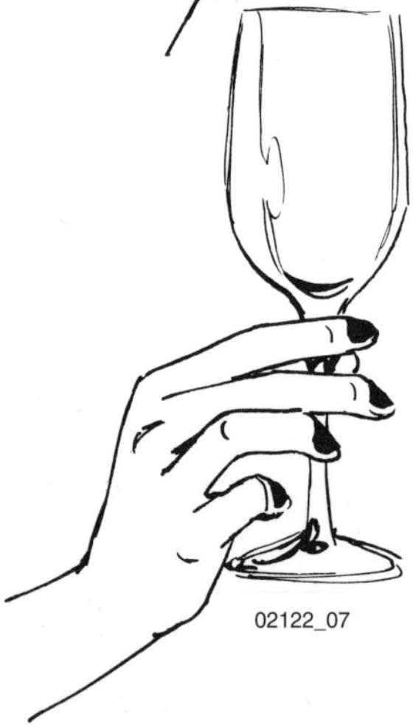
02122_07

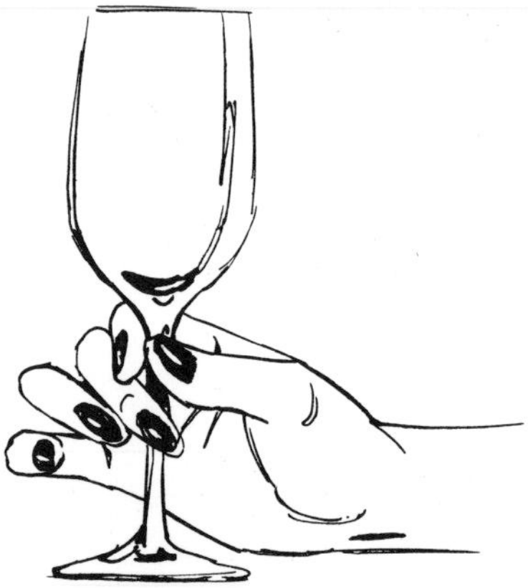
02122_08

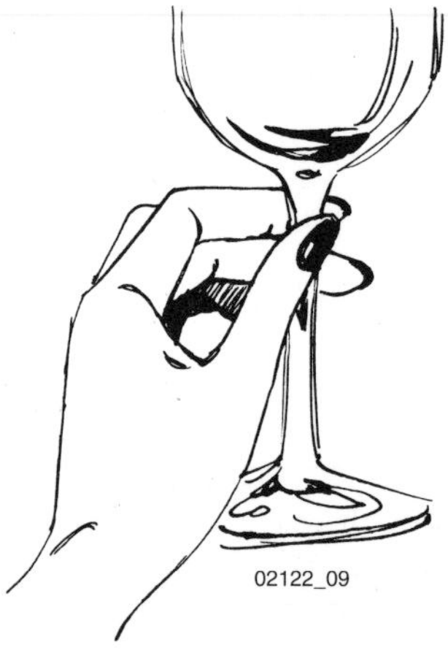
02122_09

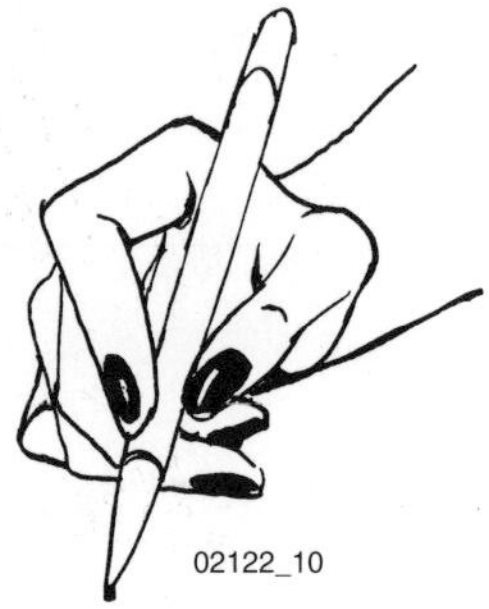
02122_10

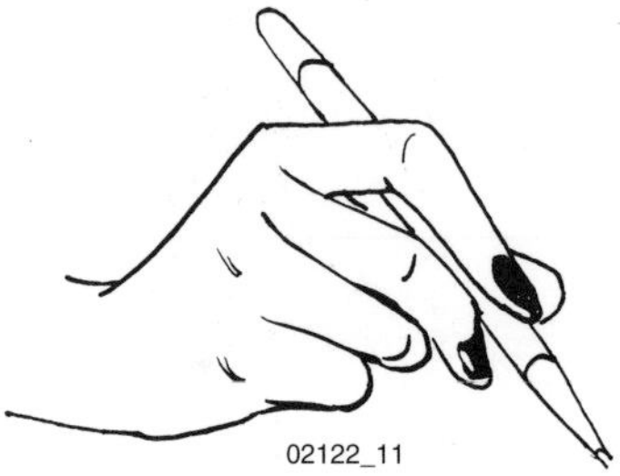
02122_11

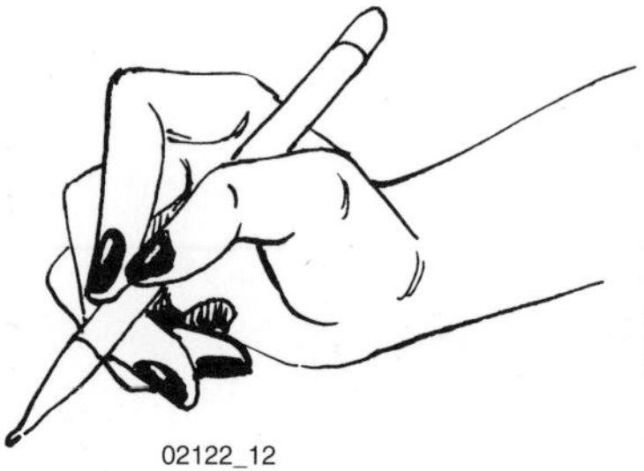
02122_12

HAND

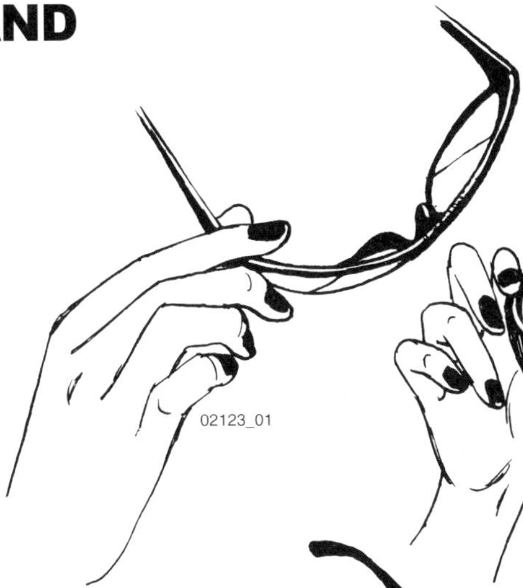

02123_01

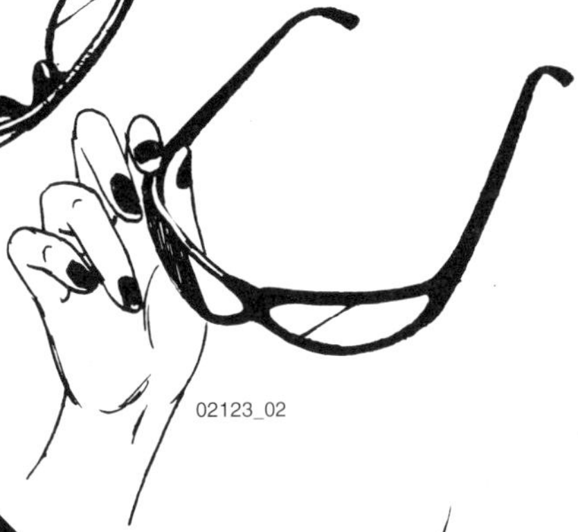

02123_02

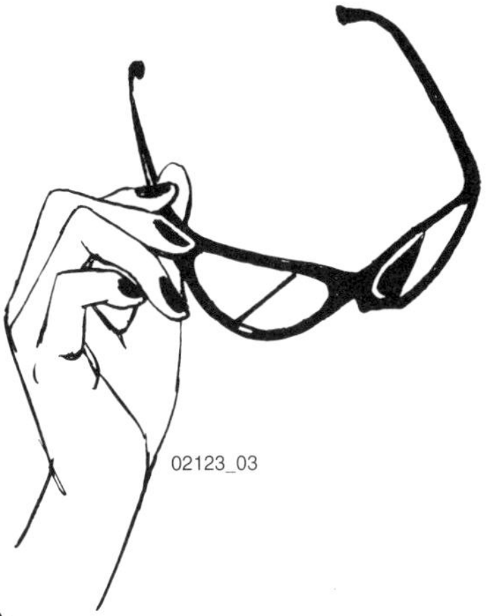

02123_03

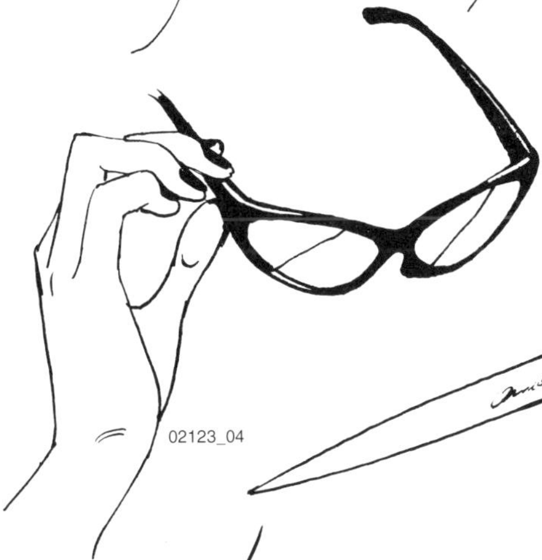

02123_04

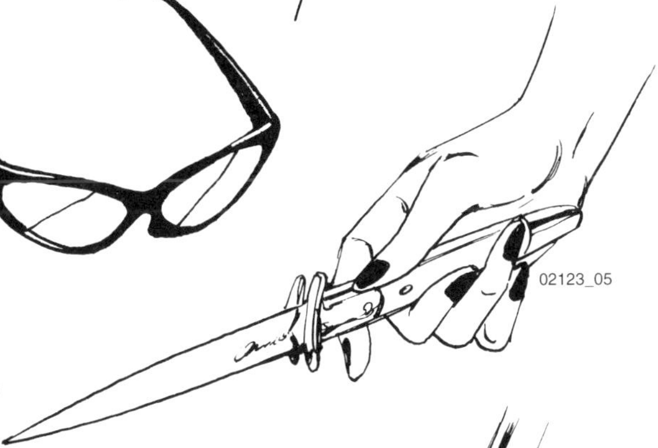

02123_05

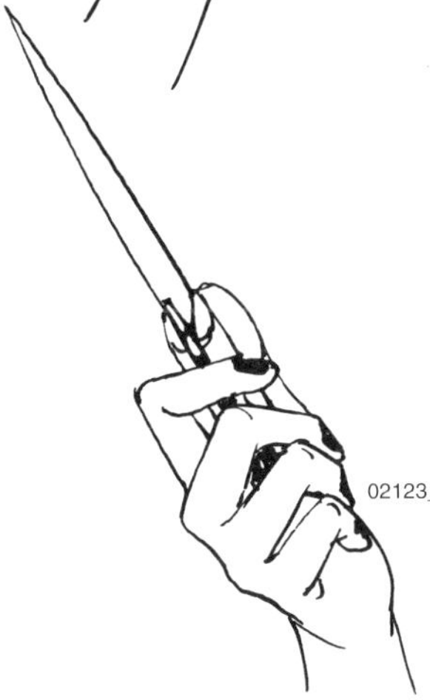

02123_06

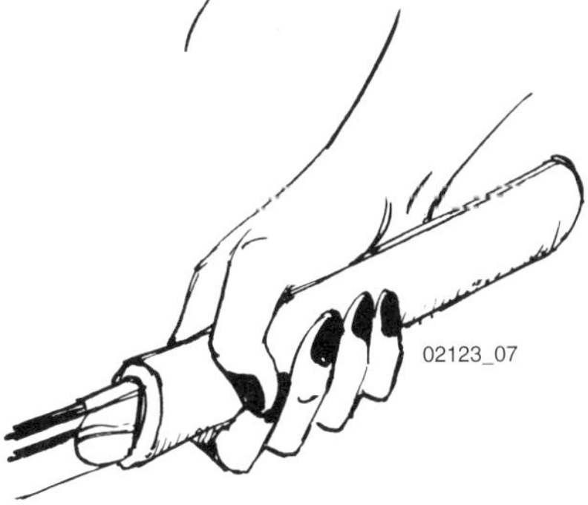

02123_07

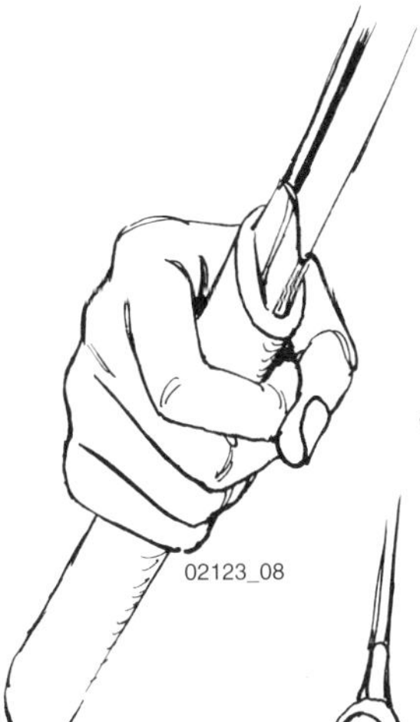

02123_08

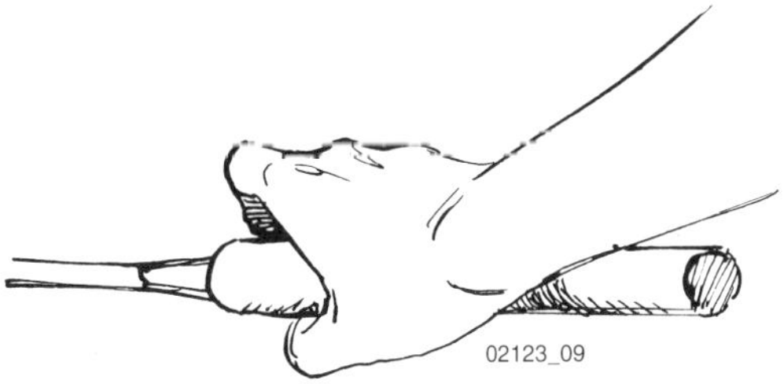

02123_09

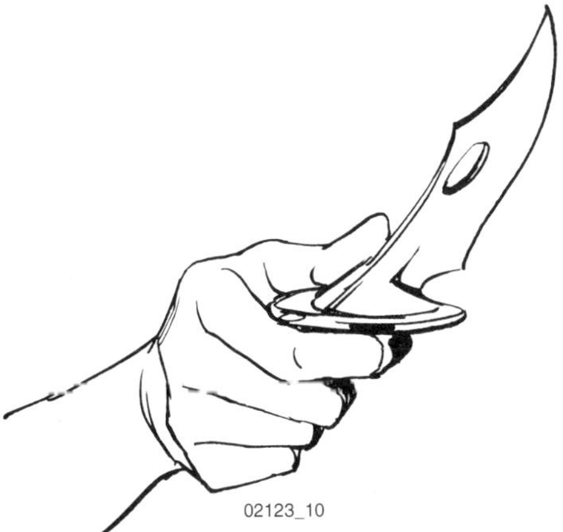

02123_10

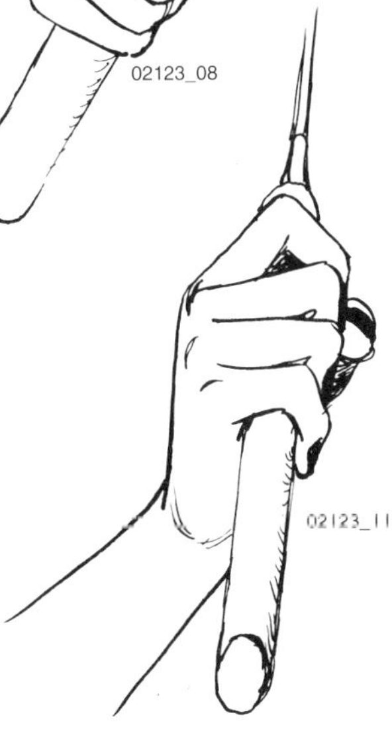

02123_11

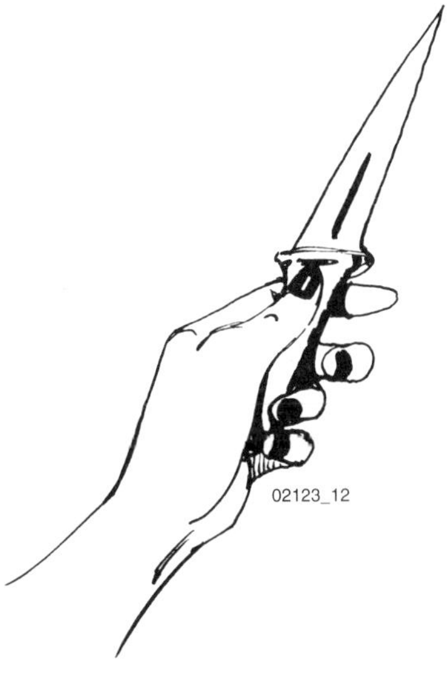

02123_12

HAND

02124_01

02124_02

02124_03

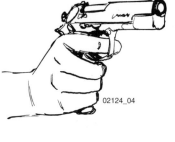

02124_04

02124_05

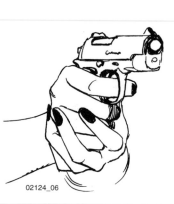

02124_06

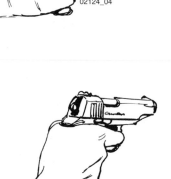

02124_07

02124_08

02124_09

02124_10

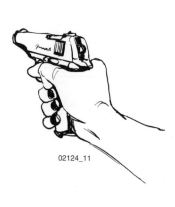

02124_11

02124_12

124

HAND

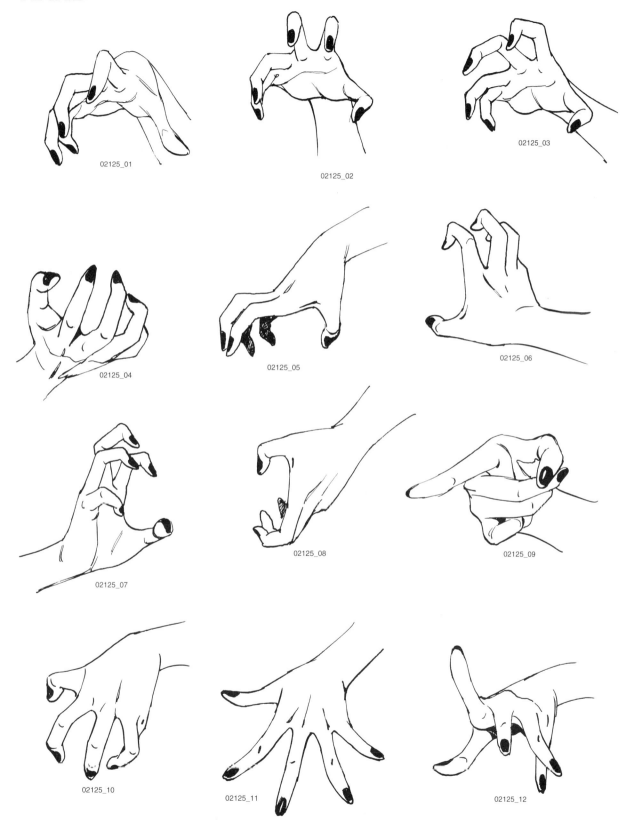

02125_01

02125_02

02125_03

02125_04

02125_05

02125_06

02125_07

02125_08

02125_09

02125_10

02125_11

02125_12

125

著作物（イラスト）使用の件について

小社では、小社の著作物であるイラスト集（CD-ROM・書籍等）からのイラスト使用につきまして以下の理由から著作権フリーという立場をとっておりません。

●イラストは商標やパッケージデザイン等に利用されるケースが多く、イラスト使用者同士で混乱を招く恐れがあるからです。特に、商標などに自由に登録されますと、使用者間で商標登録侵害の係争が生じます。過去に実際に、小社のイラストにおきましてそのような事態が起こっております。

●イラストの著作権は、著作者の死後50年までは生きているものです。著作権フリーのクリップアート集として出回っているものの多くは古い出版物であったり、または使用者間で係争の恐れのない、キャラクター性の弱いものです。小社は出版社であり、多くの著作者のお力添えで出版物を発行しております。各著作者の著作権を保護する意味から、著作権フリーの立場をとるわけにはまいりません。一旦フリーといたしますと、コピー商品の氾濫を誘発することにもつながります。

●小社では、多くのイラストレーターの著作により製品化を行っております。商業印刷物等に無断で使用されますと、著作者であるイラストレーターから直接使用者へクレームを付ける場合も起こり得ます。

以上の理由から、個人的な使用以外でご利用になる場合は、お手数ですが以下の手続きを行ってください。

○申請書の提出
※次ページの「著作物使用申請書」に必要事項を記入の上、FAXまたは、郵送で下記までお送りください。また、小社ホームページ（URL http://www.mpc-world.co.jp/）からも申請できます。

○使用するイラストの近くに「ⒸMPC＆ⒸYou Kusano」とクレジット表記する、あるいは奥付か欄外に「MPC刊『スーパー・キャラクター／デザイン＆ポーズ　草野雄著』より使用」の旨のクレジットを表記する。
※クレジット表記が不可能な場合は、使用料金をいただく場合がございます。
※使用料金等については一概には申し上げられませんので、詳細をお問い合わせになる場合も、まず申請書に必要事項を明確に記入の上、小社までお知らせください。

○印刷物（コピーでも可）を一部小社へ提出。

※社内報やプライベートでの使用については、この限りではありません。

無断使用の場合は、使用料が発生する場合がございます。

株式会社エム・ピー・シー
著作物使用管理係
〒101-0047 東京都千代田区内神田1-10-1　平富ビル
TEL 03-3291-6637
FAX 03-3295-8457
e-mail:chosaku@mpc-world.co.jp
URL http://www.mpc-world.co.jp/

年　月　日

株式会社エム・ピー・シー行

住所：〒

社名：
担当者名：
電話：

著作物使用申請書
下記の通り著作物の使用を申請します

記

使用希望イラストが収録されたMPCの製品名：

『スーパー・キャラクター／デザイン＆ポーズ　草野雄著』

使用予定イラスト（ファイル名）：

使用目的：

使用期間：

体裁：

製造部数：

宣伝・販売・発行元の会社・団体名：

イラスト使用物に価格が生じる際の定価：

商品化される場合の商品名：

使用に関する条件
1.場合によっては使用料を申し受けます
2.クレジットの明記（注・参照）
3.見本を一部提示

注：クレジット表記の仕方は、以下のいずれかの方法でお願いします。
　1.イラストの近くに「©MPC ＆© You Kusano」とクレジット表記する。
　2.奥付等に「MPC刊『スーパー・キャラクター／デザイン＆ポーズ　草野雄著』より使用」の旨を記載する。

Arts & Direction : You Kusano

Editor : Jun Itoh

DTP : Tsukuru Morita, Jun Itoh

Translation : Suzi Yamaguchi, Tsukuru Morita, Excite-kun

お問い合わせについて（株式会社エム・ピー・シー　サポートセンター）

お問い合わせは、封書かFaxまたはe-mailでのみ受け付けております。

※電話でのサポートは行っておりませんのでご注意ください。

※小社でお答えできるのは、付録CD-ROMの内容に関することのみです。

※Adobe Photoshop や Microsoft Wordなどのアプリケーションソフトの操作方法については、各ソフトの販売元にお問い合わせください。小社ではお答えできかねます。

お問い合わせの際は、お買い上げの書籍名、お名前・年齢・性別・〒番号・住所・電話番号・FAX番号・e-mailアドレスを必ず明記し、使用しているパソコン、プリンタ、OS（WindowsまたはMacintoshのバージョン）、アプリケーションソフト名とそのバージョン、パソコン歴、また、ご質問内容をなるべく詳しく書いてください。

※必要事項が書かれていないと、お答えできない場合があります。

サポート専用連絡先（株式会社エム・ピー・シー　サポートセンター）

〒101-0047　東京都千代田区内神田1-10-1 平富ビル

FAX 03-3295-8457

受付時間：午前10:30～午後4:00　休業：土曜・日曜・祭日

URL *http://www.mpc-world.co.jp/*

e-mail　*support@mpc-world.co.jp*

イラスト・データの著作権について

スーパー・キャラクター／デザイン&ポーズ2 ヒロイン編

2001年 4月29日　第1刷発行 2001年11月 1日　第2刷発行	発 行 所　**MPC** 株式会社 エム・ピー・シー

著　　者　草野　雄Ⓒ

発 行 人　後藤　文彦

印刷・製本　図書印刷株式会社

〒101-0047

東京都千代田区内神田1-10-1 平富ビル

Tel 03-3291-6637（営業部）

※本書の内容および付録CD-ROMについてのご質問は、お電話ではお受けできません。詳しくは上記「お問い合わせについて」をご覧ください。

郵便振替 00170-9-37434

http://www.mpc-world.co.jp/
